hbl, stx   F681B68

Conquest of Southwest Kansas :

3 9153 00517356 4

F
681
B68

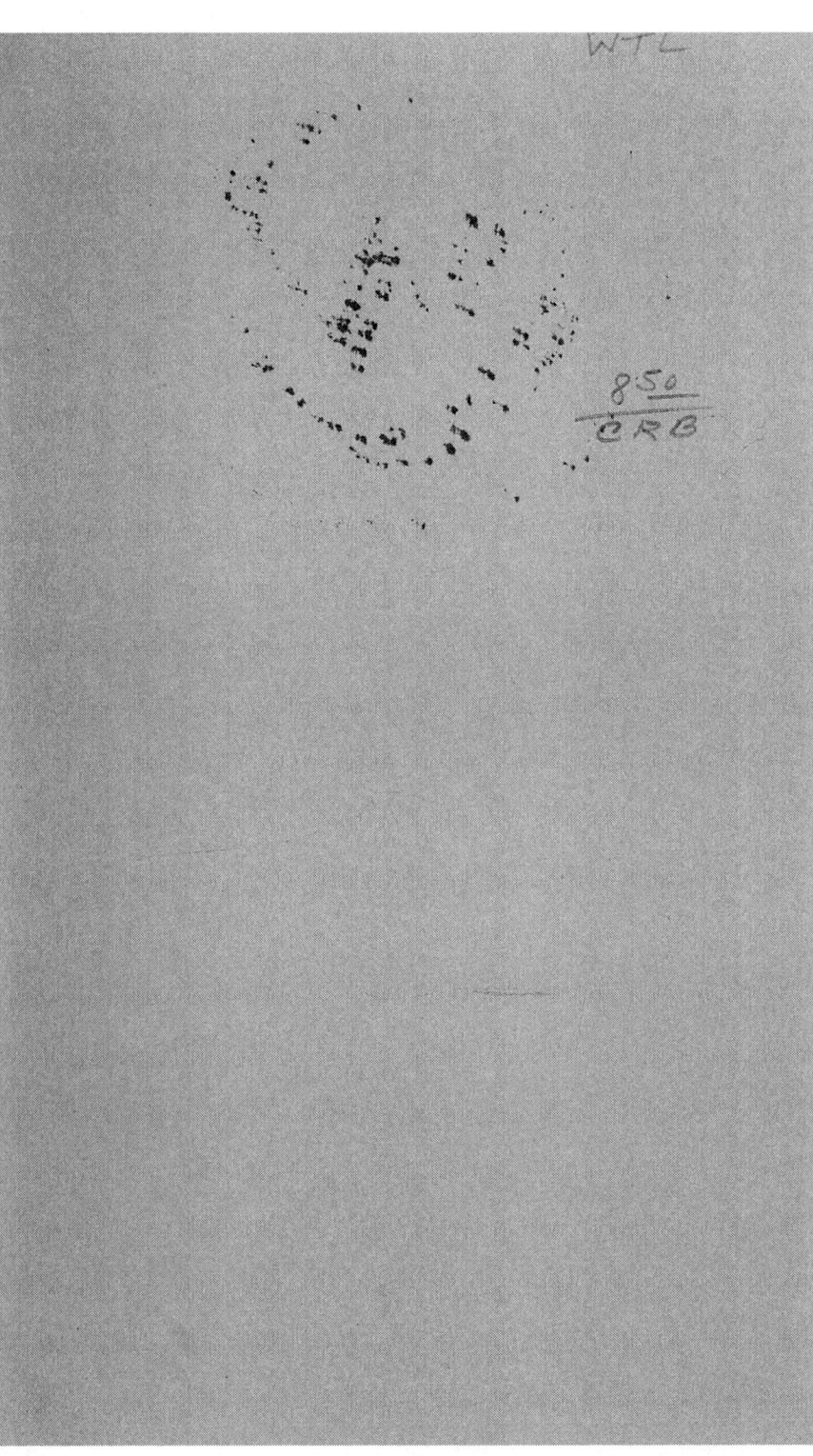

Conquest of Southwest Kansas

By
LEOLA HOWARD BLANCHARD

A History and Thrilling Stories
of Frontier Life in the
State of Kansas

PRINTED IN U.S.A.

INDEX

	Page
The Buffalo	7
The Indians	15
Mystical Land of Quivira	26
Great American Desert	30
Santa Fe Trail	33
Kansas National Forest Reserve, and Big Game Preserve	38
Garden City Experiment Station	41
Cattle Range and the Cowboys	44
Settlement of Southwestern Kansas	55
Animals and Birds of Southwestern Kansas	78
Irrigation in Southwestern Kansas	86
Sequoyah County	98
Garfield County	101
Southwestern Land District	121
Finney County	123
Court Houses	134
Beef Business	140
Official Roster	146
Schools	148
Soil, Surface and Agriculture	150
Roads and Bridges	169
Lost Towns	180
Towns of Finney County	193
Garden City	228
Post Commanders	307
Kearny County, Lakin	215
Fort Hays—Fort Dodge Trail	218
First Settler in Lane County	221
Herbert T. Hineman	354
Early Incidents at Medicine Lodge	223
Santa Fe Railroad, and Others of Finney County	320
Garden City Sugar Company	328
Scott County	335

Introduction

I BELIEVE the pioneers of this region owe it to themselves, and to future generations, to leave an imperishable record of how they found this country in the beginning; and how it was transformed by their hands into its present-day comforts and prosperity. Why people first came here, and how. What ideas they brought with them, and what sorts of people they were. Just what they did here; how they first fared in the land; and how they have gotten on since then, makes an important and fascinating study of local history, most of which will never be found in a state history.

"But, you cannot do that," said S. H. Corbett, who lived in Kearny county, when I told him I was writing the history of Finney county. "Why a lot of us old timers in these other counties had a part in making that Finney county history, and your story wouldn't be very complete if you left us out. No, you cannot write a history of Finney county alone," he added with a decided shake of his head. . . . And he was right. We cannot study Finney county as a detached and isolated experience. Its story is so inextricably interwoven with the story of the surrounding counties of Southwest Kansas, that it would be incomplete if told separately, and would loose much of its romance and glamour. And then, there is ever a certain unity in history which must be respected. No nation has ever lived without more or less contact with other nations; without having its destinies interfered with and influenced by other nations. No state of the Union was ever developed by itself alone, much less a county. So, the record of Finney county must be preceded and accompanied by a brief study in the general history of this region.

History is rarely able to preserve the names of all the

first explorers of any county. Hardy traders, trappers, hunters, adventurers, and possibly homeseekers streamed over this region, long before the persons set down as the first explorers and settlers. But the names of those old rangers and incidents connected with them are sealed in the obscurity which comes of failure to commit them to writing . . . and so are lost. For this reason, many interesting incidents, and many whose names should have a place in this record will be missed. In the various sections are the names of people who are, or have been, residents of Southwestern Kansas. Some are strong men and women who have labored and achieved. Many others have accomplished a less important part, yet they all represent a combined effort that has resulted in the building up of counties and state.

The early history of this region should have found a chronicler many years ago, while it was still fresh in the minds of the pioneers. But no one seemed to realize the romance of their lives, or the importance of leaving a permanent record of developments. Perhaps I am presuming to attempt this work, since I have never in any way been connected with this history of Southwestern Kansas. But for that very reason, I am free of all false notions concerning myself, or of others who have helped in its development. My mind is not filled with local prejudice and conceit, or undue sympathy.

My information has been gained through yellow pages of old newspaper files, public documents, books, state histories, and any written record which promised to throw light on the subject. A large amount of material has been derived from personal interviews with the men and women who have helped in the making of the history of Southwest Kansas. In fact, this story is quite largely their own. I have simply done the recording. I am indebted to many people for original contributions and reminiscences, for which I have endeavored to give full credit. These pioneers whose minds are still fresh at sixty, seventy, eighty and ninety years, have been patient and careful of truth in relating incidents. I feel very fortunate in having met them, and have been assured by those who know, that all the data herein recorded is a true basis on which future historians may build.

———o———

A TRIBUTE to the pioneers, from John A. Martin, Governor of Kansas, who delivered an address at the Southwestern Exposition, in Garden City, October, 1886:

"The loneliness and immensity of the plains had no terrors for you. You invaded their solitudes. You pushed the frontier steadily westward. You plowed and planted, and digged and sowed. You were determined to conquer the land, by irrigation if necessary. You came to stay, and you conquered. You saw the wilderness vanish, until at last every doubting Thomas was silenced and the whole world realized that here, on the western borders of Kansas, was as rich, as beautiful, and as productive a land as the sun, journeying from continent to continent, looks down upon and warms with his genial rays.

"There is something splendid in the march of civilization into and over an unpeopled land . . . something grander, even than the advance of a victorious army. It is better to build up than to destroy . . . better to redeem a desert than to make one. The march of the armies of industry and peace across the plains, peopling their solitudes, conquering the wilderness, and forcing from its soil a fatness, is an achievement romantic and inspiring. And you, people of Western Kansas, are the heroes of this conquest."

> The greater part of the printing plates used in this book were made from photographs dimmed with age and invaluable to their owners. Many are the only ones in existence. I am confident my readers will co-operate with me in expressing my appreciation to those who have made possible the preservation of these relics of the past.

The sketch on the cover was taken from an original painting made by Mrs. John A. Stevens. It depicts a true incident of pioneer life in Southwest Kansas, and the story is told on page 17.

The Buffalo

"Backward, turn backward, O time in your flight,
Knock all these big houses plumb out of sight.
Give us the frontier, with grass-covered plain,
Give us our buffalo hump-steak again."

THE earliest history of Kansas is as inseparably linked with the buffalo, as with the Indian, for Kansas was a favorite grazing land, roamed by mighty herds. The plains were carpeted with an abundance of buffalo grass, which is the most nutritious of stock feed. It is equally good, whether dry or green, and it furnished the buffalo a year 'round pasture.

The first white men to encounter the buffalo in Western Kansas were Coronado and his followers, and the following is a description written by Castenada, one of the party:

"The first time we encountered the buffalo, all our horses took to flight on seeing them, for they were a terrible sight. They have a broad and short face, eyes two palms from each other and projecting in such a manner side-ways that they can see a pursuer. Their beard is like that of a goat and so long that it drags the ground when they lower the head. They always change their hair in May, and at that season, really resemble lions. Their tail is very short and terminates in a great tuft. When they run they carry it in the air like a scorpion. Their wool is so fine that handsome clothes could certainly be made of it, except that it cannot be dyed, as it is a tawny red."

D. W. (Doc) Barton, who established ranch headquarters at Pierceville in 1872, says he has seen great herds of buffalo come sweeping across the prairie with deafening noise, and plunge into the Arkansas river with such force as to throw the water high in the air. Indeed, it looked as though the wallowing herd would throw all the water from the river bed. They would drift into this region by the thousands and Mr. Barton has ridden up on the flat north of the river when the buffalo would be so numerous that he could see nothing but a black mass as far as the eye could reach.

The buffalo herds usually followed a leader in single file, using the same trail over and over again until it was worn into a ditch. The prairies were also broken by thousands of buffalo wallows. These depressions were made by the bulls pawing the soil until it was loosened; they would then get down and roll in the loose earth until they obtained a thick coating, which would protect them from tormenting insects. They also rolled in these wallows to take off the dead hair in the spring. They used the same wallows over and over, until they became quite deep, and after a rain, held water and became tiny lakes. There were also numbers of large circles stamped on the sod. These were made by the older buffalo herding the calves and weaker ones within, while they stood with their heads out and guarded the wolves away.

In the spring the bulls would fight for possession of the herd, and they would to some extent be divided into bunches; but in the fall and early winter, when drifting south, they would be in one great herd. They were then comparatively tame, and one could ride quite close before they would move away. But when the hunters came in and began to slaughter them, they soon became wild, and would run and jump at the crack of a gun, even if fired at a great distance.

The Indians who lived in this region were dependent on the buffalo. The meat was their food; the hides were used for clothing, bedding, dishes, teepees and for nearly every purpose, even to horse shoes. The buffalo also played an indispensible part in pioneer history. The early settlers and travellers through this region were almost as dependent on the buffalo for their food as were the Indians. All the "Old Timers" in Western Kansas are familiar with the solution of the fuel problem, which was solved by gathering up the "buffalo chips".

The Indians killed only to supply their needs, but as civilization advanced, there was a systematic slaughter. The vast herds of buffalo decreased before the outfits of commercialized butchers, until all that are now in existence are those kept in private parks and game preserves. The hunters were the first to commercialize the buffalo.

C. J. (Buffalo) Jones breaking buffaloes to drive near Garden City

They waged a wanton slaughter to obtain the hides for market, but they left the carcass to rot upon the ground. When settlement began, the bones of thousands lay scattered over the plains, and the eyeless sockets of the great heads stared up in mute reproach at those who had come in to usurp their grand old range. Later, when the bones were found to have a commercial value, they were all gathered up by the homesteaders and sold for $5.00 a ton. Many of the settlers could not have lived on their claims, if it had not been for the pitiful harvest of buffalo bones.

There were few efforts made to check the destruction of the buffalo. In fact, it is claimed that the government encouraged it, in order to bring the Indians under subjection. The greatest champion of the passing herds was C. J. Jones, a man prominent in the development of Southwestern Kansas. Zane Gray says of him:

"At last, seeing that the extinction of the noble beast was inevitable, he smashed his rifle over a wagon wheel and vowed to save the species. For ten years he labored, pursuing, capturing and taming buffalo, for which the West gave him fame, and the name, 'Preserver of the American Bison'."

The historian, T. C. Hornaday, Superintendent of the Taxidermical Department of the Smithsonian Institute, said in his report to the Fiftieth Congress:

"Mr. Jones' original herd of fifty-seven buffalo constitutes a living testimonial of his individual enterprise, courage, endurance and skill in the chase. The majority of the individuals comprising the herd he himself ran down, lassoed and tied with his own hands. It was the greatest feat ever accomplished. For five consecutive years, Colonel Jones made an annual trip to the uninhabited and desolate 'Panhandle' of Texas, to secure buffalo calves out of the small herd of one or two hundred head, which represented the last remnant of buffalo that formerly roamed that region."

The buffalo captured by Mr. Jones were placed in state and national parks, except a few which he kept in Finney county. These later ones were owned by George and E. G. Finnup. A few years ago it became necessary to kill them, but the heads of the last cow and bull have been mounted and their hides made into beautiful robes and will long be preserved in Garden City.

At the time the Atchison, Topeka and Santa Fe railroad was built through this region, thousands of buffalo still grazed the plains and had regular watering places along the Arkansas river. The meat for the laborers who did the construction work of the railroad was the flesh of the buffalo which was killed by hired hunters. Many times the trains were compelled to stop and wait while a herd was crossing the track. If the train failed to stop, each individual buffalo would hurl itself in maddened frenzy at the passing obstacle, until numbers would be killed, and the train derailed.

The Last Buffalo Hunt Near Garden City

James R. Fulton was erecting a house, the third to be built in Garden City. It was a nice day in November, 1878, and two men were on the roof shingling, when one of them paused to glance over the prairie. This was an uncontrolled habit of the isolated bands of pioneers. They were always watching the horizon, hoping for something to appear which would break the monotony of the blank prairie which so completely surrounded them. To the northeast, about two or three miles, the shingler noticed a number of objects which appeared to be little haycocks moving up and down on the grassy slopes. He called attention to his discovery and all the men of the town climbed up on the building to get a view of the unusual sight. At his first glance, W. D. Fulton shouted, "buffalo" although all that could be seen was the shaggy humps.

The herd was feeding slowly, and was headed toward the river. The animals advanced majestically from the higher prairie down into the valley, seemingly unaware that man was laying the foundation of a city on one of their favorite feeding grounds. On came the shaggy monsters, numbering twenty-eight. It was a grand sight and one never to be witnessed again in Finney county.

But the men on the roof were thrilled at the prospect of a big game hunt, and wasted no time in gazing at the scene. In a short time they were off after the buffalo. Mr. Fulton had a fine saddle mare and John Stevens had a speedy young stallion. They rode in advance while

Farlow Weeks and some others followed with a wagon to bring back the game.

The chase lasted into the night, but when Weeks returned he had two fat cows in his wagon. Fulton shot both of the cows, although every one knew Stevens was the best shot. But then, John Stevens, that stalwart young Swede, was hoping to be Fulton's son-in-law, and so . . . well, "Uncle Billy" shot both the cows, and no one ever voiced any doubts about the matter. The fresh meat was a treat to the settlers and lasted several weeks.

The last buffalo seen in Finney county was in the spring of 1879. On the 24th day of April a small herd came in sight of Garden City. C. J. Jones set out after them alone. After riding several miles, his horse stepped in a prairie dog hole, and injured his leg. Mr. Jones had to abandon the chase and walked back to town, leading his horse.

On June 5, 1879, Wm. Moore, who lived north of Garden City, discovered several buffalo grazing not far from his house. He got his gun and shot at one, but the whole herd turned on him and ran him into the house, and then walked quietly off.

One of the most noted buffalo hunts in Southwestern Kansas occurred in October, 1879, and the following account of it appeared in a Topeka paper:

"Through the invitation of C. J. Jones of Garden City, Governor St. John, accompanied by Dr. Parker of Independence, Missouri; Col. D. C. Smith of Normal, Illinois, and Mayor Shreeve of Topeka, arrived in Garden City October 8. They were joined by C. J. Jones, an old frontiersman who is well versed in the ways of 'roughing it' on the plains. Many a buffalo has unwillingly responded to the crack of his trusty Creedmore.

"They went immediately to Lakin, where they overtook Captain J. R. Fulton, one of the most noted buffalo hunters of the plains. He is a brave man and they had confidence in his ability to protect them against the bloodthirsty Red Devils that come down on hunters, when least expected, to retaliate for killing 'Red Man's cattle'. The story is told how Captain Fulton once bluffed the noted chief 'Big Bow' and two hundred warriors. The chief stood over the captain with drawn knife, ready to plunge it to the hilt, but the Captain looked him in the eye, laid bare his breast, and dared him to commit the deed. The Captain is one of a thousand who can look an Indian out of countenance.

"From Lakin, the party drove about eighty miles northwest, where they found plenty of buffalo, antelope and other wild game. The Governor proved himself equal to the occasion, and many a wild beast yielded to the crack of his rifle. Dr. Parker won the laurels by killing the giant buffalo of the plains. It was laughable to see the doctor mount the beast as soon as it fell, and hear him explain, 'I always knew I had religion, now I know it.' Had we space we could give a sketch of the party creeping on all fours up to a dead buffalo and two wolves, mistaking it for a buffalo cow and twin calves.

"After enjoying the charms of the plains for ten days, the distinguished party arrived at Hawley's Station on the Santa Fe railroad, just west of the Kansas line. This was the first house or anything like civilization since leaving Lakin, ten days previously. The party flagged the train at 8 p.m. and as they stepped on the platform of the front coach, they were covered by four guards, all armed with Winchester rifles, who mistook the governor's party for train robbers. The hunters surrendered, and the facts were soon made known, and the train was again rolling down the Arkansas river valley.

"They all stopped off at Garden City and were guests of Mr. Jones. After spending the day hunting antelope and jack rabbits, the Governor's party left for their homes, delighted with their trip."

Gone are all the buffalo that once ranged in Western Kansas, except the small herd which is kept in the game preserve. They of all the animals were best constructed to endure the fitful climate of this region. Their heavy robes protected them from the terrible blizzards when all other animal life perished. Gone forever are those grand old monarchs of the prairie, they, and all evidences of their habitation have been erased from the Great Plains by the hand of civilized man. Even their very bones have been carted away; their trails and wallows have been leveled by the "sod busters", but their memory will always be a fixed feature in the early romance of Southwest Kansas.

Lines to a Buffalo

Far out upon the prairie,
  Today I idly roam;
This erst was called the hunters' range,
  The noble bisons' home.

Here proud of man, he grandly strode,
  A monarch in his might.
Fearless he scanned his vast abode,
  With keen, far-reaching sight.

Too soon, alas! the whistling ball
  Sped swift, upon its way.
Brave to the death, I saw thee fall
  And marked thy closing day.

Again thy trail I cross, Alas!
  'Twas here I saw thee die.
And here beneath the tangled grass
  Thy bleaching bones, espy.
          —Mrs. L. C. Hopkins. (1879)

The Indians
Indians of Western Kansas

FROM a period extending far back into the past, far back of any written record, perhaps thousands of years ago, these plains were inhabited by a primitive people. They were the original Americans and were called Indians. Many generations failed to develop much individuality or any great degree of cultural progress, but their hunting grounds extended over all this region. Numerous wandering tribes coming up from the south and west or in from the north and east, infested Western Kansas during the centuries. However, they were not in any sense occupants of the country, so cannot be identified with the history of the territory.

So far as records show, the Pawnee and Wichita tribes of the Caddoan Linguistic families were the original owners and occupants of the greater part of the soil of Kansas. They held possession until down to about 1780. The Caddoan tribe encountered by Coronado and other early Spanish explorers were the Wichitas. Their country was called Quivira and they were the Quivirans. But long before the period of land cessions, the tribes of the Caddoan family had departed from Kansas and their land had fallen to other tribes. There was little left to show for the ancient glory of the Caddoans.

At the period when treaty making began in the west, tribes of the Siouan family occupied, or claimed to occupy by far the greater part of Kansas. The two divisions of the Siouan family, the Osage and the Kansa, had been drifting westward from the Alleghany mountains since the earliest date known by white men. It may be supposed that the original Caddoans were driven out by the advance of the Siouans from the east. The Kansa Indians rank first in historical importance of all the Kansas tribes.

The Algonquin family was divided in two tribes. They were called the Arapahos and Cheyennes, and they were the Indians who claimed and inhabited this territory in more recent times, even after the country was partially settled. They came originally from what is now Minnesota. Both were important plains tribes, roaming from the Black Hills to the Arkansas river, and always at war with other tribes. They were fierce and daring riders and were the most dreaded foes of the early Mexican traders and

travellers over the Santa Fe trail. They would lay in wait along the trail and suddenly swoop down and circle unprotected emigrant trains. If defeated in the onslaught, they would vanish over the barren prairies in clouds of dust. Too many times, however, they left evidences of victorious brutalities upon their victims. The "Point of Rocks", which is located eight miles east of Garden City along the Arkansas river, is reputed to be a favorite base of attack. Many arrow heads and Indian curios have been found there. The Santa Fe Trail passed directly below it.

The treaty of 1867 was supposed to end the term of

Indian occupancy in Western Kansas. However, it continued to be a favorite hunting ground for numerous tribes for the next ten years. In fact, a great many Indians still remained here the year 'round and made no pretense of living on their allotments. The pioneer cattlemen ranged their stock among them, and they were never known to bother the herds. They much preferred the meat of the buffalo to domestic cattle. There was very little trouble between them and the early settlers, although there were many Indian scares.

Pierceville is the only town in Southwestern Kansas ever attacked by the Indians. The story of how they destroyed that place in 1874 is told in the history of Pierceville.

John Stevens was ambushed by a band of renegade Indians out in the Pawnee region. He gave the following account of his encounter to R. J. Churchill:

"It was along in the seventies, before the settlers had started coming in. We were out here hunting wild horses, and our main camp was somewhere north and east of where Garden City is now located. I wanted to look over the Pawnee valley, so I left the camp and rode out alone. At noon I stopped to eat my dinner in a creek valley, probably the Walnut. I knew there were some Indians in that region, and I realized I was placing myself in an ideal position for an attack. But here was water and plenty of good grass for my horse, and not a sign of an Indian. I decided to risk it, and was not disturbed during my meal. However, they had evidently been watching, but they wanted me out where they could employ their usual tactics. For as soon as I had mounted my horse and was riding in the open out on the high prairie, they were after me, and soon they were around me in a circle. And then they shot my horse. Until then, I had not suspected that the Indians meant mischief. Never again will I give them a chance to circle me, if I can prevent it. They were after my guns, and intended to kill me to get them.

"After killing my horse, I guess they thought they had plenty of time to use me for a target. They all withdrew behind a knoll two or three hundred yards away and held a pow wow, but directly an Indian came riding out on either side while one from behind the knoll began to shoot. After each shot, the ones stationed on the sides would ride in to report where the bullet had struck. They kept this up for six hours, firing about every half hour and each time the bullet came a little closer. Finally one just grazed the tip of my elbow and injured my hip, and at once the Indians set up a great Ki-yi-ing.

"As yet, I had not fired one shot in return, but right then and there, I made up my mind it was time to act. That Indian would not get another chance at me. The Indian, before shooting, would raise up from behind the knoll and take considerable time in sighting and expose his body down to the waist. So I got ready, and when the Indian raised up and I thought he was about ready to shoot, I turned my Sharp's Needle gun loose on him. He dropped from sight and didn't come up again. I waited awhile, and having seen nothing of the Indians since I had shot, I decided I had better get to moving, for the sun was getting low."

"Which way did you go, Stevens?"

"Well, Dick, it was getting late. My horse was dead, I had been wounded and it was up to me to walk six miles to camp. The nearest way lay directly toward where I had last seen the Indians. I got my rifle ready and started toward the knoll, but when I reached the top, there wasn't an Indian in sight. They had all pulled out, and I have always been uncertain whether I hit my Indian or not."

The last Indian raid through Kansas was the famous expedition of Dull Knife and his band of Cheyennes in the fall of 1878. The Cheyennes had long been the most dreaded of the fierce, fighting plains tribes, but their power and numbers had been greatly diminished, and they had been placed on a reservation in the Indian Territory. It was crowded and unhealthy, and it was clear their extinction was but a matter of time. The fall of 1878 found them famished and dying. Their tribe had been reduced from 235 warriors to 89, and the women and children in like proportion. There was but one way out for them, and that was to flee to Canada. Dull Knife was the hereditary chief of the band, but he was old, and a young, fearless warrior called Little Wolf was elected as war chief. A great council was held in the teepee of Dull Knife on the night of September 8, '78. No one knows what was said, but the next day they began to carry out their plans and they immediately set out on one of the most hazardous marches recorded in history. There were five great military barriers to be passed, and the soldiers were re-inforced by hundreds of cowboys and settlers.

The greatest need of the Cheyennes was for horses and arms. Little Wolf ordered his men to pick up every horse and every weapon in the region through which they marched, and as they advanced they swept the country clean of both. But they had positive orders not to kill any people unless it became necessary to protect their own lives. Most of the settlers fled before them, but a few ranchers fought desperately to save their property, and were killed. Along the line of the Santa Fe railroad was a line of soldiers commanded by General Pope, and the news of Dull Knife's escape spread like wildfire, and filled all the settlers of Southwestern Kansas with terror. Word was brought to Fort Dodge, "that the Cheyennes, riding like madmen, were headed north, killing and burning as they rode, carrying fresh scalps and herding stolen horses with them."

After entering the state of Kansas, the Cheyennes travelled west across Clark county, into Meade county, and then north to the Arkansas river. They crossed the Santa Fe railroad east of Pierceville, where a trestle was built over a draw. No one witnessed this crossing, but they left a dead squaw laying on the railroad track, and there were numerous hoof prints of ponies visible on either side. Little Wolf had left none of his people behind. Their march was encumbered with the aged, and the sick, and the helpless, and all were in a famished condition. In their flight, they had no time to dispose of their dead, and they were left to rot by the wayside. There were so many of these grim markers that it was easy to follow their course. With the crossing of the Santa Fe, they had passed the first of their military barriers. That night they made camp on the Pawnee creek in Finney county, near the present site of Kinney dam.

W. D. Fulton, in company with Tom Hurdle and Mr. Hopper who were visiting him from the east, were out on a hunting trip in that region, and that night they were surprised to see a great many campfires. Mr. Fulton knew at once that Indians were camped there, but he had always been on friendly terms with them and was not in the least alarmed. But his tenderfoot companions from the east were badly scared and expected the worst. They were snugly wrapped in their blankets, but they could not sleep. They insisted that their families still needed their protection, and they had no right to lie still and let themselves be massacred. About midnight they got up and headed toward Garden City. They arrived at daybreak, under the impression that the Indians were in close pursuit. They alarmed the town, declaring they must prepare for an early attack, but the Indians never came.

The next morning the Cheyennes were seen by a government scout, but long before he reported their location to officials at Fort Dodge, the Indians were on their way north. They travelled as much as seventy miles a day, and the United States troops were never able to overtake them.

There were few settlers in this region at that time and they were always on the lookout for Indians. Sometime later in the fall of 1878, someone reported that Indians were approaching Garden City over the sand hills from the south. Instantly the people of the town gathered in a small group and stood watching the hills intently. A single rider appeared and then suddenly dropped from sight in a dip in the hills. A little later a rider appeared at another point, but he soon dropped out of sight. They could not determine whether it was a different man each time, or the same one, but finally they agreed that it was a party of advance Indian scouts. The citizens were very much alarmed, except the Fulton brothers; they were sure they could handle the situation. They hastily collected all the fire arms in town, which amounted to seven guns, one of which belonged to Emanuel Schnars and the other six to the Fultons. The guns were passed out to the men. David Menke begged to be left out of the gun deal, declaring he was more afraid of the gun than he was of the Indians, but he took the gun which was thrust into his trembling hands. James Fulton gave the orders and they all marched down to a high place on the railroad grade. Concealing themselves behind the embankment they were instructed to shoot the first Indian who stuck his head up on the other side, and they laid their rifles across the rails. The Fultons were on the lookout, but before long they let out a shout of laughter, for a lone cowboy had emerged from behind the last obscuring hill, and was waving his sombrero.

Mrs. Dan Larmor recalls an incident which occurred about 1880. A party of riders were observed approaching rapidly toward Garden City, from the west along the river banks. They were enshrouded in clouds of dust, but to those watching, it was plainly visible that their bodies were bedecked with flowing feathers. The citizens began at once to make hasty preparations to defend the little village against an Indian attack, and the women and children sought shelter in an adobe house. On came the riders and with a whoop, drew rein on Main street. But when the clouds of dust had subsided, the wary storekeepers, looking through the front windows, beheld only a band of gay cowboys ensheathed in sage brush. The mosquitos were very bad in those days, great swarms of big ones tormented man and beast. The cowboys had tied on the brush to protect themselves from the stings of the insects. At that period, when Indian warriors were still more or less free to range this region, it was very natural to mistake the brush for feathers.

R. J. Churchill remembers the Indian scare of 1882. The report came to the people on the Pawnee that the Indians, a thousand of them had broken out of the reservation and were headed north. This made the settlers in that region very anxious, for when the Cheyennes had broken out in 1878 their route north had been across the head of the Pawnee. The trail left by the government wagons of the pursuing troops was still plainly visible on the north side of the middle fork. Mr. Churchill says:

"At that time, John Spicer, a son of Admiral Spicer, U.S. Navy, was out as a government scout and was making headquarters at my place. In the hurry of preparing for a possible raid, one of the shells that Spicer was reloading, exploded and mashed the end of his little finger. Well, it was up to me to go for the doctor, so I climbed on my best bronc, and as no one knew just where the Indians were, I wasted no time in getting to Garden City.

"When I arrived at town, I learned that the Indians were still south of the railroad, but no one knew just where. I also learned the state had sent guns and ammunition to the city. I did not learn whether the brave men of the east were unwilling to risk themselves, so just sent the guns, or whether the men of Garden City just wired for the guns, thinking they could do the rest.

"It didn't take long to get Dr. Lowrance, and we made the return to the ranch in quick time.

"'It means a little ether, John,' said Dr. Lowrance, after a glance at the wound. The bunks were built against the wall, and not convenient for operating tables, so we made Spicer a bed on the floor. I assisted the doctor, and he kept me busy, but he did a good job. His charges for driving forty miles out to the Pawnee and back was $25.00. One could afford to be sick in the '80's.

"In a few days after that, we heard that the Indians had crossed the railroad west of Garden City, but the troops had surrounded them, and persuaded them without violence to return peaceably to their reservation.

"The last Indian scare in Southwestern Kansas was in the summer of 1885. John H. Whitson, who was living northwest of Garden City, says that a band of Cheyennes and Arapahoes, held on a reservation at Anadarko, Indian Territory, broke from their reservation and headed northwest toward their old stamping ground in the Dakotas. There was great excitement all along the border. It was thought the escaping redskins would strike across the Arkansas and the Santa Fe railroad close to Garden City. Messengers were scurrying all over the plains warning the settlers. Yet not one came near us until after the danger was passed, and we were perhaps the only persons in the whole country who were at that time out in the 'danger zone'."

The following telegram was sent out to W. D. Fulton from the governor's office:

Topeka, Kansas, July 7, 1885.
W. D. Fulton, Garden City, Kansas:

The Sheriff of Kingman telegraphs me that the Indians are reported in Pratt and Comanche counties, killing and burning. The report may be exaggerated, but it is important that the people be warned and organized for defense. Please see that the news is spread and effect the best organization possible.

John A. Martin, Governor."

PROCLAMATION

"I, W. D. Fulton, sheriff of Finney county, Kansas, by virtue of authority vested in me by law, in view of the fact that there is an insurrection now prevailing in the southwest portion of the state, do hereby call upon all able-bodied men of Finney county to come foreward at once and enroll and hold themselves in readiness to preserve the peace of the state. All are called upon to meet at the Rink in Garden City, at 2 o'clock p.m., July 8, 1885."

The Sheriff telegraphed the Governor to send 100 stands of arms, and 5000 rounds of ammunition.

A letter from the Governor followed, which said:

"An ample force of United States Cavalry is now on the southern border, and posts will be established at Kiowa and at the point where the old road from Dodge to Supply crossed the Cimarron. The posts will be instructed to maintain scouts east and west and guard our border against any possible invasion of the Indians. For the assistance you and those who co-operated with you rendered in this work, I desire to express my grateful thanks.

John A. Martin, Governor."

At that time militia companies were organized at Garden City as follows: Company A, Captain, J. W. Weeks; First Lieutenant, Judge H. M. Wheeler; Second Lieutenant, N. J. Earp; Company B, Captain, D. A. Mims; First Lieutenant, J. J. Munger; Second Lieutenant, John Lowry; Sergeant, Dr. Frank Cartwright; Dr. A. Sabine was appointed battalion surgeon; Hon. C. J. Jones, Quartermaster, and I. R. Holmes, Commissary of Subsistence. Company A was made up principally of the G.A.R. boys; Company B, of volunteers.

Mayor Holmes said to a Topeka Capital reporter:

"Should the Indians come on Kansas soil, the whole Indian question should then be left to the settlement of the people who are in danger from them. And they will settle it, too, without asking the permission of the general government. The old settlers who know about Indians have made up their minds that they will not put up with any more nonsense, and their perfect organization and determination has given them confidence in the settlers. The government better take care of its pets if it does not want them killed."

Within a short time after this, Hon. C. J. Jones received the following telegram from the governor: "My latest and most reliable advices are that the reported Indian raid is a scare without foundation. John A. Martin, Governor."

The year 1884 perhaps marked the close of the great epoch of Indian myths and romances which dominated the lives of those first inhabitants of this region. That year under government escort, they camped for some time in the Pawnee valley. They roamed over the prairies and traded peaceably with the settlers; for the last time they hunted the antelope in a primitive manner, which was by relay. They would surround the animal, and then keep it running in a circle until it fell exhausted. They fished in the waters of the Pawnee, and teased and captured the turtles. Once more they visited their burying grounds along the bluffs of the spring branches, and then they were gone forever. Nothing now remains but a few stories of their habits and savage depredations. Or on the other hand, stories told by sympathetic pioneers who witnessed the heartless treatment of the Indians by the soldiers and greedy whites who desired to possess their happy hunting grounds.

The Mystical Land of Quivira

IT is customary to think the history of our country began in the east and travelled westward, but in some respects Kansas and the Southwest are older than New England and Virginia. Older in the sense that the battles of the white man with the Indian on this continent began here, rather than in the forests of the Pequot and Powhatan. In this region occurred the first bloodshed between the Indians and the whites. Padilla, the priest, was slain by the Indians, and the Indian guide, known as the "Turk", was put to death by the Spaniards. Southwestern Kansas has the right to use the march of Coronado in 1541 as a basis for its history; and it is thrilling to know that the first white men to ride over these plains were dressed in glittering armor, and were the select noblemen of a powerful nation.

Francisco Vasquez de Coronado is reputed to be the first white man to visit Kansas. His expeditions in 1541 gave the Spaniards the prior title to the land by right of discovery. But no claim of proprietorship was ever established to any portion of Kansas except the southwest corner. The Spaniards were seeking gold and precious jewels. Failing in this, they withdrew in disgust, back over the shortest possible route to New Spain.

Volumes have been written about Quivira and its location. Many claim to have figured out the exact routing of Coronado's expedition, but no one knows and it is not likely they ever will know the exact spots visited by Coronado. Sufficient data to determine these matters does not exist. There never existed, even in New Spain, any definite knowledge of the location of Quivira. It was to them a half-mystical land, to the eastward, abounding in gold and great wealth. It was a land of grassy plains, roamed over by rolling herds of wild oxen and inhabited by a wild, brutish people. But it does not matter about exact boundaries for there were no rigidly defined lines between the primitive nations in that far-away time, and their hunting grounds overlapped. It is not essential to know every mile of the route travelled by Coronado. Statements recorded in the old Spanish Chronicles, mapped portions of the route, and fragmentary remains that have been discovered, prove that Coronado did visit Quivira, and that Quivira was in Kansas—that Quivira was Kansas.

There is proof that Coronado and his band of select men followed a primitive trail across the counties of Southwestern Kansas. The detailed account they gave of the country, the climate, and the rivers, are authority for the claim. Another proof is the famous "Coronado Sword" that is now the property of the State Historical Society at Topeka. This sword was found in the year 1886 at the head waters of the Pawnee, near the north line of Finney county, nearly due north of the town of Ingalls. It evidently belonged to Gallego, one of the principal men of the Coronado expedition, for it bears his name graven in the metal. On it is also an inscription:

"No me Saques Sin Razon
No me Enbaines Sin Honor'."

Translated:

"Draw me not without reason;
Sheath me not without honor."

In 1930 a Spanish lance and the elaborate bit of an ancient Spanish bridle were found in a box canyon near the Beaver river. A line drawn between these archeological findings cuts across Stevens, Haskell, and directly through the center of Finney county. These findings and their location are a strong indication that the route of that famous march led across this region, either when they entered the country or when they retreated.

For two generations after Coronado's expedition, the Spaniards sent various explorers to the Great Plains, still seeking gold and silver. But countries holding only possibilities of trade and agriculture were not considered of much value by the Spaniards. They finally abandoned hopes of finding riches, and left it for a stronger people to explore and develop the land they had discovered. They made no property claims and it was all but forgotten by them, except their historians, for two hundred years.

The early development of the "Great West" was due to the French. Robert Cavalier de la Salle was the first man to comprehend the magnitude and possibilities of the great valley of the Mississippi. Different from the Spaniards, he dreamed of establishing an empire that was to rest on commerce; and which would depend on the settling and developing of the country. He resolved to secure the land for France; and to develop the trade for himself. He succeeded in establishing the French Province of Louisiana April 9, 1682, which included almost the entire area of Kansas.

No detailed account of French and Spanish explorations can be given in this work; nor shall I explain the conditions which brought about the various changes in the sovereignty of the Territory of Louisiana, except as it affected this region. It remained a part of the Dominion of France until November 3, 1762, at which time it passed into the possession of Spain. October 1, 1800, Spain agreed to retrocede the territory to France, which agreement was consummated by the treaty of Madrid, March 21, 1801. Two years later it became a part of the United States of America, by purchase from France, April 30, 1803. In the year 1812 this part of the territory was separated from that of Louisiana and incorporated into the Territory of Missouri, whose western limits were the Mexican border, and its capital city was located at St. Louis, Missouri. In

1830 congress erected all the territory west of the present state of Missouri into lands for the Indians and it was called the "Indian Country" until it was organized as the territory of Kansas in 1854.

The early governmental history of the territory included in Southwest Kansas is unique as far as proprietorship is concerned. The Arkansas river was used as a dividing line between nations until 1845. That part north of the river was successively under the governmental control of France, Spain, France again, and then the United States.

The part laying south of the river was a Spanish possession until Mexico won its independence in 1821. It remained a part of Mexico until 1836. During that year, Texas seceded from Mexico, and the southwest corner of Kansas was held as a part of the Texas Republic during the nine years of its existence. It came into the possession of the United States in 1850. It was made a part of the territory of Kansas, which included all the lands between the state of Missouri and the Rocky Mountains, when it was organized in 1854.

On January 29, 1861, Kansas was admitted as a state with its area covering practically the same territory which was claimed by the ancient Quivirans before the coming of the white men.

The Great American Desert

SOON after the acquisition of the territory of Louisiana by the United States, expeditions were sent out by the government to explore the region west of the Mississippi. The first reliable information as to climate and general features of the country was from the report of the Lewis and Clark expedition in 1804-5-6.

So far as is known, Lieut. Zebulon M. Pike was the first explorer to visit this part of Kansas. In 1806 he followed the course of the Arkansas river through this valley and his explorations embraced a larger range than any before made. The beginning of commercial intercourse with Mexico via the Santa Fe trail dates from the first publication of his journal which was published immediately after the return of Lieut. Pike.

The government also sent out Major J. C. Long on a scientific exploring expedition in 1819-1820.

The reports from these expeditions were not flattering to this country. According to their opinion, most of the state of Kansas was unfit for habitation by civilized people, especially the Western portion. And on the early maps, Western Kansas was included in that great area marked "The Great American Desert". The following report was recorded by Zebulon Pike in his journal concerning this region:

"The border of the Arkansas river . . . is the paradise of our territories for the wandering savages. . . . I believe there are elk, deer and buffalo sufficient on the banks of the Arkansas river alone, if used without waste, to feed all the savages in the United States territory one century, but the region could not support white men in large numbers even along the rivers. The wood now in the country would not be sufficient for a modern share of population more than fifteen years. But possibly time may make discoveries of coal mines which would render the country habitable."

Lieut. Pike evidently did not discover the fuel value of the "buffalo ship" which lay so thickly scattered over the prairies and like the manna of old, required only to be gathered; neither did he know that the native sod could be converted into houses far more comfortable than the ones made of logs. And never did he dream of the treasure which lay buried beneath the sod, the natural gas, which is of greater value than the treasure sought for by Coronado. Nothing but time could change the minds of the people in regard to "The Desert".

As the years passed, innumerable caravans of prairie schooners began moving westward, but they were in search of fairer lands and brighter fortunes, which they believed lay far beyond the so-called desert. It was a motley throng and the travel was sufficient to imprint clear-cut trails across the mighty plains. Traders to Santa Fe; Mormons fleeing into the wilderness to set up their temples of worship; gold seekers to California; emigrants to Oregon; soldiers; travelers and adventurers. It is estimated that ninety thousand persons passed through Kansas in 1849-50. But of all this moving host, none drew aside to settle in this beautiful region. This was a territory occupied only by Indians, a few traders, trappers and hunters.

With the organization of Kansas Territory in 1854, came a simultaneous effort to extinguish the Indian title to the lands and thus open them to white settlers. Stealthy treaties with the various tribes began. Immigrants began settling first in the eastern part. Those who came in from the north wished to have it a free state; those from the south determined to own slaves. The result was that Kansas became a battlefield for the two opposing parties, and was known as "Bleeding Kansas". The western part of the state was scarcely disturbed by events of the rebellion. It still remained largely in the possession of the Indians. There was no attempt made to settle or develop the resources of this part of the "Great American Desert" until after the close of the Civil War; and even then there were no settlers in this region until after the building of the Atchison, Topeka & Santa Fe railroad in 1872.

The records of the Department of Missouri for 1874 show the following garrisoned posts in Kansas: Fort Dodge, Fort Wallace, Fort Larned, Fort Riley and Fort Leavenworth. Summer camps were established on Wild Horse Creek and near Grinnell Station.

The records also show that small detachments of the 19th Infantry were stationed at the following points, guarding railroad stations, mails, contractors, trains, etc.: Lakin, Kearny County; Cimarron, Gray County; Syracuse, Hamilton County; Bluff Creek Mail Station; Pierceville, Finney County; Sun City, Barber County; Wild Horse Station on the Kansas-Pacific Railroad; at Aubrey and at Sargent.

The Santa Fe Trail

THE Santa Fe Trail in days of prosperous Santa Fe trade extended from Independence, Missouri, to Santa Fe, New Mexico. It was a natural route and was old and well trod by primitive inhabitants long before the early Spanish explorers followed portions of it. The first Americans to follow it were the pioneer hunters and trappers. Pike was the first American explorer who followed it up the Arkansas river. The first successful venture to Santa Fe over the trail was made by Captain William Becknell in 1821, and this date marked the beginning of Santa Fe trade.

The upper Arkansas river route followed up the north side of the Arkansas river from the Cimarron crossing, through the counties of Gray, Finney, Kearny and Hamilton, and is today represented by the main line of the Atchison, Topeka & Santa Fe railway. It was used by those desiring to stop at Bent's Fort, in Colorado, Trinidad, Raton Pass and to Santa Fe. In Finney county there was only one place of historic importance, and that was the United States government crossing, which was made by the survey of 1825. The route recommended by the government crossed the Arkansas river to the south side and entered Mexican territory at a point about six miles up the river from Garden City, near Holcomb. The following is the original description of the crossing as given out by the government surveyors:

"Crossing of the Arkansas river at the Mexican boundary of the 100th degree, just below the bend of the river, at the lower end of a small island with a few trees. At this place there are no banks on either side to hinder wagons. The river is here very shallow, not more than knee deep in a low stage of the water. The bed of the river is altogether sand and is unsafe to stand long on one place with a wagon or it may sink in the sand.

"The upper route is more safe for herding stock and more commodious to the traveler as he will always be sure of wood and water and a sure guide and in general it is easier to kill buffalo for provision."

From this crossing, the trail followed south of the river to Chouteau Island, near the present town of Hartland, which was a place of historic importance. It was to this point that the disastrous expedition of Chouteau (1815-1817) retreated and successfully resisted a Comanche attack. Many things marked this place so strongly that the traveler could not mistake it. It was the largest island of timber in the river and on the south side of the river at the lower end of the island was a thicket of willows.

In 1829 Major Bennett Riley was ordered to take four companies of the 6th Infantry and accompany a trader caravan to the western frontier. He escorted the caravan to Chouteau Island without any molestation whatever. He camped on the north bank of the Arkansas and watched the American wagons disappear in the desert wastes of Mexican territory. They had gone but a short distance when they were attacked by Indians. Major Riley went to their assistance, although he knew the gravity of taking his troops on foreign territory. The Indians retreated, but he went one day more with the traders. He camped at Chouteau until their return and was beset by Indians all summer.

From Chouteau Island the route turned south to "Wagon Bed Spring" of the Cimarron. This was a much safer and better watered route than the one by way of Cimarron crossing.

The Cimarron crossing was a shorter, but more dangerous cut-off to Santa Fe. There was less water and fuel and the Indians were more hostile. It crossed Haskell,

Grant and Morton counties to the southwest corner of the state.

During the first years the trade was largely carried on by detached parties who used pack animals to carry their merchandise. But the loss incurred from the raids of hostile Indians soon made it necessary to join for common safety, and they began moving in trains.

There was a gradual growth of the Santa Fe trade from 1821 to 1843. At the close of that period, the Santa Fe trade was brought to a sudden stop by the closing of all Mexican frontier ports of entry by a proclamation of Santa Ana. He believed the Americans were aiding and sympathizing with the Texans, who had declared their independence of Mexico.

It was not until the trouble with Mexico was settled, or until 1850, that this great overland trail again became the path of a constantly increasing tide of trade and travel. During the early years the trail which the wagons followed was strewed along with the bones of horses, oxen and men, who had died on the way from hunger, thirst and exhaustion or from attacks of Indians. But after the restrictions of the Mexican trade were removed and New Mexico and California became a part of the Union, the trade and travelers again increased in volume until caravans of emigrants and traders moved along the trail through Southwestern Kansas in almost as continuous a line as the trains of the Santa Fe railroad of today.

D. W. Barton states that the famous Cimarron crossing on the Arkansas was at Ingalls, and he pointed out the exact place, just west of his home where he had seen many caravans cross the river. The old ruts made by the trampling of ox teams, the wheels of government wagons, prairie schooners and pack mules, are still visible at points on the hills, both north and south of the river at Ingalls. He says there was not much traffic on the Santa Fe trail after the Santa Fe railroad was built. The Indians were still hostile toward the caravans and he recalls how they utterly destroyed the last wagon train which attempted to cross his range in 1873.

The same general route of the old Santa Fe trail, as it crossed this region, is still used as a national highway. But, the new trail has been straightened, the ruts graded up by modern machinery, and the soil covered over with a lasting grade of cement, or gravelled. The trail of today winds like a white ribbon through fields of grain and pastures of blooded stock. Its stream of traffic is immensely greater than ever in olden times, resembling more the thoroughfare of a city than it does a country road.

Thousands of travelers pass along this famous overland avenue every year. Luxurious, high-powered passenger buses, great trucks, and vans loaded with merchandise. The sad part is that it has lost its identity and is now called U.S. Highway 50 South. There is nothing in the state of Kansas that has more historic importance than the Santa Fe trail. It is many years older than the state itself. Millions of American people would be delighted to travel over "the old national highway" if they were rightly directed. It should stand distinctly as a marked highway across the state, and spots of particular interest should be so marked by fitting monuments.

The old John Beatty ranch on the Cimarron River south of Richfield, Kansas, was the scene of a tragedy on the Santa Fe Trail in the early 50's. A man by the name of Alexander, grand uncle of J. T. Alexander of Mullinville, Kansas, in company with four other men, left their homes in Illinois and followed the Santa Fe Trail from Independence, Missouri, to Santa Fe, New Mexico, with three wagons loaded with dry goods. They arrived safely and sold their calico for $2 a yard, and were paid with silver ware and silver bullion. On their return trip they got as far as the Cimarron river, where they made camp.

That night, Indians came and drove off their horses. They buried their silver, piled their wagons on top of it and burned them, and then started for their homes on foot. Their ammunition was used up before they reached Independence, Missouri, and they were in a famished condition when they reached that point. The buried bullion has never been discovered.

The Kansas National Forest Reserve and The Big Game Preserve

IN the spring of 1906 the government set aside an area consisting of 165,000 acres as a National Forest Reserve. This was a part of the government's reclamation work in Western Kansas. The land lay south of the Arkansas river in the sand hill area of Finney, Kearny, Hamilton, Grant and Haskell counties, to the Colorado line. This land was set aside for the purpose of experimental tree planting, with the idea of transforming the almost bleak sand hills into a forest which would be a blessing to mankind in the next generation.

Orders were issue by the government in the fall of 1905 to commence work preparing the ground, and the next spring 1,000,000 trees were planted. For several years a like number were planted and the original plans were to continue until the entire tract should be planted. A federal nursery was established in 1908 two miles west of Garden City, where the poor farm is located. Another nursery was established in 1911 on Section 26, Township 24, Range 33 West, which is now within the present State Game Preserve. The reason for the establishment of two nurseries was for the purpose of testing out trees grown on a heavy soil and on a sandy soil. Experimental plantings were tried out for a period of years with pines, spruce, cedars and hardwoods of different age stock.

In 1906 the administration of the reserve was under Forest Supervisor C. A. Scott of the Nebraska National Forest Reserve. H. R. Shockley of the same forest was in charge in 1907 and until July 8, 1908. These men were only here at certain periods of the year. On July 8, 1908, the government established an office at Garden City with B. R. H. d'Allemand in charge as forest supervisor. He had two assistants, one in charge of nurseries, and the other had charge of range administration.

Mr. d'Allemand was selected for this reserve because of his experience in both forestry and grazing administration. He was a graduate of the University of Nebraska, having specialized in forestry. He helped with the nursery and planting operations in the Nebraska National Forest Reserve in 1903-4-5. From there he was transferred to the Pike National Forest in Colorado to assist in the nursery and planting operations of that forest. In 1906 he was transferred to the Santa Barbara National Forest Reserve of California, to take charge of the nursery and planting operations of that forest.

A short time after Mr. d'Allemand took charge of this reserve, the whole grazing area was put under the administration of the office in Garden City, and all cattle and horses were grazed under permits issued to the stockmen. Fifty cents was charged per head for the six months grazing period. Twenty-five per cent of the grazing receipts reverted back to the counties in which the government land was located, to be used for road work, and an additional ten per cent was spent through the government also for road improvement in the counties. L. E. Thomas, who lived in this county for many years and was well versed in range problems, was selected as Forest Ranger and had charge of the reserve range from Garden City to the Colorado line.

Under the Act of June, 1906, any land that was tillable within the reserve was restored to entry as it was applied for.

Every other section of land south of the Santa Fe railroad right of way for a distance of ten miles belonged to the various stockmen and ranchers, they having bought it from the railroad. In 1912 the government passed an act which allowed the blocking of their lands which were within the boundary of the Forest Reserve. This was much better for the ranchers and simplified matters of range administration.

The success of tree planting in the Western Kansas sand hill area did not prove very satisfactory. At that time the region was more arid and the evaporation too great and the government decided to abandon the project. In December, 1915, it was all restored to homestead entry, except five sections held as a State Game Preserve.

In a short time every acre in the forest reserve had been filed on, but in most cases as soon as final proof was made the land was deeded to ranchers and other land owners. When people first began to settle in Finney county the sand hills were barren of all vegetation except soap weeds and some sage brush, the reason no doubt being because of prairie fires which burned over the area. Now it affords excellent grazing. Mr. d'Allemand and Mr. Thomas have found as many as thirty different grasses growing on one section.

In 1915 five sections, or approximately 3,200 acres, were deeded to the state as a "big game preserve," the rest of the reserve having been homesteaded. Its closest point to Garden City is about one mile south of town and from there extends a distance of three miles back into the sand hills. It is the home of nine head of buffalo and a variety of game birds, and is supervised by a deputy game warden.

The Garden City Experiment Station

THE Garden City Experiment Station is located four and one-half miles northeast of Garden City. It was established June 14, 1907, for the purpose of carrying out experimental and demonstration work adapted to climatic and soil conditions of Southwest Kansas. Since 1910 the Federal Investigations in Dry-Land Agriculture and the State Experimental work on irrigation, crop variety testing, nursery work and other minor experiments have been in charge of a Federal employee and the station superintendent.

The superintendents since the beginning of the station in 1907 have been: J. E. Payne, 1907; H. R. Reed, 1908-1910; E. F. Chilcott, 1911-13; M. C. Sewell, 1914-15; G. S. Knapp, 1916-19; and F. A. Wagner, 1919 to the present time.

The federal men in charge of Dry-Land Agriculture investigations have been: Ralph Edwards, 1911-12; J. G. Lill, 1913-14; C. B. Brown, 1915-17; F. A. Wagner, 1918-19; F. E. Keating, 1919-21; E. H. Coles, 1922-28; and R. L. Von Treba, 1929 to the present time.

On June 21, 1912, the state board of regents secured a ninety-nine-year lease on the land which is owned by Finney county. The Garden City Station comprises 320 acres of land, forty acres of which was broken in 1907. At that time the remainder was covered with native buffalo grass, but at the present time approximately 190 acres are under cultivation. Of this 40 acres first broken, 148 tenth-acre plats were appropriated for experimental work in dry-land agriculture in co-operation with the United States Department of Agriculture.

During the year 1911 a pumping plant was installed by the Garden City Commercial Club, county commissioners of Finney county, the State Agricultural College and the irrigation investigations of the United States Department of Agriculture. The installation was completed in December, 1911. The purpose of the pumping plant was to carry on experiments as to amount and seasons of watering. The investigations are still being carried on. The station now has a new pumping plant under construction, and a large reservoir to hold surplus water from pumps.

The experiments now being carried on are on sorghum varieties and types such as combine and silage, wheat varieties and alfalfa and a few minor crops. The dry-land projects include rotation methods of planting and cultivation.

The buildings on the station include a house for the superintendent, one for the United States Department of Agriculture Agronomist and three tenement houses for the station help. An office, implement shed, dairy barn, hay barn, horse barn, silo, milk house and hog house. The station has seven head of horses and four head of mules for field work. Also a varied number of hogs and Holstein cattle but these are not used for experimental purposes.

On the dry-land project, there is a weather instrument yard which records the daily temperature, wind velocity, precipitation and evaporation.

Southwestern Kansas

IN 1855 the "Bogus" Legislature of Kansas formed Washington county. It included all of Southwestern Kansas, and much other territory. Washington county was attached to Allen county for judicial purposes. (Laws of 1855.)

The Legislature of 1857 cut down Washington county almost to its present size, but there was no provision made for the territory in this part of the state, and it was left nameless. (Laws of 1857.)

Eight new counties were created by the Legislature of 1860. Among these was the county of Peketon, which included all that part of the state west of the sixth principal meridian to New Mexico, and south of Township 16, i.e., the entire area of Kansas west of the present Marion County and south of the present Saline county. (General Laws of 1860.)

The Legislature of 1865 wiped out the county of Peketon and enlarged Marion county to include all the territory in Peketon. In 1867 Marion was reduced to very nearly its present form, and the southwest corner of Kansas was again left without a name.

During July and August of 1872 this region was surveyed. The first selection of land was made by the Santa Fe railroad, which occurred January 18, 1873. That same winter the entire area of Southwest Kansas was divided into counties and named as follows: Hamilton, Kearny, Sequoyah, Stanton, Grant, Arapahoe, Kansas, Stevens, Seward, Scott, Wichita, Greeley, Lane, Gray and Meade. A land office was located at Larned in 1874 for this part of the state.

With the building of railroads through Western Kansas the Indians were finally driven from the plains and herded into reservations; and the buffaloes were soon all slaughtered by the hunters. Practically all the land thus vacated belonged to the United States government, or to the railroad companies. The Santa Fe land grant in this region comprised a strip twenty miles wide and one hundred thirty miles long of alternate sections, extending from near Dodge City to the Colorado line. Most of this grant west of Dodge lay in the Arkansas river valley, the most favorable between eastern Kansas and the Rocky Mountains. The Indian and the buffalo were gone, and here lay thousands of acres of good grazing land waiting only for cattle. The cattlemen had the free consent of both government and railroad to use the range, and they hastened to take possession. Almost immediately this big expanse of pasture was covered with the longhorn Texas cattle and cowboys. The "long trail" from Texas was the means of stocking this vast area quickly.

The Cattle Range and the Cowboys

"'Twas good to live when all the sod
  Without no fence nor fuss,
  Belonged in partnership to God
  The government and us."

The real history of all Western Kansas began with the cattle which were first driven up over the trail from Texas. Those drives marked the beginning of that brief period during which the cattlemen reigned supreme; and was one of the most interesting epochs in the development of this region.

The story of those veteran cowmen of the south who dared to drive their cattle over the long trails to shipping points in Kansas is full of thrills and romance. But the life of the drovers and cowboys who accompanied the herds was by no means an easy one. They endured constant exposure and privations. Their life was always in danger. Accidents, stampedes, marauding bands of Indians and horse and cattle thieves harassed them continually. Those cowboys were the real pioneers of the prairie, and their charge, the long-legged Texas cow, has been dubbed "the mother of the West".

The noted firm of Barton Brothers introduced the cattle industry into the western third of Kansas. They left southern Texas in February, 1872, with 3,000 head of

D. W. (Doc) Barton, who arrived in Southwestern Kansas in July, 1872, with 3,000 head of Texas cattle. He was the first man to establish a ranch west of Old Fort Dodge.

long-horn cattle and headed for the Arkansas river in Western Kansas. However, there were many tribes of hostile Indians and gangs of Mexican desperadoes between them and their destination. They were forced to abandon their original plan of crossing the Indian Territory, and follow the western or Pecos trail, whose course was up the Pecos river valley in New Mexico and on north to Colorado. Striking the Arkansas river at Pueblo they followed its course down to the present town of Garden City, and camped beneath a big, old cottonwood tree. Its giant trunk had been half burned and almost stripped of branches to furnish fuel for Santa Fe trail travellers, but it furnished a marker for their camp site that could be seen many miles out on the range by the cowboys. They remained at this location until fall, when they established ranch headquarters for the winter in dugouts built in the bank of the Arkansas river at Pierceville. From that time on their cattle range was south of the river, between Pierceville and Cimarron, and south to the Red river of Texas. The personnel of the Barton Brothers company in charge of cattle at this time was D. W. (Doc) Barton, Al Barton, D. Eubank, and Tom Connell. They were assisted by twelve drovers and cowboys.

Indians of different tribes occupied the country; some just hunting while passing through to other reservations; others out scouting around for mischief and on the warpath. But some of the tribes lived here the year 'round. In the year 1876 Mr. Barton kept a herd of one hundred and sixty good saddle horses up on Pawnee creek. That winter the Northern Sioux Indians were also wintering on the Pawnee. They were out on the warpath and short of horses, but they did not bother Mr. Barton's herd, and his herds of cattle were never at any time molested by the Indians.

Mr. Barton was here with his cattle before the first structure of any kind was built in Dodge City, and he has lived in or near there during all these years, and has witnessed every step in its development. He knew all the famous characters of Dodge City and the frontier and many of them were employed to work in his outfits. The "Slaughter Kid" worked for him three years. He had a bad reputation, but Mr. Barton says he was a good hand. Ben Hodges, the reputed desperado and horse thief, also worked for Mr. Barton for a few years. He was well acquainted with the Daltons, Billy the Kid and all the so-called bad characters that made Dodge City famous. But he says there was just one cowboy buried on Boot Hill, the rest were gamblers and a rough element that ran the town.

Mr. Barton gradually bred his herds up until he had a good grade, and his cattle business prospered until the blizzard of 1886. At that time he lost eleven thousand head of grade cattle and eight hundred that were registered. Mr. Barton still lives at Ingalls, Kansas, and is eighty years of age, but he appears to be many years younger. For many years he has been engaged in wheat ranching.

Those men who made cattle raising their business in the early days were forced to live always on the edge or just beyond settlement. This was necessary in order that they might graze their stock on the uninhabited wilderness beyond. Very few of those early ranchmen owned much of the land they used. They usually owned the land on which the ranch buildings were located and also the watering places on their range. They obtained this by homesteading or buying it from the railroad company. In this way each held a monopoly within the agreed boundary limits of his range. They paid no taxes; they paid no rent; their range was free. About the only expense was the wages paid for help. The grass was very nutritious and they depended entirely upon it for feed. In this semi-arid climate it cured upon the ground and became as good for winter grazing as for summer use. Unless the winters were too severe, cattle grew fat without other feed.

A few years after the Bartons arrived in this region with their first herd of Texas cattle, trails were opened up through the Indian Territory to Dodge City, and at once it became the most popular of all the shipping points in

Kansas for the Texas trail herds. At first the herds were allowed to feed along the trail only in passing. They soon found, however, that it was good business to arrive at the shipping point early and allow the cattle to graze on the Kansas grass for a month or two before putting them on the market. Many times they were forced to hold them on the prairie for quite a period waiting for a buyer.

There were different ways of disposing of a herd when they arrived at the shipping point. They might sell to eastern buyers, or ship on their own account. Or they might drive them on into open territories and sell direct to ranchers; but they much preferred to sell to buyers on the prairies. In the beginning of the drives the Texans sold their cattle by the head, and they had to be paid in gold. As they became better acquainted with the buyers, they accepted exchange on Kansas City, St. Louis and New York and learned to sell by the pound. Cattle of any age or condition above four years of age was called beef.

Some of the buyers were Indian agents who contracted for herds to be delivered to the reservations. Other government contracts were for the use of soldiers who were garrisoned at various places on the prairies. In those years of the cattle trade herds were being moved continually by the various owners and buyers in all directions across Western Kansas. During these drives a number of the cattle would always break away from the main herds and were left behind on the range. These were the so-called "wild cattle" which the early settlers found roaming free on the prairie.

The Texas cattle of trail days had long slender legs with the backbone prominent. The bones were covered with little flesh and still less fat. The face was narrow with a pointed nose, but the heads were invariably topped with long, sharp horns. The average length of the horns was between five and six feet. It has been said "the old-time Texas ranger was about fifty-fifty on horns and the rest of him". The horns were so long that the drovers experienced the greatest difficulty in getting the animals through the car doors when the shipments were made.

The eastern buyers began early to place yearling steers on ranches surrounding Dodge City. At the end of two years they would market them at a big profit. Many of the cattle driven up were bought by ranchers who used them to stock this country. And many men went to Texas

Trail Herd

and bought and drove up their own herds. It took but a short time for all the available grazing lands near Dodge City to be taken up. As others came in desiring range they began to reach out in surrounding territory. Before 1880 the entire area from Dodge City to the Colorado line had all been parcelled out, and was claimed by various ranchers. Their branded herds mingled more or less together as they ranged over this territory.

The cattlemen usually lived comfortably at ranch headquarters or in town. But the cowboys who took charge of the herds were scattered day and night over their vast range of prairies.

They were always on patrol, forming an army of volunteer mounted guards, and were a big aid in protecting the frontier. This region was not sufficiently organized to have much protection by the law, and the carrying of deadly weapons was a prevailing custom of that day. The cowboys were always armed and were forced sometimes to be a "law unto themselves", especially when it came to dealing out justice to cattle and horse thieves and other notorious offenders of the law. The warnings of the Indian outbreaks were swiftly carried by them to the settlers, and also to the military authorities. Many times the cowboys could settle Indian troubles themselves; it was a well-known fact that the Indians had more fear and respect for the cowboys than they had for the soldiers.

The cowboy holds a prominent place in American history and will always be a favorite character in American literature. The original cowboys of the far southwest may have been the toughs they were pictured, but after the civil war the cowboy was certainly a different character. Northern men of all classes joined the ranks of the cow-punchers. Farmers' sons, college men and sons of noblemen from across the seas; but it didn't matter who they had been or what they had done, they won a place on the plains as "cowboy" after they had proven what they could do.

The qualities of a genuine cowboy were good horsemanship and a skillful use of the lariat. He suffered more hardships than any other type of pioneer. His work kept him always in the open and he was forced to endure constant exposure and fatigue. He did not desert the herd to protect himself even in the worst blizzard, tornadoes or hail and thunder storms. He may have been rough acting, but not a desperado. He was always mounted on a well-trained horse, and in his work with the cattle on the range controlled only by the voice and never used a whip. During a threatened stampede they would circle the herd and hold them together by singing.

It is impossible at this late date to collect all the names of those first venturesome men who dared to carry on their business among the Indians and the outlaws. The country was inhabited only by wild beasts and deadly rattlesnakes. Those men gave no thought to preserving historical data. They knew little and cared less about the political and geographical divisions of the region they were occupying. They rode from Dodge City to Colorado and from the Arkansas river to the Red river of Texas, but the distance was not gauged by miles. Their saddle horses were not equipped with modern mileage registers; they travelled by time. They had no idea how many miles it was between certain points, but they knew exactly how many hours, or days, or weeks it would take to get there, barring unexpected delays.

The following information concerning the various cattle, horse and sheep ranchers was secured from old files of the Garden City newspapers. Each issue contained a directory of the various ranchers and their range:

The Hardesty brothers were among the very earliest to range cattle in this territory. During the '70's they ranged from Dodge City to the Colorado line. Later they had headquarters on Beaver Creek in "No Man's Land." Their main brand was lazy bar S on left hip, and lazy bar W on left side.

One of the first cattle and sheep ranches to be established was that of Meyers, who had headquarters at Lakin and his range was between Lakin and Sherlock. The earliest known horse ranch was that of H. Porter. His headquarters were on the river south of Sherlock. In 1881 Fred Harvey bought the range of both Porter and Meyers, which gave him the entire range between Lakin and Garden City, and his round-up covered the territory between the Arkansas and Canadian rivers. He brought his cattle down from Wallace, Kansas. Major Falls was in charge of his cattle operations and S. H. Corbett was one of the cowboys. The brand was X Y, and it was known as the X Y range.

N. J. Earp, post office Garden City. Brand, N E high on right side. A mark in left ear with under and upper slit. Range at Point of Rocks.

A. J. Shorb, post office Garden City. Brand, X S high on left side. Range on Pawnee.

D. R. Menke, dealer in thoroughbred sheep. Range three miles northeast of Garden City.

A. F. Lee, Deerfield, Kansas. Range on Arkansas river between Sherlock and Deerfield.

W. H. Herford, Garden City. Range on Pawnee with Churchill brothers. Cattle branded with flying H on either or both sides. Ear mark, swallow fork left. Under stop right. Horse brand flying H on left shoulder.

D. W. Barton, post office Pierceville. Brand OS on left side, crop off the right ear.

M. L. Lavender, post office Felix, Finney county. Range on Pawnee. Horses branded ML connected, on left shoulder. Cattle branded on the left side.

A. S. Van Patten, Finney county. Cattle branded VAN on left side. Horses branded VP connected, on left shoulder.

Henry Barton, Pierceville, range on south side of the river opposite the town. Branded on the left side and hip with flying V.

Alex M. Kinkaid, post office Garden City. Range twenty miles north on Pawnee. Cattle branded XK on left side. Ear mark, slit in left ear.

August G. Wolfley, Pierceville. Range on Crooked creek. Cattle branded AW on left side; increase brand on neck; horse brand AW on left hip.

Churchill brothers, post office Loyal, ranch on head of Pawnee. Cattle branded on left side J-C. Additional brands, J on left hip. Horses and mules branded C on left shoulder.

F. E. Despres, post office Garden City. Cattle branded O on right hip and 4 on right shoulder. Horses branded

F. D. on right shoulder. Range four and a half miles north of Garden City.

W. L. Curtis, post office Garden City. Range twenty miles north on Pawnee. Cattle branded WLC on left side. Horses branded C on left shoulder.

Halloway Cattle Company. Peter Van Os, manager. Address, Garden City. Range at Point of Rocks, near Sidney, Finney county. Brand HC on left shoulder.

D. C. Sullivan, Spring Ranch, Hamilton county, post office Lakin.

Barkley and Gregory, Garden City. Thoroughbred and graded Cotswold and Merino sheep. Range on Sherlock section, northeast.

Keyser brothers, post office at Garden City. Range north side of the Arkansas river, eight miles east of Pierceville. Cattle branded bar H on left shoulder and bar H on left hip. Ear marked with swallow fork in right. Additional brands, leg, double H on left hip; ear mark, crop right and under slope left. Also bar T on left side and — on thigh; ear mark, swallow fork and under bit in left.

S. A. Bullard, post office address Dodge City. Range south side of Arkansas between Pierceville and Garden City. Cattle branded cross ++ on left shoulder and circle on left hip; also some with bar on shoulder. Horse brand bar on shoulder; others were branded with cross on shoulder.

The Union Cattle Company. A part of the cattle ranging on the Pawnee, 20 miles north of Garden City, in charge of M. L. Lavender. Balance of the herd was in the Indian Territory. All cattle branded UC. B. Haskell was the general manager, Atchison, Kansas.

A. B. Boylan. Address Lakin. Range, Arkansas river and on the Pawnee with Cranston brothers. Cattle branded B.

E. E. Evans, address Cowland, Kansas. Cattle branded cross ++; also figure 2 on right hip. Horse brand, figure 2 on left shoulder. Range at Hackberry Springs in Finney county.

Isaac Hurst and Sons. Post office Garden City with range north. Cattle branded and owned, viz: those branded IH on left shoulder by Charles Hurst; IH on left side by Wm. Hurst; IH on left hip by Isaac Hurst; those branded with lazy V (<) on left side just back of shoulder, and (Λ) on side and hip, owned by Albert Hurst.

Moss and Moss, post office Loyal, Finney county. Care of Churchill Bros. Texas cattle branded J on left leg.

D. H. Atwater, Sherlock, Kansas. Range near Sherlock. Branded A on left shoulder and T on left hip.

John O'Laughlin, Lakin. Range at Wagon Bed Springs, on the Cimarron thirty miles south. Cattle branded (pig pen) on left side. Ear mark crop off and two splits in right.

D. Fay, Cowland, cattle branded FAY. Range at Hackberry Springs, Finney county.

Dr. A. Sabine, range five miles north of Garden City. Joe Beeson, foreman. Brand Λ-S. Also owned all UC bar cattle in Kansas.

X Y ranch, H. M. Falls, manager, Deerfield. Cattle branded X Y on left side. Left ear cropped.

Lock Locke, post office Lakin. Range on north side of Arkansas river, between Hartland and Coolidge. Cattle branded IXL bar on left side.

Inge Brothers and Vinzant, Garden City. Brand I N on left side and V on left hip. Range south and east of Deerfield.

Phi Norman Horse Ranch. Headquarters ten miles north of Garden City. Brand, Greek letter Phi on left shoulder. The Phi stud comprises the following stallions: Duke of Monmouth, Lord Balfour, Lafayette, Jim, Frank.

B. F. Smith, Garden City. Breeder of short-horn cattle. Brand box S on left hip.

Cimarron and Crooked Creek Cattle Company. R. E. Steele, manager, range on Cimarron river. Brand, crooked L on left shoulder and hip.

I. R. Holmes, Garden City. Range northwest. Cattle brand T cross on left side.

Goff and Morgan, Garden City. Range north of Arkansas river. Brand D G - on left side.

B. L. Stotts, dealer in thoroughbred and grade sheep. Range Point of Rock.

Settlement of Southwest Kansas

For several years after Western Kansas was being opened for settlement, the counties in this region remained unorganized and had no population except the cattlemen. They were the lords of the land, but had no interest in it except as it provided grass and water for their stock. They ranged their cattle over thousands of acres without the restriction of a single fence, but they were doomed to witness a marvelous change in the country.

The supremacy of the cattlemen was of short duration. The railroad company, which had been the prime means of beginning the cattle industry, was also the chief inducement for people to come in and homestead the land. Just as soon as it was known that the Indians had abandoned this region people all over the United States began to study the maps of Western Kansas.

The spring of 1878 opened with plentiful moisture. As far as the eye could reach the short-grass plains were covered with a carpet of green, unmarked by roads and highways. Not a sign of civilization except the iron rails of the Santa Fe railroad. Not a tree or a shrub was here to break the vision, nothing in sight but the great herds of Texas cattle grazing at will in this vacant "back yard" of Kansas settlement.

But the eyes of the cowboys who guarded the herds began anxiously to watch the distant horizon, for they had heard the rumors of coming settlers. As the days passed, sure enough, tiny dust clouds appeared far to the east and grew, and soon they could discern covered wagons lumbering slowly, but steadily advancing over the maze of cattle trails. As the hours passed they could hear the shouts of the drivers above the creaking wagons urging their sweating horses or ox teams and tired domestic

Ship of the plains at anchor

cattle toward the valleys of the Pawnee or Arkansas rivers. And they could see written across the canvas tops in crude letters, "WESTERN KANSAS OR BUST".

The vanguard of grangers had arrived. They were hardy pioneers, looking for a home, a place to settle and rear their families. They were not daunted by the great vacant expanses of rolling prairie and level plains. Even though it looked like a barren waste, they knew it held possibilities. They were not dismayed by the fact that it was sparingly watered by the few creeks and the Arkansas river, which was usually dry several months of the year. Scarcer and scarcer grew the timber as they made their way west, until all that there was grew on the islands in the river, beyond the reach of annual prairie fires.

But they did not complain because the land before them lay bare to all the garish sunshine of the year, without the shadow of a tree or the seclusion of primeval forests. Their eyes roamed in every direction and they were not dismayed when they saw only the townsites of ants and prairie dogs rising in dwarf mounds above the level height of the close-curled buffalo grass. They were thinking of a time in the future, when the buffalo grass would be replaced by tame grasses and by fields of golden grain. They dreamed of cities which would spring up to replace that debris of animal and insect architecture, which alone had littered the landscape for centuries.

To the landless it seemed a great boon to have the opportunity to settle upon government land and acquire fee simple title to a quarter section of land for a mere living upon it. Even many who had farms or places of business in the east decided they could better their conditions by disposing of their property and settling upon the cheap, yet fertile land of the west. Briefly, it may be stated that the heads of families, or persons over 21 years of age, were entitled under the acts of congress to 480 acres of land, 160 as a homestead, 160 as pre-emption, and 160 as timber claim. Only 320 acres, however, could be entered at the same time. Five years' residence was required on a homestead claim before patent could be issued. The settler had six months after he filed on land before establishing a residence and commencing his improvements. He might also be temporarily absent six months. Pre-emption required immediate settlement. After six months, by paying $1.25 per acre, patent could be secured. Within limits of railroad land, $2.50 per acre was paid. No settlement was required under the timber culture act. The claimant was required to break five acres of land during the first year, five acres during the second year, and cultivate the first five, and the third year plant five acres to trees, tree seeds or cuttings. All this could be done by an agent, and a non-resident could acquire title to land under the provision of this act. Since there was only one timber claim in each government township, and it could be owned by a non-resident, this class of claims were soon all taken up. But the job of plowing and cultivating the timber claims supplied some of the settlers with money so they could stay on their homesteads. In many cases, in lieu of payment for their labor, they were given title to the timber claim.

Naturally, the cattlemen were resentful of the coming of the settlers and homesteaders who kept arriving singly and in groups during the years of 1878 and '79. Coming in wagons, or dropping off the trains along the railroad sidings of the Santa Fe, they were met by the cowboys, who did their best to discourage them from settling here.

"Say, let us tell you something," they would begin. "It never rains out there and you will starve to death. Dodge City is as far west as civilization will ever go, and that place is hardly a fit place for a civilized man with a family." From that time on there was a struggle between the grangers and the cattlemen as to who would occupy the land.

In 1878 there was a sprinkling of homesteaders scattered over the prairies, and the next year, 1879, many more filed on claims. Nature seemed to favor the efforts of those first settlers, even if the cattlemen didn't. Everything planted that first year yielded bountifully, and the country gave out every promise to those desiring to make permanent settlement. Towns were established and dugouts and sod houses of homesteaders dotted the plains, where they lived as snug as "wasps" in their mud houses. James Craig came to Garden City in March, 1879, and he tells how they located the claims:

"I found Buffalo Jones and Bill Stapelton on the job ready to show people over the country, and locate them on government land, and for some time after my arrival they did a thriving business. I remember driving around with Jones and Stapelton locating people. The land office

Home of Ira J. Wolf in Finney County. Mr. Wolf and R. E. Stotts in the foreground.

at that time was located at Larned, and Jones received a report every day of all land located the previous day. We would start out in the morning with perhaps six or eight people who wanted to locate. It was my job when we started from a known corner to count the revolutions of the wheel of the vehicle we were riding in. A handkerchief tied to a wheel and knowing the distance around the wheel was a quick way to measure between the corners, and of keeping track of the section, township and range. We could tell the prospective settler just how far we were from Garden City."

It has been said of that first year that it was a "will o' the wist which lured hundreds of homesteaders into this region, only to have their hopes blasted by drouth during the next succeeding years." The dry weather set in the fall of 1878, continued all through the year of 1879, and with little intermission during 1880-81-82.

In those years, in spite of the fact that the settlers congregated to pray for rain and for relief from climatic conditions, it never rained, and the country looked like a parched desert. The very grass would crunch and fall to powder beneath the feet of the settlers. At the end of four years, few of the first enthusiastic people who had taken claims were left. Even as the "Arabs quietly folded their tents and moved away", so did the first settlers, but instead of folding up tents, they unfolded their old canvas tops and spread them back in place over the weather-beaten wagon bows. Beneath the old sign "WESTERN KANSAS OR BUST" they scrawled in bright new letters, "Busted by God", and the heads of the famishing horses that were hitched to those "ships of the Great Plains" were headed back east toward "wife's folks".

It has been said that all who remained did so because they couldn't get away. But that is not true. Those who kept on did so because they could, and because they wanted to. They had a persistence born partly of faith in the country and partly of a dogged determination to stick to their possessions to the end. They refused to be beaten by climate or any other circumstance.

Many had come into the country well dressed, but after two or three years their clothing was worn out and they had not the means to buy new. Socks became a luxury. Blue jeans covered the worn cloth trousers of the men and they were not particular as to the style of their coats. Their stiff derby hats were dented and battered but continued to do service. The women made over the good clothes they had brought with them for their growing children, and for themselves made new cotton dresses. And then as their plight became known boxes and barrels of clothing began arriving from relatives and benevolent organizations in the east. These donations were hailed with delight, although the housewives were often filled with despair and disappointment when they tried to fit out their families with "used and discarded clothing."

But it was not so much a question of what to wear, as what to eat? The Rev. A. C. McKeever, a pioneer of

Gathering Chips

Finney county, recently said in an address to the old settlers at Garden City:

"There were times when the flowers did not bloom, the grass did not get green, and the larder was low. If it had not been for the jack rabbits and the wild ducks and geese, a great many of the early settlers would have found it much harder.

"I remember hearing about a case in the early days of a man who had come out west to make his fortune. He had faith, he was ambitious, and he worked hard. The report went out through Ohio, Indiana and Illinois that the people were starving to death on the plains, and the good people of Ohio sent a young man out here to investigate, and provided a purse whereby the suffering might be relieved. This young fellow from Ohio came to the man who had staked his all to make his fortune. Of course he did not want to turn over the money to anyone who was not in need, so he was very careful in his investigation and cautious in his movements. He asked the settler how he was getting along, and true to the policy of the early settlers, he was told what a wonderful country it was, and how delightful to live in such rarefied air, and told about the beautiful sunsets. Then the would-be-benefactor asked him where they got their provisions, and told him that word had gone out that the settlers were starving and that a carload of provisions had been sent out for those in need, but he was so glad to learn there was no need here. The settler was silent for a few minutes, then he said, "Well, you know, we got along fine last year and expected to this year; but our dog died, and you know, it takes a damned good dog to catch rabbits.'"

There was little money in the country among the settlers, except the pension checks received from the government by the civil war soldiers. The chief industry among the homesteaders was picking up buffalo and cattle bones of which there appeared to be an inexhaustible supply all over the prairies, and hundreds of loads were brought in to points along the railroad to be shipped, for which the settlers received five or six dollars a ton.

Mrs. H. W. Crow recalls how her husband and Sim Buckles would go far out on the prairie to gather bones. There were no roads or trails to follow and in order to find their way back to Garden City, they would tie a log under the wagon low enough to drag on the ground to make a mark, so they could follow it home. They would also haul in "buffalo chips" and rick them up like hay stacks to keep them dry for winter fuel.

Another source of income which was obtained in a hard but thrilling way was the catching of wild horses, which were shipped east. In 1880 two men from Pennsylvania came out to Garden City to buy up wild horses to take backeast and sell at retail. They had no difficulty in buying two car loads of fine horses, but a difficulty arose when they offered a $1000 bill in payment. It was im-

Deer shot by Bob and Sam Craig in an early-day hunt in Western Kansas

possible to get it changed, and they finally had to go to Larned where the United States land office was located.

In those days C. J. Jones, the Craig brothers and others would go out antelope hunting. They would fix up sleds so they could get over the ground quickly and it was an easy way to haul in the game. They usually returned with a few, or perhaps a number, and would ship them to Topeka or Kansas City, receiving four or five dollars apiece for them.

N. F. Weeks, who with his brother, J. W. Weeks, located at Garden City May 3, 1878, has left a written record of some of those early hunting trips:

"About 1879 white-tailed deer were more or less plentiful in the sand hills, and Jones and others made frequent trips into the sand hills. Jones was always accompanied by his favorite stag hound. On one of these trips I accompanied him, and reaching a place where the Dan Larmor ranch was afterwards located, a fine buck was sighted and the hounds took up the chase. We were riding in a platform spring wagon, Jones driving and I holding the gun. As the chase warmed up Jones kept urging the team to greater speed. It was a mad rush across the hills, the wagon swayed and bounced and at times it almost upset. The deer headed for the Island in the river. Finally we struck some particularly rough and boggy ground and we both took headers from the wagons. Jones managed to land on his feet and kept on running. Just how I struck the ground I have never been able to tell, for it was like being hit by a cyclone, but I saw Jones plunging into the water and heard him shouting to bring the gun. I finally reached the island where the dog was holding the deer and Jones dispatched it with a bullet.

"Parts of the wagon and pieces of the harness were scattered for miles down the river and the wagon had to be sent to Sterling for repairs. That did not bother Jones in the least, he got what he went after and did not count the cost. Jones always had a lot of hunting dogs and when he was unable to supply them with meat they formed the habit of raiding the butcher shops of Halsey and Butts, and frequently would carry off a whole quarter of beef, for which Jones would pay without question. One of his favorite hounds disappeared once and he went to Colorado in search of him, thinking he had followed some emigrant wagon off, but the dog was never found.

"Early in the fall of 1879 Jones suggested a hunt in the Cimarron river country for buffalo. At that time he had a large number of wolf and stag hounds, and others of like character, and recently having secured a high-grade pup, he wanted to try it out on big game. So accompanied by my brother, Joe Weeks, and George Edwards, son of Jesse Edwards, we left Garden City with two wagons. I rode with Jones and we traveled southwest toward the Cimarron. Antelope were plentiful in the sand hills, and we soon sighted a large herd. I shall never forget that sight. The sun was just coming up and its first rays fell on the brownish-red and white of the grazing animals. Immediately the hunting instincts were aroused, every muscle became taut, every nerve in the man seemed to quiver with excitement, and his eyes snapped and glittered as only a man's will when the instincts of the true hunter are aroused.

"On getting within fair shooting distance he could have bagged several easily, but he wanted to see his dogs perform, and suggested that he would cripple an antelope, and then the dogs and the pup would be turned loose. This was done, the leashes were unloosed, and with loud baying the dogs took after the startled and fleeing antelope. Some time elapsed and the older dogs returned to the wagons, but much to Mr. Jones' anxiety the pup failed to show up, so telling the other men to continue their journey to the Cimarron we started in search of the pup. All day we kept up the search, but the pup was never seen again.

"Our water supply gave out and late in the day we headed for the Cimarron where we expected to find water. About nine or ten o'clock that night we came up to the other members of the party. Their supply of water was also exhausted and the river was entirely dry. This was a serious situation. Our horses were already in an exhausted condition, and it was a two days' drive to the Arkansas. There was no water on the way, nothing but the sun-scorched prairie sage brush and withered grass. Early the next day we started and our progress was necessarily slow.

"We made camp the first night, and fortunately there

occurred that rare phenomena of the plains, a dew fell, and eating the dew-covered grass our horses were somewhat refreshed. We were all suffering from thirst, and we ate nothing but crackers all day, and by eating them slowly, a saliva would be started in our dry and parched mouths. Late in the day what a glorious sight unfolded itself. There ahead of us was the Arkansas river, and the water glistened in the sunlight. It was a joyous, life-inspiring scene, and man and beasts quickened their steps. Reaching the water, all rushed to partake of its blessed relief. It was warm and unpalatable, but it quenched the burning thirst. The horses drank with avidity, and when they had had enough for the time, they could not be forced from the river, and finally one of Edwards' horses died. During the torture of those days, Jones was the guiding spirit."

Those pioneer men of Western Kansas who came and who remained in spite of drouths and discouragement, really enjoyed that life as they first found it here. But it was hard on the women, the majority of whom had been reared in homes of comfort and culture in the east. They tried to be optimistic and worked out their part nobly, but they suffered loneliness and privations. Mrs. B. L. Stotts came with her husband to Garden City in 1881, and has since learned to love the country, but she almost shrinks from any mention of those first years. She says:

"I never took any credit to myself for being a pioneer, having gone to Colorado in 1870, when the Indians were still making periodical raids on the settlers. There was some spice in that life, but being a pioneer in Western Kansas was different. The spring and summer we came here, 1881, was very dry. For nine consecutive months there was not a single drop of rain. There were no trees. Some cottonwood cuttings had been set out along the streets of Garden City, but as yet furnished no shade, and the soap weeds, the largest thing here, furnished very little.

"Each day the sun arose in a blaze of glory, each succeeding day more dazzling than the one before. We kept our eyes turned heavenward looking for clouds, not being so presumptious as to expect rain, but merely seeking a dimmer for the intense sunlight. We saw in the mirage limpid lakes of sparkling water, buildings which might have been churches and theaters, and beautiful groves of stately trees, but it all kept just out of reach and the blazing sun shone on. The certainty that it would be on the job again in the morning took away the pleasure of its setting.

"We drank water from driven wells not more than eight or ten feet deep, and rank with alkali. We suffered for ice, though in case of sickness we were sometimes able to get it from the passenger trains.

"The awful monotony was killing. There was nothing to do, nothing to see and no where to go, and should we have attempted to go anywhere we would only have become lost, for there were only a few dim trails leading to the claims of a few settlers, so we women crept about from house to house. There was no use to hurry; we had all the time there was. Our conversation each day was a repetition of that of the day before and always concerned the awfulness of living in such a desert, where the wind and the sun had full sweep.

"Frequently on wash day, a line of clothes would be seen sailing through the air. On one of those occasions after a woman had rescued and washed her clothes for the second time, she was heard to repeat language similar no doubt to some she had heard her husband use. It was a time to try women's souls. I never heard the men complain, and as a sect, I was sure they did not require much to satisfy them. I am sure the children were sensible of their hardships. One day my little son came into the house, threw himself on the floor in the abandonment of grief, and howled out, 'Mamma, will we always have to live here?' and when in my desperation I told him that I thought we would, he, with a more desperate howl, cried out, 'and will we have to die here, too?'

"We old timers smile now when we meet, and it's a knowing smile the newer population does not understand, for we are rich in experience."

The following sketch was written by C. A. Loucks of Lakin, Kansas:

"Probably no woman in the history of the pioneers of Western Kansas has contributed more to the welfare and happiness of humanity during that period than Amy M. Loucks. She was born in Pennsylvania in 1843. She received a high school and academic education. Through association with a brother who was a physician, she became interested in the science of medicine and surgery.

"In 1866 she married William P. Loucks, and in 1879 they moved to Lakin. At that time Kearny county was unorganized territory, as was most of the western part of the state. It was entirely a cow country, there being no substantial settlement. There was no school, churches or other organized society. The nearest doctor was at Dodge City, seventy-five miles away. Lakin was on the Santa Fe railroad and consisted of a depot, an eating house, the house in which the agent lived, a store operated by John O'Laughlin, who supplied cattle ranches, buffalo hunters, and the travelers on the Santa Fe trail, and the town had a saloon.

"Mrs. Loucks ability and helpfulness made her a friend to all who were in distress. She treated their injuries, nursed them to health, or said a prayer at their death. To show her resourcefulness and ability, we may relate a few instances: A man had been scalped by the Indians and left on the prairie for dead. He was found and brought to Lakin. The scalp had not been entirely removed, but was pulled down over his eyes. She replaced the scalp, stitched it with a fiddle string and a common needle, and nursed him back to health, communicated with his relatives in the east and sent him to them. Although the poor fellow lived for many years, he never regained his sanity.

"A posse summoned her to treat a badly wounded prisoner. With a small vial of carbolic acid as an antiseptic, a knitting needle as a probe, and a pair of common pincers, she removed the bullet and saved the man's life.

"At another time, with a razor as a lance and her embroidery scissors, she removed three fingers from the crushed hand of a railroad brakeman.

"In those days the railroad ran immigrant trains. One day the conductor telegraphed Mrs. Loucks to meet the train on its arrival at Lakin. She found a woman who was about to become a mother, and before she could be removed to a private place, it was necessary for Mrs. Loucks to perform the act of mid-wifery on the freight truck on the depot platform.

"A railroad wreck occurred near Lakin in which several employees were killed, and many passengers were injured. Mrs. Loucks administered first aid to a score or more, awaiting the arrival of a special train from Dodge City carrying their railroad surgeon. In appreciation of this act, H. R. Nickerson, the Division Superintendent, and later president of the company, gave her a pass, which courtesy was extended as long as he was connected with the railroad.

"Not only did she minister to the afflicted, but she was always doing those things which promote the general welfare and happiness of the country. In 1879 she organized and taught the first school in Kearny county. This was a subscription school and there were but 17 pupils enrolled, including her two sons. She was instrumental in organizing the first church in Lakin."

The only schools in Southwest Kansas in those early years were financed by private subscriptions. As for text books, they were odds and ends from as many states as there were families represented. Garden City became an organized district the fall of 1880, and was the first to employ a teacher with a certificate. No other districts were organized until 1884.

Churches and Sunday schools were few and far between and were held in private homes or barns, until later years when school houses were built and used for that purpose. Garden City, Sherlock, Pierceville, and all points along the railroad had men who were able to preach and conduct religious services. These were attended by all classes and by a much larger per cent of the people than today, when there are many fine churches.

Services in Garden City were first held in the Landis and Hollinger building, which was built in 1879, or the Red Lion Livery stable. The Rev. H. S. Booth was conducting a service on Sunday in the Red Lion Livery stable when a bunch of drunken cowboys came in and sat down by the stove. They began to feel good as they got warmed up and tried to break up the meeting. B. L. Stotts was sitting pretty close to them and he raised up and asked them politely to keep quiet. But the cowboys took it for a joke and opened up, louder than ever. Mr. Stotts then got up and walked to the front. He asked the minister to let him have the floor for a minute, and he proceeded to address the cowboys.

"Now, if you fellows want to remain in here you are welcome, but if you stay, you will have to behave like men."

He was answered by a drunken twitter. Mr. Stotts then picked up a chair and placed it by the side of Rev. Booth, and he continued.

"The first fellow who makes any disturbance will have to be carried out that door."

The drunken laugh was smothered for Mr. Stotts had calmly sat down by the side of the preacher, and across his knees lay a big six shooter. His fame as a crack shot had never been doubted by anyone. Thus he sat through the service, and the audience remained deadly quiet, if not appreciative.

The early settlers were left entirely on their own resources for amusements. The literary was perhaps the first organization and the programs consisted entirely of "home talent", but they were very interesting and heartily enjoyed. Picnics and dances were common, and holidays were all observed. The first Fourth of July celebration in this region was held at Garden City in 1879. People came in wagons and on horseback for many miles, and they were all surprised that there were so many people really living in the country.

The following was the order of the program.

National salute at daylight, 38 guns.

Military parade led by the band at 10 o'clock. Then the program continued at the new Finnup building, which Frederick Finnup donated for the occasion.

Vocal music; Prayer.

Declaration of Independence, read by C. J. Jones.

Music by the band, and the speeches.

Thirteen colonies represented by thirteen little girls.

Basket Dinner.

Music by the band, responses, and music, Star Spangled Banner.

Then followed contests, sack races, horse races, etc.

A dance was held at night with twenty couples present.

Captain Fulton was chief marshal of the day. The personnel of the band was: Levi Wilkinson, E♭ cornet; Frank Wood, 1st; N. F. Weeks, 2nd; Amos Baim, tenor; R. N. Hall, baritone; L. C. Reed, tuba; J. N. Collins, tenor drum; Chas. Weeks, bass.

The Kansas "breezes" and the hot winds succeeded in driving many out of the country in a rage of disgust. Andrew Rinehart, a carpenter who had come from Indiana, declared with appropriate expletives that more than once he had put a weather board in place against the side of a house, and the wind had held it there while he nailed it in position.

The elements seemed to be favoring again the cattle industry and the cattlemen viewed with satisfaction this clearing of the range. The free range law was still in effect and there were cattle and cowboys every where, and the few remaining settlers found it difficult to homestead on the open range. George W. Finnup recalls conditions of the winter of 1880-81:

"That winter was just one snow storm after another. Antelope were thick in those days and drifted in to the edge of town; and cattle drifted down here from the Smoky Hill river, and other localities in northwestern Kansas and western Nebraska, Colorado and Wyoming. Many cattle companies had representatives at Garden City to look after their cattle. After a severe storm there would be some nice weather for several days and the boys would say, 'Well, we'd better get out and look after the cattle.'

"They would first go east and west up and down the river and haul sand over the ice so that the cattle could cross without danger of injury from falling. They would then gather them up and cross them to the south side of the river. This was necessary in order to protect the interests of both cattlemen and settlers. There was no one living south of the Arkansas river, and the cattle could drift and graze wherever they pleased, but north of the river was a scattering of settlers, all up and down the valley. These had small crops and a few cattle of their own. They had little feed and very little fencing, and they showed no mercy for those strange, storm-driven cattle from northern ranges that would swoop down and destroy and devour all their feed in a night's time. Naturally they were driving them day and night, chasing them with dogs, shooting at them, and of course they always had plenty of fresh beef on hand.

"It was also necessary to keep the range cattle on the south side of the river on account of the Santa Fe railroad tracks. They would get on the tracks and bunch up in the cuts, and the trains would plow through them and kill many every few days. The Santa Fe paid out thousands of dollars for cattle killed in this way during the winter of 1880-81, and in order to protect themselves in the future, they fenced their right of way. They fenced the road bed that spring on each side from Dodge City to La Junta, Colorado, a distance of 200 miles, using heavy round cedar posts, eight feet apart, and four galvanized wires.

"After the cattle were crossed to the south side of the river they would travel day and night, up and down, and you could hear them bawling by the thousands. In a few days another storm would come and every head would be gone, drifting on south with the blizzard, but a fresh bunch would come down from the north to again torment the settlers, and the whole crossing process had to be repeated. Thousands died that winter from starvation, as many had been brought up late from Texas and were pretty thin, and they were not used to such a severe climate. Many of the cattle companies went broke that winter.

"The men who were here looking after the cattle were often the managers of the cattle company and were above the average cowboy. Some remained here and married girls they met; among several others were John E. Biggs and Ed L. Wirt. While they were waiting to cross the herds to the south side of the river so they could drift with the storm and get away from the railroad and settlers, the cowboys would pass their time by playing pool or billiards during the day, and at night it would be cards, if there wasn't a dance in town. These dances occurred frequently and they would generally have Chalk Beeson and others to play, from Dodge City.

"That spring dozens of cow outfits came through Garden City and on to the Canadian river of Texas, where they gathered up what was left of their herds. Along in May they brought them back to the Arkansas river, where they camped, in a big round up. For days they were busy cutting them out, and separating them so the different outfits could take their cattle to their own range."

There was never any very serious fueds between the cattle rangers and the homesteaders in Western Kansas. Perhaps the cowboys tried to discourage settlement on their ranges, but they were not desperate about it, and they were always very respectful toward the pioneer women. Mrs. L. E. Thomas, who lived on the range, remarked recently of the cowboys: "Many a time I served meals to cowboys. Did they sit back and let me do all the work? No, they rolled up their sleeves, washed, and then went to work like good fellows. They were always gentlemen as we found them."

After the long drouth period ending in 1882 climatic conditions improved so that immense crops favored the farmers all during 1883-84-85. C. M. Johnston came to this county the spring of 1882, and he recalls the climatic conditions of that year:

"Never having been in a semi-dry climate, I could not get accustomed to the dryness. There was scarcely anything here but distance, and that was only half clad in short grama and buffalo grass. However, when fall set in, it was followed by rains aplenty and there was abundant moisture all during the year of 1883. The summer months of that year I used to ride up on the flats carrying a good-sized basket, returning with it filled with mushrooms, some as large as saucers. That year along the railroad right-of-way the horse weeds, cockle burrs, etc., grew to immense proportions, requiring constant attention of section hands to clear the track for vision. Draws and fertile spots were miniature forests. We tenderfeet were at a loss to figure how, if the country was put under the plow, the crops would be. I have only seen a few seasons like it since."

The word that Western Kansas would produce a big yield of grain and vegetables traveled swiftly. Homesteaders came by thousands, and in a short time there was a shanty on every claim, and speculators began arriving from every state in the Union.

This was all fine for the country and the settlers, but it was a blow to the cattle rangers. Many of the ranchmen had by this time fenced large areas of the government land. The following article appeared in a Dodge City newspaper in the spring of 1885:

"It cannot be denied that the present season thus far has been favorable to the growth of agricultural products. Ranchmen must survey the situation squarely in the face and make preparations to meet it. The days of free range in Kansas are numbered among the things of the past. Ranchmen must hereafter own their grazing lands. All of the government land in Kansas will soon be occupied by settlers or owned in fee simple by individuals. The stock industry will in the future, as in the past, be the main reliance of our people for support. Its character, however, must change. The herds must be in less number and the cattle of a better grade and shelter must be provided during winter months and stock feed should be raised here."

On July 2, 1885, the land commissioners made decision that persons must remove all wire and posts from the government land.

An article which appeared in a Garden City newspaper in the spring of '85 gives a little idea of the intensity of feeling which existed between the settlers and cattlemen:

"Many newcomers are building and plowing on the south side of the river who are hoping that Major Falls will be persuaded not to bring his 20,000 head of cattle here to be branded this summer, but keep them on the Cimarron range. The stock will annoy the settlers and destroy their crops, so that they will soon become discouraged and leave. . . . It is said that stockmen are setting the prairie on fire so we will have a dry season, and the 'cussed granger' will be a thousand miles away."

By the spring of 1885 the settlers were coming in so fast as to break up and destroy the range and make it impossible to manage large herds. Boom towns sprang up all over the old range, and boasted of populations they have never had since. John H. Whitson says, "The spring we moved in, 1885, the big cattle ranches were almost gone and the settlers had a song which they sang gleefully:

"It was the tenth of May, God bless the day,
When the X Y cowboys went away."

"There was no good feeling between the cowboys and the newcomers. And the cowboys of the big X Y ranch, getting intoxicated in Garden City, would race their horses past the sod houses or humble homes of the settlers, emit blood-curdling yells, and fire off their revolvers in order to scare the women and children and intimidate the settlers into leaving."

The last blow to the free-range cattle industry was the blizzards of 1886, which destroyed thousands of head of livestock and financially ruined many of the biggest cattle dealers. It seemed as though the elements and the law had joined forces which brought about a complete victory for the homesteader, for the herd law became operative in Finney county and others of this region June 24, 1886. The effect of this law was to prevent the running at large of all cattle, horses, sheep and other domestic animals. This law is still in effect.

The day of open range and that wild life has passed, but not yet has the last of those old-time cowboys ridden his bronc into the "sunset". A few of the men who made that history are still living and they recount with startling clearness, tales of round-ups, Indians, and the chuck wagon comforts of range life. They picture vividly the terrible blizzards; and at last the tragic fate of their herds, which they found piled in cuts and ravines and frozen to death in deep snow, during the blizzard of 1886.

The Animals and Birds of Southwest Kansas

THIS vast prairie lay practically unbroken by rugged craigs and hills, or deep canyons. And owing to frequent prairie fires, not even trees or bushes grew along the water courses, except on small islands in the Arkansas river. There was very little natural protection which make attractive haunts for many species of wild animals. However, this region was inhabited by an abundance of wild animal life at the time of early discoveries and explorations. The Arkansas valley with its grassy uplands rolling down to the broad, moist river bottom, and its ever-flowing stream of water, was a meadow which attracted and fed innumerable numbers of buffalo. The antelope thrived here in herds and bunches, and also a few deer and elk.

Of the smaller animals which roamed the prairie, were the thousands of big gray wolves and coyotes, and the little swift, similar to a fox in shape but much prettier and so fleet they could outrun anything. Skunks were numerous and their bite was very fatal. There were many badgers and some bob-cats, also beaver and mink. D. W. Barton recalls that during the winter of 1873, trappers caught six hundred beaver on the Arkansas between Dodge City and the present site of Garden City. The Pawnee creek with its many spring branches sheltered immense numbers of skunks, mink, muskrat, badger, civits and coons. Of course there were hosts of prairie dogs and rabbits, rattlesnakes, terrapins and ground squirrels harboring all over the surface of the prairie. So entirely does civilized man sweep the wild beasts from his presence as soon as he gains opportunity, that most of these animals became extinct soon after the country was opened for settlement, and but few others have immigrated into this region to take their place. The opossum and tree squirrels which are quite common now have come here in late years. The wild horses and cattle found here by pioneer settlers were not native, but were strays from southern herds.

Hunting wild horses in Western Kansas was the chief occupation of the first settlers in this region. Not for

Rabbit hunt, January 31, 1894, at Garden City. The men holding the guns are, from left to right: E. J. Pyle, E. B. Stotts, Val Rice, Sam Craig, R. J. McClurkin, J. S. Griggs, Jake Collins, Chas. Bogart, Mark Cox, G. H. Bronner, M. F. Griggs, Paul Nichols, Lew Raney, Bert Hopper, Clyde Hopper, Ben Neal, G. K. Bass, and E. E. Jenkins.

sport, but as a means of livelihood. Richard J. Churchill says of the wild horses:

"There were numerous bands of wild horses that roamed the high prairie and came into the Pawnee valley to water. These gave us trouble to keep our own from mixing with them. It was very interesting to watch the strategy and the generalship of the wild stallions. In traveling the mare always took the lead, while the gentleman stayed behind and kept up the stragglers. Only by doing this was he able to keep his harem together. If by chance two bands were near each other, they would bunch up on different sides while the two stallions, like gladiators of old, would meet between them and fight it out. Kick, strike, bite, no holds barred. Finally one of them would decide he was getting the worst of it and would hike out for his own band and whoop them away as fast as possible to prevent the other stallion from getting his mares away from him.

"Many of the settlers made money by running the horses down and selling them. The first death among the

Wild horses in Western Kansas. The monarch of the herd on guard.

settlers occurred at one of these wild horse roundups. It was the first day out, and camp had been made for the evening. They were unloading their stuff from the wagon when Charley Goddard pulled a Winchester rifle to him by the muzzle. The gun caught in a buffalo robe and was discharged, shooting him in the stomach. He lived only a few hours. Another young man and I stayed with him while a rider was dispatched for a doctor. The others went to the valley to tell his family. I will never forget that night. The dead man sleeping so peacefully, the mournful howling of the coyotes spoke of earthly things. Yet the vast dome of the sky set with glittering stars, the silence, the hush of nature, had in it the sublime. It made me feel as though we were in God's own cathedral. At sunup the next morning his folks found us, and we buried him in the valley in a rude pine coffin, hastily made. It was pioneer life."

There is a draw in the southeast part of Lane county just across the line of Garfield known as Wild Horse Canyon. In the early days it was walled up at the ends so horses could not get out, and the sides were so steep they could not climb up them. One end was left partly open with a strong gate for closing. The hunters, after following a bunch of wild horses until they would be almost famished for water and so tame they could be driven, would head them into this corral, close the gate and capture them.

James Craig recalls the wild horses that were here when he first arrived: "Early in the spring of 1879 hundreds of wild horses were roaming the country. The ground was bare of vegetation, and parties were formed to run them down while they were almost starved and without water. Their plan was to take food and grain and camp at some water hole, and round up eight or ten small bunches, and with their grain-fed and shod horses run them all day. Then round them up at night and keep them close to camp without food or water. At the end of the week with such treatment, the ponies were so worn out that they could be driven to some good corral and roped. A forked cottonwood stick about 15 inches long was tied with rawhide to one front foot, they were then turned out to graze and corralled at night. In a very short time they would be shipped east and sold. I remember Link Fulton and a man named Johnson drove sixty wild ponies to Garden City and corralled them. I bought five of them and soon broke them to work and ride. They were all colors, bays, blacks, buckskins and roans."

John H. Whitson says: "We got much amusement and service out of a pair of ponies we bought from W. R. Hopkins in 1885. They had been caught by wild horse hunters out of a wild herd. But they were runaways before joining that herd, as they bore brands. One brand was that of an Indian owner; it showed a buffalo and a bow and arrow, the bow and arrow as big as the buffalo. These ponies ran away with me, tried to throw me, and cut up all manner of tricks. But they pulled a buggy and buckboard for me over many leagues of the flat lands of Western Kansas."

James R. Fulton and W. D. Fulton and his son Link were the most famous of the wild horse hunters in Western Kansas. John Stevens and Emanuel Schnars, both young men, were connected with their outfit. For several years prior to any settlement west of Dodge City they spent their time in capturing wild horses in this region. It was while on one of these trips that they conceived the idea of founding a city, and the next March, 1878, they returned and filed on land and staked out Garden City. But they still continued to hunt wild horses. Mrs. E. L. Wirt, daughter of W. D. Fulton, said recently: "We camped by the river on the present site of Garden City until some building material arrived, and to me, then a young girl, it was a very thrilling adventure. Antelope came near our house to feed. There were buffalo and wild horses in large herds in the surrounding country. And the wild horses still proved to be a very profitable business for my father. The summer of 1878 he captured and corralled over one hundred. They were beautiful animals with long mains and tails, roaring like lions, and almost climbing over the corral for freedom."

From the Garden City Paper in 1879. "Messrs. Fulton and Stevens have opened a livery stable. They are at pressent negotiating for some buggies and propose that the one hundred wild horses they caught last summer shall pay for their oats."

The following account was written by Link Fulton, just before his death in 1927: "During the summer of 1880 a Mr. Roberts came west for his health. He had some money, so he and I formed a partnership and equipped an outfit and started out after wild horses. After being out twenty days we drove a bunch of twenty fine wild horses into Garden City. There was a good corral near the present entrance to Finnup Park. We had considerable trouble in getting them into the corral, but finally succeeded. In a short time all the people in town and several emigrants came down to see the horses. C. J. Jones climbed up on the fence and some stranger was with him. C. J. asked what we would take for the herd, and we finally closed the deal, through the help of Jones, selling to the stranger for $400. This was an almost unbelievable amount of money at that time. The next day we helped the man as far as Pierceville with the horses."

The methods used to capture wild horses seemed cruel, since it was accomplished by starving them for food and water. Many times it was necessary to kill the stallion to keep him from running the mares away. Accidents were quite common in handling the wild horses, resulting in their being killed. James R. Fulton caught several fine horses on one trip and tied them out on the prairie. During the night it rained causing the ropes to shrink around their necks and one of the horses was found choked to death in the morning.

A fine young colt which had been captured by W. D. Fulton was hobbled and turned out to graze. A large gray mule running loose caught it by the neck and carried it about 30 yards, at the same time shaking it like a dog would a rat, killing it almost instantly.

At this date there are very few wild animals for

hunting or trapping in Finney county. Badgers, skunks, a few civits and coyotes are about all that are left. The hide markets in this region depend now for business chiefly on domestic cattle and old horses.

FISH

This is not considered a natural fishing section of the state, but in the years before irrigation the Arkansas river and the Pawnee with its many spring branches all carried good streams of water and many fine fish were taken from them. The Indians and pioneers were well supplied with bass, channel cat, and their favorite was a certain specie of river trout. At this period there is scarcely any fish in the streams, but a great many private lakes and irrigation reservoirs have been stocked with fish from the state hatchery. The best known are McKinney's dam, north of Deerfield, and Kinney's dam, near Kalvesta.

BIRDS

Before the occupation of the white man this country was the nesting place or feeding grounds for many varieties of game birds. The prairie abounded in prairie chickens, long billed and golden plover, quail and wild turkeys. The bayous along the streams were covered with immense swarms of many varieties of ducks, geese, heron, snipes and cranes. A story is told that even after Garden City was founded, "great flocks of cranes would hover over the town, and the pioneer business men would sit in their private office and shoot through the windows, killing great numbers." Some are inclined to discount that story, but there was a corn field just back of the office of the "Garden City Paper" in the fall of 1879 which was a feeding place of a large number of cranes, and furnished considerable fun for hunters and a number were killed.

There were many carrion birds, black ravens, buzzards, hawks, crows, owls and eagles. But at that time about the only bird that could be classed as a song bird was the meadow lark. The western meadow lark, which is native to all parts of Kansas, has been unanimously chosen as the state bird.

The cultivation of the soil always means a loss of certain species, but on the other hand many birds are quick to follow in the path of agriculture. The planting of fruit and shade trees have attracted many birds of the nesting variety to this region.

H. W. Menke published in October, 1894, at Lawrence, Kansas, the first list of Kansas birds ever collected. His list is of great value.

A list was made from observations of B. R. H. d'Allemand and S. C. Bruner covering the period from May, 1913, to January, 1915. The data in their report was mostly taken at the Garden City and Kansas nurseries, and in their immediate vicinities, including the river bottom which was between the two nurseries. Their list contains 116 birds and they have given both the common and scientific names. The data was based on studies with field glasses and no collecting was done.

G. B. Norris, of Garden City, has spent much time in observation of bird life in this region and he has done considerable collecting. His list is available but has never been published, although it is considered the most complete yet to be compiled.

Irrigation in Southwest Kansas

"When it rains we are happy. When it does not, we need not be wholly miserable, for we have hundreds of acres susceptible of irrigation at the minimum of expense and labor."
—Irrigator, 1885.

THE semi-arid character of the Great Plains, long known to stockman and Indians, but denied by land agents, and discredited by eager and hopeful settlers, asserted itself shortly after the first settlements were made, and with unmistakable emphasis. Not an acre of crops was harvested in 1879. The prairie schooners set sail and steered for other parts, and Garden City threatened to dwindle away. A few settlers remained to rake amid the ashes of their ruined hopes. Among them were some men who had learned the methods of irrigation while living in California and Colorado. They wanted to try it here.

The following letter, which was written by G. W. Hollinger, was received by George Finnup in 1922:

"Your letter came duly to hand asking for data concerning the building of the first irrigation ditch.

"Landis and Hollinger had a store of general merchandise at Garden City, with Levi Wilkinson as manager, in 1879. We also put a stock of lumber there with W. H. Armentrout at the head of that enterprise. He conducted the lumber business on the shares. I want to say that both men were all right in every way.

"Our first experience was with a severe drouth, and all early settlers know what that means. I remember very vividly that toward the end of the season we received a doleful letter from Mr. Armentrout stating all facts concerning the situation caused by the drouth; that settlers are very much discouraged and about ready to abandon the country unless we did as suggested by two settlers, one from Colorado, the other from California, who are familiar with irrigating lands and had farmed in that way. So the writer made a trip to Garden City to look the situation over. Went over the ground with Mr. Armentrout about three miles west along the Arkansas river. At that point there was an island in the river, not far from the north shore, where it would not cost much to make a dam and turn the water into a ditch and extend it to Garden City, and then farther east. We figured the expense to make the dam, cut the ditch to Garden City, and a few laterals would cost about seven or eight hundred dollars. We told Mr. Armentrout to go ahead, cut the main ditch and a few laterals. He went to work, put in the dam, cut out the main ditch and a great many more laterals than we first figured on. When we had everything paid for we had invested $2,000 to $2,200. Rufus Holmes, of Sterling, a real estate agent, sold it for us about six months after it was completed to a farmers' organizations. We got all the money out we put in but no more. We built the ditch to hold and encourage the settlers. Some years ago I had a letter from Mr. Hutchinson on this same subject. I told him that if you people intended to build a monument in memory of the first ditch built in Kansas, to build it in memory of Wm. H. Armentrout, as he did the hand work. And again I tell you the same thing."

Mr. D. R. Menke has written concerning the first irrigation ditch:

"The 'Garden City Ditch', which was the first to be constructed in Western Kansas, was built by Mr. W. H. Armentrout the latter part of 1879. The headgate was located on section 16, township 24, range 33, and ran down the valley through section 15, 14, and in section 13. It was then turned loose on the old Santa Fe trail. The first ditch ended at the northeast corner of the Finnup homestead. Later on it was extended to the Dan Larmor land on section 20-24-32. The next year seventeen farmers who lived along the ditch bought it from Landis and Hollinger, and extended it across the railroad and down toward the Doty farm, and then later to our farm (Menke) northeast of Garden City. It remained in the farmers' hands until the Sugar Company came in, or about 1905. While the farmers owned the ditch they all had equal interest, and paid but a small amount for their original shares. After that no assessments were made except for a superintendent, and all other assessments were for work only. History should show that Armentrout really was the father of irrigation in Western Kansas."

The soil which had produced nothing in the previous summer responded in 1880 to the new method of cultivation with enormous crops of all varieties of products. In quality they surpassed anything previously grown in this region. As these facts became known it was a revelation to the thoroughly disheartened settlers. The Garden City "experiment" became the mecca of students of irrigation throughout the wide territory which had hitherto depended upon uncertain rainfall. The extension of irrigation was urged as the price of prosperity, and at once began a revolution of the industrial methods of the Arkansas Valley region in Western Kansas. Under the irrigation system, Squire Worrell had the model farm of the county in 1882. The editor of the Irrigator, O. H. Knight, published an account of his visit to the farm that summer:

"As we approached Mr. Worrell's house, we were invited to jump out of the buggy for a stroll. We did so, and passed through one of the most beautiful fields of alfalfa (Chilian clover) that we have ever seen. Mr. Worrell informed us that during 1881 he gathered five crops. He estimated the average of his crops last season as follows: Irish potatoes, 400 bushels to the acre; sweet potatoes, 600 bushels to the acre; onions, 600 bushels to the acre; cabbages, 4,000 heads to the acre; melons, 8,000 to the acre; turnips, 1,000 bushels to the acre; and wheat, 20 to 25 bushels to the acre. Mr. Worrell has farmed here two years, having come here from Colorado."

The following history of canal work and irrigation was written by James Craig, who had more to do with the first irrigation canals than any other one man:

James Craig

"On the strength of what Squire Worrell had done, the Kansas Ditch Company was organized. C. J. Jones, always on the lookout for something to do, took out a charter to construct a ditch from a point on the Arkansas river in section 7, township 24, range 34. We were all poor financially, Jones included. However, a meeting was called to see about constructing a ditch to cover the valley around Sherlock, and east to Garden City. Also the country north of Garden City. It was agreed at the meeting that a survey should be made, and if it was found that water could be brought to the land west of Garden City and north, the farmers would build the ditch for half interest. Jones was to furnish money for the head gates, machinery, etc., for the other half interest. It was also agreed, since money was scarce and tools limited, that we would take turns so that such tools as we had could be kept busy.

"The survey was made for fifteen miles, where the ditch is now located. A branch ditch was surveyed down through Sherlock. It left the main line in section 2, township 24, range 34. When everything was ready, the farmers were reluctant to start work. My neighbor, Isaac Hurst, the best-fixed man financially of any of us, agreed with my brother Bob and myself that we would take the first turn. Having had some experience moving dirt while working on the railroad in Illinois I was somewhat of a boss to the outfit. My team plowed the first furrow where the head gates were to go. Jones held the plow, I drove the team. When we had worked a month others who had promised to take turns refused to do anything.

"We had a meeting with Jones, and it was agreed that Hurst and his boy and brother Bob and I would continue the work for a half interest in the Kansas ditch. The work was started in June, 1880, and was pushed until cold weather stopped us. We began again early in the spring of 1881 and by July of that year we had water to our farms. We continued to operate the Kansas ditch until the summer of 1882, when Jones sold out his interests in the Kansas ditch to Latham Hudson and McCord.

"The ditch was enlarged and the head gates moved west to their present location in Kearny county. I took charge of the construction work, late in the fall of 1882. Brother Bob and I were stockholders until Latham Hudson and Company sold their interests, including ours, to the Pelham, Denney Dewey outfit in 1889. It was operated by them until it went into the hands of the receiver. T. E. Dewey was appointed receiver. It was operated by him until it was bought by the farmers, and it is now known as the Farmers Ditch.

"Prior to the taking over of the ditch it had been leased by Dewey to C. E. Sexon, and had filled up to such extent that when the farmers bought the ditch from the receiver it was necessary to clean out the entire ditch. I was appointed to cross section the ditch and let contract to the water-right holders. During the fall and winter of 1901-02 we took out 100,000 yards of dirt and put in new head-gates. The work was all done under my supervision.

"I was chairman of the Farmers Ditch organization when the government conceived the plan, under the reclamation service, of pumping water from the sand of the Arkansas valley. I helped, together with C. A. Schneider, to purchase right-of-ways for the ditch and right-of-ways for the pumping plant at Deerfield.

"C. J. Jones, always scheming and ready to promote anything he thought there was money in, took out a charter for what was known as the Minnehaha Ditch. In fact, Jones had a dozen charters for irrigation ditches along the Arkansas river. He surveyed the ditch himself, and did some work for about two miles. He got a little money from the south side people for what he had done. The ditch was taken out on the south bank of the Arkansas in 1880, about two miles west of Lakin. It was abandoned without ever being used.

"The Southside Ditch was taken out on the south bank of the Arkansas river in section 16, township 25, range 37, in Kearny county, opposite Hartland. It was built and operated by C. H. Longstrath for a number of years, representing an Ohio company. Afterwards it was operated by Mr. Linn for the Ohio owners. It was later purchased by the sugar interests of Colorado Springs at the time they were promoting the Sugar Factory at Garden City. It covered all of the valley south of the river to Sherlock, and north of the sand hills.

"The Great Eastern Irrigation Company, another of Jones' charters on the Arkansas river, was conceived by Jones and promoted by him in 1881. He induced a number of business men at Lawrence, Kansas, to go in with him and construct a canal, starting at a point on the Arkansas river in section 16, township 25, range 37, opposite Hartland. During the summer of 1881, a surveying party from Lawrence, with F. O. Marvin of the University of Kansas, a professor in the engineering department, in charge of the work. We made several surveys, and finally decided on the present location. Sometime later it was agreed that the Great Eastern Canal should be constructed. I was instructed to cross section the canal and get it ready for construction. In September and October, 1881, we laid out the work about thirty miles. The canal was to cover the valley land west of Lakin, the land south of Deerfield, and from where it turned north just east of Deerfield, and to cover all the land north of Sherlock (Holcomb) for ten miles, and all the land north of the Kansas Ditch.

"In November, 1881, I was instructed to proceed with the work of construction. Fourteen head of mules with harness and other equipment were shipped to me at Garden City from Lawrence, Kansas, November 5, 1881. We moved to Hartland, Kansas. The work was heavy, and we camped all winter on Sand Creek and did most of the heavy work from there. When spring opened up we bought a New Era grader. We pushed the work rapidly and by October, 1882, the work of construction was pretty well along. The summer of 1882 we constructed waste gates and head gates in the canal, also a flume over Sand Creek, west of Lakin. Water was brought through the canal that fall some distance east of Lakin.

"The Canal company had some agreement with the A.T. & S.F. railroad company that they were to receive certain sections of land north of Deerfield, and east of there, when the canal was in a certain state of completion. They did not think the canal was complete enough to warrant their turning the land promised over to the Canal company. In the spring of 1883 I was instructed to turn the canal over to the farmers to operate through the summer. No charges were to be made for the use of the water.

"I was told to take my outfit to the Crooked Creek cattle ranch in Meade county, and to remain there all summer. In September I was ordered to take the outfit back to Lakin and proceed with the work there. I found the farmers had neglected caring for the head-gates and the canal. The head-gates had sunk into the river. New ones had to be constructed and the banks repaired. In 1884 the first water was sold to the farmers. New laterals were built. The Boyd lateral, the Abbot lateral and the Craig lateral. Also the Deerfield lateral, which started just west of Lakin running east and north to the country north of Deerfield.

"I was in charge until the spring of 1886, when I quit and recommended Ed Blankenship for superintendent. He was followed by Percy Russell. It was operated by the Great Eastern Irrigation Company until it was purchased by the Denny Dewey people in 1889. They improved the system and constructed the underflow system at Hartland in 1890, which was a failure. The underflow system was started at the bottom of the main canal, some distance from the river bank. Then running up stream and parallel with the river with a fall of one foot to the mile. The river has an 8-foot fall per mile at this point, so at the end of a mile the underflow canal was seven feet below the river bed. The canal was 20 feet wide on the bottom. About 20 cubic feet per second of water was recovered. The river broke in and the underflow was abandoned.

"Like the Kansas Ditch, which belonged to the same company, it went into the hands of T. E. Dewey as receiver. It was sold to the Sugar Company who improved the ditches and added Lake McKinney to the system in 1906.

"The Amazon Ditch was another of Jones' charters on the Arkansas river. The headgates are located at the Slate Cut about five miles west of Hartland on the north side of the river, and parallel to the Great Eastern Canal for about twenty miles and irrigated the country north of Deerfield. Construction work was started in 1889. At the time the charter was taken out, Jones certainly saw big things. The ditch was intended to cover all the country out as far north as the old town of Terry and as far east as the head of the Pawnee. Some of his ditches are to be found on the high lands northeast of Garden City. Any person should have known that the ditches already constructed and in use added to the ditches in Colorado would take the full flow of the Arkansas river."

PUMP IRRIGATION

During the past fifty years, and especially during the first twenty-five of those years, long periods of drouth were experienced. The effects of dry years in the earlier history of the Southwest were more noticeable than in

Windmill demonstration at Finney County Fair, held in Garden City in 1895. Held in interest of pump irrigation.

older sections of the country because in the Southwest crops had not been developed that were suitable to an arid climate. More adaptable crops and varieties of crops have been developed in recent years, and more efficient and timely farming practices have come into use; these offset in a measure the effects of periods of dry weather.

Irrigation was the first remedy applied in the Southwest to overcome the effects of lack of rainfall, and after years of experimental work on the part of the earlier farmers, efficient and economical means of pumping water from underground sources of water have been developed. Large areas of Southwestern Kansas are underlaid with streams and other underground bodies of water at comparatively shallow depths. This is particularly true in the Arkansas valley in this part of the state, where water is found at various depths from eight to sixty feet. In many localities there are several underground strata of water-bearing gravel, one below the other. Water is lifted from this supply of underground water which flows down from the mountains of Colorado, by centrifugal or turbine pumps. Most of these pumps are operated by electric motors, but in places where electricity is not available other kinds of power are used. In some places water is lifted more than 100 feet for irrigation with these pumps, but the shallower the "lift" the less power required to obtain the same amount of water. There are many such pumping plants in the Arkansas valley between Dodge City and Syracuse which pump from 1,500 to 2,000 gallons of water a minute. Some pump as much as 4,000 to 5,000 gallons per minute, and these larger plants will furnish enough water to irrigate from 320 to 640 acres of land a year, depending on the type of soil and the kind of crop raised.

While the cost of irrigation from pumping plants is generally greater than it is under a ditch taking water by gravity flow from a river or reservoir filled from a river, the certainly of being able to get water whenever it is needed by the owner of the pumping plant is valuable and enables him to grow more abundant crops as a rule, than if he depended on river water which is not always available.

Dams have been built in a number of the smaller streams in Southwestern Kansas to store water for irrigation. Pawnee creek has several of these dams. Pumping plants are sometimes used to lift the water from the creeks to the higher land in the valleys. Gardens are irrigated on many Western Kansas farms from small reservoirs which are filled from windmills or engines.

Doty's Irrigation Reservoir, Finney County, Kansas

In 1905 the government undertook to put in a pump irrigation system near Deerfield to supply water for the Farmers Ditch (the old Kansas Ditch). A series of twenty shallow wells, each with an individual motor and pump, was put across the Arkansas valley. They pumped the water into the Farmers Ditch. There was no lack of water, but the expense, under government operation proved too great, and the project was abandoned after a few years. Now the Farmers Ditch takes water directly from the Arkansas river. Some of the best improved and most productive farms in this part of the state are under this ditch.

Among the pioneers in the development of pumping plants for irrigation in Western Kansas were the Carter Brothers. In 1889 W. O. Carter and E. N. Gause put in a pumping plant in the southwest corner of Stevens park in Garden City. A windmill was used for power and a suction pump with a five-inch cylinder was used. Later a suction pump with a ten-inch cylinder was used. Gaso-

Type of individual pumping plant installed about 1912.
C. A. Schneider and W. O. Carter.

line engines were the next step in the development of power, and now most plants in the western part are run by electric motors. S. Schulman, an early day settler in Western Kansas, was also closely identified with the development of practical irrigation systems in this part of the Arkansas Valley. Many plants now in use were installed by Mr. Schulman.

The largest pumping plant installed by Carter Brothers is on section 8-24-33. This plant has a capacity of 5,000 gallons a minute. I. L. Diesem bought the first commercial job installed by Carter Brothers. Other early users of pumping plants were T. J. Dyke, Ed Hall, Lee Doty, father of D. D. Doty, and Bob Grace.

It is estimated that more than 400,000 acres of shallow water land suitable for pump irrigation surrounds Garden City.

Sequoyah County

SEQUOYAH county was named by the Kansas Legislature in 1873, before it had a single white inhabitant. It was named in honor of a Cherokee Indian, who was the most remarkable man of his race. His memory is still venerated by his people, for he was the inventor of the alphabet of their language.

Many have wondered why a Kansas county was named for a Cherokee Indian. Joseph B. Thoburn, secretary of the Oklahoma Historical Society, feels sure the name was suggested by Colonel William A. Phillips of Salina, who was elected to congress at the time Sequoyah county was created. During the civil war he was in command of an Indian brigade in the Union army. After the war he represented the Cherokee nation as its attorney at Washington. Some of the pioneers of this county were not pleased when the name was changed to Finney, but the majority favored the change since it was much easier to spell and pronounce.

Sequoyah county was attached to Ford county for judicial purposes and was never organized. It was described as follows:

"Sequoyah county is 864 square miles in area, being twenty-four miles from east to west, and thirty-six miles from north to south. This is a treeless region. The Arkansas river runs in a southeasterly direction across the county. The points in the county are Pierceville, Garden City, and Sherlock."

A petition praying for the organization of Sequoyah county into a municipal township was examined by the board of county commissioners of Ford county July 8, 1879. It was found to contain the required number of signers. The request was granted and an election ordered to elect township officers to take place on July 25, 1879, at Garden City, Sequoyah county.

"Dodge City, Kansas, July 26, 1879.

"A special meeting of the board of commissioners of Ford county met pursuant to call for the purpose of canvassing the votes polled at a special election of township officers. The following parties received the highest number of votes and are declared elected. The county clerk is ordered to issue certificates to the same:

"Township Trustee, J. R. Fulton; Treasurer, J. R. Spencer; Clerk, Amos Baim; Justice of Peace, N. M. Carter, of Garden City; Justice of Peace, Morris R. Logue, Pierceville; Constable, J. C. North, Garden City; Constable, Alban E. Moore, Pierceville. Each received 67 votes. votes.

"Signed,
"A. J. Peacock."

For the next four years, Sequoyah county remained under the jurisdiction of Ford county. Pursuant to law they met each year to levy a 10-mill tax on Sequoyah township for county purposes. People wanting a marriage license had to go to Dodge City. The school teachers were examined at Dodge City and all court matters were handled there. An election was held in the township each year and the results taken to Dodge City where the results were canvassed by the Ford county board of commissioners. The elections each year, as recorded in Commissioners Journal A of Ford county, were as follows:

FEBRUARY 10, 1880
Votes Cast, 49
Jas. R. Fulton, Trustee
Wm. D. Fulton, Treasurer
J. L. Williams, Clerk
Joseph Weeks, Justice of Peace
Morris R. Logue, Justice of Peace
J. B. Smith, Constable
L. A. Collins, Constable
H. M. Wheeler, Road Overseer

FEBRUARY 8, 1881
Votes Cast, 54
Levi Wilkinson, Trustee
Wm. D. Fulton, Treasurer
George H. DeWaters, Clerk
N. C. Jones, Justice of Peace
Morris R. Logue, Justice of Peace
N. J. Earp, Constable
J. W. Wallace, Constable

FEBRUARY 14, 1882
Votes Cast, 64
Jas. R. Fulton, Trustee
Wm. D. Fulton, Treasurer
Geo. H. DeWaters, Clerk
N. J. Earp, Constable
H. M. Wheeler, Justice of
 Peace
J. A. Stevens, Constable
D. R. Menke, Road Overseer

FEBRUARY 6, 1883
Votes Cast, 56
J. J. Erisman, Trustee
L. C. Pierce, Treasurer
N. J. Earp, Constable
B. B. Black, Clerk
J. S. Edwards, Road Overseer
J. H. Pierce, Justice of
 Peace

The making of homes, the foundation of towns, and laying the basis for all future development of a great county were begun in old Sequoyah. The domestic experiences of those first pioneers are full of interest, yet under the most favorable circumstances they found frontier life plenty disagreeable. They were beset by drouths, prairie fires and blizzards. There was a struggle involving patience, self-sacrifice and industry, but they elected to stay on. But when better years came they lost their little empire, and Sequoyah county disappeared forever from the map. October 1, 1884, it with other unorganized territory was organized as a county, and called Finney.

THAT part of Finney county now called Garfield township has had an interesting historical career of its own. When it was first created in 1873 it was called Buffalo county. It was never organized and in a short time disappeared from the map. At various times during the next fourteen years parts of its area were annexed to Hodgeman, Finney, Gray and Lane counties. In 1887 Garfield county was created out of six townships from the northeast corner of Finney and six from Hodgeman county, which was practically the original territory of old Buffalo county. It was named in honor of President Garfield, and was organized July 16, 1887.

A committee was appointed to locate the county seat. Thomas Rowe was the chairman. The center of the county was in section twelve, but it was hard to get water there, so they decided on section thirteen. C. J. Jones and Mr. Pickerin had purchased the townsite and at once made a plat and had a lot sale. The post office from Cuyler was moved to the new location, but they called the town Creola. However, when the name was sent in, they were informed there was already a town in the state by that name, so it was changed to Eminence. But the location for the county seat which was selected by the committee did not suit the people living in the east part of the county. Those citizens under the leadership of John

Bull contended that the county had been cut to make Ravanna the county seat.

The Governor appointed John Bull, G. M. Goff and J. E. Dixon for commissioners and Clarence Van Patten was appointed county clerk. The first meeting of the commissioners of Garfield county was held in Ravanna on the 22nd of July, 1887. The first business attended to was to receive sealed bids for county record needs as per list furnished by the commissioners. The bid of M. M. Murdock & Company of Wichita, Kansas, was accepted, the amount being $1,676.64. and a 16 2/3 discount to be allowed if paid for in one year.

At a meeting September 9, 1887, Mrs. M. L. Ramsel was appointed county superintendent; J. M. Knapp, surveyor; W. C. Coulson, sheriff; F. A. Hutto, county attorney; J. E. Turner, court clerk. The county was divided into six townships: Michigan, Garfield, Essex, Lorenz, Kalvesta, and Center. Eminence was not allowed a precinct.

The board of commissioners met pursuant to call of chairman John Bull, at Ravanna, October 8, 1887. On motion the following order was made: That a special election be held on November 8, 1887, for the purpose of locating the permanent county seat of Garfield county, and to elect a full set of officers.

There was bitter feeling between the Eminence and Ravanna factions in the county, and the sober-minded citizens (J. A. Goodman says there were no sober-minded ones) were worried over possible rioting on election day. Both sides anticipated trouble and made preparations to protect their interests, and both were well armed. C. J. Jones of the Eminence forces hired Bat Masterson and twenty deputies to come from Dodge City to keep order. Several have said that the presence of Masterson and the famous gunmen he had with him was the only thing that prevented the worst gun battle that ever took place between citizens of a state. Both sides were organized and took turns in voting. First a Ravanna man, and then he would be directly followed by an Eminence booster. They watched each other suspiciously, in brooding silence, but feeling was so intense that one word of insult would have thrown them into a maddened, fighting mob, resulting in the loss of many lives. Bat Masterson and his men stood back and quietly watched every movement as the voting proceeded, but they at least had in such a bluff that the men of both factions felt that the first man to raise a disturbance would be shot down. For this reason, to all outward appearances, the election went off smoothly.

Ballot boxes from the outlaying precincts were rushed under guards into Ravanna in the shortest possible time. J. A. Goodman drove a team hitched to a light spring wagon at break-neck speed across the prairie trail from Michigan township, while J. E. T. Kephart sat on the ballot box to keep it from bouncing out of the back end. Another man rode along on a horse as guard. They fully expected to be robbed of the ballot box at every dip in the trail by one faction or other. "But, pshaw," said J. A. Goodman, "we didn't even see a soul."

Eminence received 432 votes and Ravanna received 467 and was declared to be the county seat. There was a wild celebration at Ravanna that night, and according to C. J. Jones it was helped along by a "jugful". In fact, someone said that a whole barrelful stood in the corner of a certain barn. The following officers were elected on that day:

John Johnson, Representative; Clarence Van Patten, County Clerk; Frank W. Dunn, Register of Deeds; Lewis Y. Thompson, Sheriff; J. E. T. Kephart, Probate Judge; Theo. W. Craig, County Attorney; M. L. Ramsell, County Superintendent; J. M. Knapp, Surveyor; Austin Connett, Coroner; Chas. Donart, Commissioner; M. A. Johnson, Commissioner; William Moore, Commissioner.

During the next year Ravanna boomed and the population soon reached about seven hundred. But the Eminence boosters were still at work and the county seat fight was still on. A law suit began at once which ended in the supreme court. There it was proven that the ballot box had been stuffed at the county seat election and 46

The Garfield County courthouse, built at Ravanna in 1889. Ravanna lost the county seat before it was completed and it was never used for a courthouse.

ballots favoring Ravanna were thrown out, and the decision was in favor of Eminence.

The next election was held at Ravanna November 6, 1888. The following were the officers elected:

W. M. Speck, Representative; D. W. Herman, County Clerk; F. W. Dunn, Register of Deeds; W. T. Williams, County Treasurer; W. H. Alleman, Sheriff; L. W. Fulton, Court Clerk; J. E. T. Kephart, Probate Judge; T. W. Craig, County Attorney; M. L. Ramsell, County

Superintendent; D. B. Huffman, Coroner; N. Cheroweth, Surveyor; C. H. Winters, Commissioner 1st District; T. C. Sale, Commissioner 2nd District; W. S. Rader, Commissioner 3rd District.

On October 7, 1889, the board of commissioners met in regular session for the last time in Ravanna. C. H. Winters, T. C. Sale and W. S. Rader, commissioners, and D. W. Herman, county clerk, present. On motion the board adjourned until one o'clock, to meet at Eminence, which was now the accepted county seat of Garfield county. But many of the citizens of Ravanna were not in favor of allowing the county records to be taken to Eminence. They did not stand guard over the court house, but were ready for action should anyone try to take the records out of the building.

Just after dark on the evening of October 7, Fred Smith and John Rader from Eminence, drove a team of race ponies hitched to a spring wagon through the streets of Ravanna and stopped at the court house. They entered and then managed to secure the county records. In a few minutes they had started on a wild flight across the prairie, headed back toward Eminence. Their action was discovered and an alarm sounded before they had hardly gotten started. The Ravanna men, headed by Tom O'Toole and Michael Hainey, followed in hot pursuit and kept shooting at regular intervals.

It was dark and the road was broken by draws which made it difficult to travel, but it helped to cover the movements of the men in the spring wagon. They dashed straight ahead until they came to the trail that cut across country into Eminence, but instead of taking it, they turned off into a dry draw. The Ravanna men continued on the trail that led directly into Eminence until they reached the hitching posts in front of the Bryan Hotel, a three-story building. L. W. Fulton heard the commotion and ran down stairs with his 44 revolver cocked, and called "hands up". He did not intend to shoot, but the gun was accidently discharged, and it killed one of the horses. Fulton marched the men upstairs and locked them in a room. He gave his wife a gun and told her to guard the door, and to shoot the first man who tried to get out. He and some other men then went out to where Smith and Rader were hiding, and informed them that it was safe to come on into town. And so Eminence became the county seat.

The commissioners met in regular session for the first time in Eminence, Kansas, October 11, 1889. About the first motion made was to lease a building, lot 7, block 62, in the town of Eminence for one year at $30 per month, to be used as a court house. The building belonged to Frederick Finnup.

The next general election was held in Eminence November 5, 1889: L. J. Gilson, County Clerk; Eugene Rall, County Treasurer; A. T. Irvine, Register of Deeds; George Hewes, Sheriff; H. D. Collins, Surveyor; L. V. Minor, Coroner; Thomas Rowe, Commissioner, 3rd Dist.

Election of 1890: R. J. Churchill, Representative; J. V. Killion, Probate Judge; D. W. Herman, unexpired term of Probate Judge; G. W. Harvey, County Attorney; L. W. Fulton, Court Clerk; H. D. Collins, County Superintendent; J. E. Dawson, Commissioner of 1st District; W. M. Blair, Commissioner of 2nd District.

Election of 1891: Eugene Rall, County Treasurer; S. S. Axten, County Clerk; A. J. Irvine, Register of Deeds; James Phelps, Sheriff; Thomas Morris, Surveyor; D. H. Mandigo, Coroner; Julius Johann, Commissioner 2nd District.

Election of 1892: F. A. Milton, Representative; C. V. Chalfont, Probate Judge; John Hatch, Court Clerk; M. L. Ramsell, County Superintendent; George L. Sigman, County Attorney; A. J. Knox, Commissioner.

The new officers elected in November, 1892, held one

meeting after they took their office, that was January 9, 1893. At the conclusion of the meeting, on motion, the salaries of the following county officers of Garfield county were fixed for the year 1893, and allowed in full: Probate Judge, $125; County Attorney, $125; County Clerk, $500; County Treasurer $500.

A motion was made that the board be adjourned, sine die. A. J. Knox, Chairman. Signed, (Finis)

After Ravanna lost the county seat, they had the county resurveyed and discovered that it had less than the 432 square miles which is required by law, and the Supreme Court decided it was illegally organized. In 1893 it was annexed to Finney county. The organization of Garfield county was a costly experience, and the county seat fight created enmity between its citizens, but no lives were lost, as was the case in some other county seat fights of Western Kansas. While Ravanna was the county seat, bonds were voted to the amount of $10,000 to build a court house. The building was erected of native stone, but never entirely finished, and it was never used, but it had to be paid for. There was much graft and extravagance. The citizens and most of the officers were honest and conservative, but they allowed the affairs of the county to be swayed by a few "political bosses" who were out for greedy gains.

When Thomas Rowe became chairman of the board of commissioners, he cut the salaries of county officers and ran it inside the tax levy, and when the funds were exhausted, he refused to allow any more bills.

Tax Rolls		Warrants	
1887	$ 7,604.53	1887	$ 650.45
1888	15,545.66	1888	34,171.07
1889	23,346.50	1889	23,656.44
1890	19,662.11	1890	18,963.03
		1891	7,643.05
		1892	4,041.25

EARLY DAY HISTORY OF OLD GARFIELD COUNTY

H. D. COLLINS

Many interesting events are connected with the early history of the Pawnee country which are well worthy of being recorded. Having lived in Pawnee Valley for twenty-five years, and during that time witnessed many things that were of interest to me I kept some data, thinking that sometime I might help someone write the story of the Pawnee country. I am indebted to my friends for help in giving information on different subjects and also relating to me numerous incidents, some amusing, some pathetic.

Thomas Alderice, who was a government scout and later lived at Eminence, tells me the scouts frequently rode over this county and were acquainted with the numerous watering places. There were thousands of buffaloes and droves of antelope roaming over the country. Wolves, prairie dogs, rattlesnakes and other denizens of the prairie were here in abundance. Also there was an occasional mountain lion, the bob-cats were rather numerous in the bluffs, beaver were to be found along the creek edge from where Ravanna now stands, and were trapped as late as '79 and '80, and a very few snow-white wolves were seen among the gray ones.

This territory was included in what was known as the Great American Desert. That was somewhat strange as there were numerous springs bursting out of the draws and the Pawnee creek then always had running water. Besides this, there were numerous trees in the east part of the county along the Pawnee and in a few other places, such as Parker's Grove, Hay Canyon, Petrie Draw and the last one toward the west was Hoadley's homestead, near Loyal townsite.

I do not find that Indians remained in this valley with any degree of permanency, and yet it would seem an ideal place for them. The Pawnee Indians were given a reservation extending perhaps from Larned west to the state line and from the Arkansas river north to beyond the Pawnee Valley. The creek was no doubt named for this tribe of Indians. It is also claimed that a number of the Pawnees, including their chief, are buried on the bluffs on the north side of the creek. Numerous bands of Indians from Colorado, Oklahoma and New Mexico were often seen passing through and hunting, during the '70's. These were harmless. But the winter of '75 and '76 there was a bunch of northern Cheyennes, estimated at ten or twelve thousand, that wintered in the Pawnee Valley, in the vicinity of White Mound. These were all well armed. The warriors each had a government Springfield rifle, two Colt's revolvers, with plenty of ammunition which had all come from government agencies. Some of the Indians died that winter and were buried on White Mound, and at another point a short distance east of there. There is also another Indian burial ground about four miles west of Eminence. At that place, F. M. Harper was quarrying stone in 1888 when he dug up skeletons, trinkets, beads, spoons and ornaments made of twenty-five and fifty-cent silver coins.

Early Settlement on the Pawnee

The first settlement was made in the eastern part of Garfield. One of the first filings on a homestead was made by Clawson Parker, in sec. 8-22-27, in the spring of 1878. A little later, Matt Smith, Semer Mason, the Coulsons, Griswolds, and in the fall of 1878, James Gross settled on sec. 11-22-28. Also about this time, came John Bull, G. M. D. Goff, Silas Halsey, Philip Miller, Bert Williams, Thomas Patterson, Meirice Lane, and others. These people were all located east of the line running north and south through Ravanna, mostly on Pawnee creek; but Goff, Halsey and Miller located at Hay Canyon.

(1) The Original Home of John O. Loyd. (2) Home of H. N. Hascall, built in 1903. (3) Customary sod house used by many young ladies while homesteading. Miss Alta Smith, 1901, near Eminence, Kansas.

Rev. H. S. Booth, who settled near Ravanna, Kansas, in 1879, and organized the First Methodist Church in Garden City.

D. W. Herman, abstractor, land attorney and real estate broker

Old settlers of Garfield township. Reading from left to right: H. J. McKeal, A. C. Gingrich, Daniel S. Carl, Richard J. Churchill, H. D. Collins and Thomas Rowe.

Cyrus Brown and his family, David Fay and family and William Steele and Crel Brown filed on land south and west of Ravanna, in what is now known as the Brown Draw. Other settlers were now coming in and locating at the springs and water privileges. Ames put up what was then a large house and stock corral. This was later known as the Peterie Spring. Ames also built a large house at Twin Springs. O. W. Crow located at the Crow Springs, now known as the Deal Springs. McVay located a short distance east of Crows Spring where there were several good springs. Those who lived at the headwaters of Pawnee creek in 1879 were: James R. Chapel; M. L. Lavender and wife and their children Nora and Minnie; Will Hazelton; C. Hoadley and wife and Ida, Myra and Charlie; George Recker; Dr. O. W. Crow; Van Patten and wife; Ted Freeman and Clarence; Ames and wife; Charlie, Dave and George Goddard, all with families; Schofield and family; William Moore and family, and R. J. Churchill.

Among those who settled at this time was Elder H. S. Booth from Boston, Mass. His family soon followed him and they located three miles north of Eminence. There being no water on his claim he moved to a claim two miles east of Ravanna where there was a spring. Like other settlers he began at once to pick up a few head of cattle and soon had a herd. At no time did he forget his high calling and was always busy preaching and building up new churches. He preached whenever he had an audience, whether in a sod house, hay loft of a livery barn or in a cowboy's camp. With the Booth family came Mrs. Mary L. Ramsell with her family. She was one of the very first persons to teach a school in Pawnee and was county superintendent of Garfield during its period of organization.

During the years of '85, '86 and '87, there was a wild rush for land. People seemed to think this was the Garden of Eden. By the spring of 1887 the county was well filled with settlers and there were seven towns in the county: Kalvesta, Lorenz, Ravanna, Essex, Eminence, Loyal and Silver Lake.

Garfield county was organized in 1887 and there was a county seat fight between Ravanna and Eminence. While there was much bitter feeling between the two contending sides and each called the other ugly names, there were no killings, and I now remember but three fights. Cicero Phelps and Wm. Speck were the first to enter the arena; but it was a bloodless affair. Speck could not hit Phelps and Phelps could not hit Speck.

No. 2 was between Dr. Miner and John Bogle and was not altogether bloodless but nothing serious resulted.

No. 3 was between the sugar bond fellows and the anti bond. It was a light skirmish with C. F. Hoadley, G. A. Deal, J. R. Bricket and others on one side and L. W. Fulton, D. S. Carl and others on the other side. It occurred in a little office in the south part of Eminence and when it started, J. R. Bricker took to his heels and ran for shelter.

We had now "400" socially in the county. There was more genuine sociability among the people than is generally found in older communities. We had preaching; Bull, Simons, George, Foster, Oliver, Gay, Studley and others took turns in preaching for us. We attended Sunday School and picnics. We had literaries and had some eloquent speakers. I now recall some of them: Dr. Suess, C. C. Showalter, J. T. Showalter, J. A. Bricker, D. W. Herman, Thos. Rowe, George McWhorter, Jacob Swaim, J. H. Ledgerwood, N. F. Hack and others. There was baseball, foot races, turkey shoots and other sports and Lee D. Price, who performed on the tight rope on special celebrations.

The report came to Ravanna that the Eminence people would raid the town on a certain night. They put out guards. The main place to watch was the bridge south of town. It was a cold night. The boys persuaded Mr. Hart to watch the bridge. He came in after a while to warm and see what report of the invaders. Mr. Hart said, "Boys, have you got any spirits?" The boys gave him some spirits. He then showed them a revolver and said, "Boys, if you hear this crack you will know that I have found something." Then tapping an old musket loaded with buckshot, said, "If you hear this go off, you will know that I have got something." These scares amounted to nothing but they were factors of a county seat fight.

During the five years of the county's existence, the schools were well looked after by Mrs. Ramsell, county superintendent. At one time there were probably thirty school districts and during the life of the county, at least fifty teachers.

The school teachers hoped to build up a great school system in Garfield county. Others dreamed of a county seat close to their farm. Others pictured fine farms with good buildings, groves, orchards and fine stock farms.

In 1882 the Jewish committee at Cincinnati, an organization whose mission seems to be to succor the poor Jewish immigrants, located twenty-four families on claims in the Pawnee district east of Ravanna. This committee paid the filing fees on the homesteads and sent supplies of food and clothing every sixty days for one year. Each family was furnished two cows and for every two families one team of horses, wagon and farm implements. These were Russian Jews, and were what we call orthodox Jews, having their Rabbi who killed their animals for meat, but ate no pork. It seems these Jews did not make a great success of farming, but were rather quiet, peaceable people and managed to live three or four years until the boom when they could prove up and mortgage their land, which it seems they all did, and most of them filed again on pre-emptions and mortgaged them. These two mortgages gave them enough money to start stores. Goldforb, Golden, Cohn, Buckwalter and others, went into business at Ravanna. Julius Wolfsohn and Maurice Eihlen, nick-named "Jay Gould", Friedman, and others at Eminence. However, they all scattered and by 1890 there was probably not a Jew left in Garfield county.

The disappointments, discouragements and defeats were many. A few persons stayed and prospered. Most of them left and have now forgotten the trials they went through. Some still feel the spirit of revenge when they think of the wrongs, imaginary or otherwise, they were subject to during the five years of the county seat war.

From the time of the organization of the county in 1887 until it was disorganized in 1893, there were more than one thousand families who had lived in the county. At the present (1931) there are only about three hundred. Of all those who cast votes in the county seat election in 1887, only four remain in Garfield township. D. S. Carl, R. J. Churchill, John Goodman and Walter Chapel. The others are all gone and they would hardly recognize the Pawnee Valley should they come back. Graded highways have replaced the cow trails. The boom towns are all gone and will never be rebuilt. Hidden away among the breaks of the Pawnee are contented ranch families. Dotted over the great level expanses are prosperous wheat and corn farms, and no one longs for the good old days.

C. L. Brown came from Cherokee county, Kansas, with his father, Cyrus Brown, in May, 1878. They both filed on claims in Garfield township, which was then called Buffalo county. Two bachelors, whose names were Parker and Johnson, had filed on land in the southeast corner of the county and were the only settlers when the Browns arrived.

In 1880 Mr. C. L. Brown returned to Baxter Springs and married Miss Charlotte Gibbons. They returned at once to the claim, but there had been no rain that spring and the grass was dry, and it did not rain all summer. They were persuaded by relatives to return to Chautauqua county. They stayed there two years and managed to get a few cows, but at the end of that time they returned to Buffalo county. Mrs. Brown drove the team and wagon with a baby in her arms, while he followed behind to drive the cattle. New calves that came on the way were loaded into the wagon along with Mrs. Brown and the baby. And this was the beginning of their herd of cattle on which they have always depended for a living. At one time they had a fine bunch of horses, but horses got cheap, and luckily, the cows were still on the job.

Their first house was a typical "palace of the plain", a dugout, 10x16, built in a bank of a spring branch of the Pawnee. Mr. Brown said, "We lived there until the family got so big they couldn't all get in, so we enlarged it by laying up sod 24 feet back of the dugout. We then lived in that until we were afraid it would fall down." In 1902 they built the house that is now on their eight-hundred-acre ranch.

Mr. Brown was never away long from home. Once, however, he went up by Scott City to help a friend fix up a ranch. He left his wife alone with the babies and nine cows to milk. "You know what we had to burn in them days?" Mr. Brown remarked. "Well, I had a pile of 'em gathered up as high as the house when I left, but it rained every night about milking time, all the time I was gone, and when I came back, wife was without fuel, for that pile had just naturally melted."

While Ravanna boomed and the county seat fights were the popular pastime, he and his wife were at home milking cows and making butter. He always took time to vote, but did not desire political honors. For nine years they sold milk to a cheese factory in Ravanna which was operated by John Bull on a co-operative system. The first summer of its existence, however, left the Browns with nothing to show for their work and a one hundred dollar grocery bill. Mr. Bull's idea was to store the cheese through the summer and let it season until fall. When fall came, he had a house full of cheese, but he couldn't find a market. It seems that no one wanted cheese that had gone through the "seasoning process". Mr. Brown had to take cheese for a dividend. He succeeded in trading some for a half barrel of sorghum, which made a change in diet, at least.

The most disastrous things in their early day experience were the blizzards of which there were several, and the hot winds of summer. There was never any bad hail storm in their vicinity, but once they could see great sheets of it that had fallen farther down in the Pawnee Valley. And it was reported that it piled so deep in the creek that the fish were all frozen.

Richard J. Churchill was born in Portland, Connecticut, April 12, 1858, and settled in old Buffalo county in April, 1879. Mr. Churchill says:

"I have lived on the middle fork of the Pawnee for over fifty-one years, which begins to look like some endurance test. I first settled on a timber claim on the level land of the main valley. The year 1879 was very dry, first and last rain was June 16. The county all burned off, and there was no grass for work horses. I began to follow up the forks of the Pawnee and found good grass and water on the middle fork, so I left my tree claim, and took preemption there, and have resided continuously on that fork since. I decided that farming was too risky, so in 1880 with two neighbors, went down into New Mexico and Texas and got a bunch of sheep, paying six dollars a dozen with all the goats you wanted thrown in.

"For mildness and beautiful weather the winter of '79 and '80 has not since been equalled. The winter of '80 and '81 was a fright. It set in the middle of November and finished up in March. The only break in it was the week from Christmas until January 1st. Cattle from the north drifted down by the thousands. Cattle outfits were on the Arkansas river crossing the cattle on ice. The next spring they gathered them down in Texas. When spring came, half my sheep were in the sweet hereafter.

"The spring of '81 my brother, John Churchill, came out. He was afterwards president of the Kansas State Board of Agriculture. We enlarged the sheep business and sold out in the fall of '83 to J. M. McVay, who settled on the north folk of the Pawnee. We then went into the cattle business, shipping out well-bred shorthorns from Missouri. In 1885 my brother sold out his interests and moved to Dodge City.

"I remember well the morning of January 18, 1883. The sky was overcast and the air still and warm. A few large flakes of snow were falling. I was sitting at a table writing when suddenly there was a roar outside. 'Now what,' I thought as I rushed to the door. On opening it, I was met by a blinding, swirling mass of dust-like snow so thick that I couldn't see six feet in front of me, while the roar of the storm would have drowned that of Niagara Falls. It was our first blizzard. It came without an instant's warning. Not a settler had met that kind of a monster before. None knew its danger. I thought as I watched its uncontrolled fury, such force cannot last— it's a squall, in a few minutes it will pass. Yet it did not pass for six hours. That night it was thirty degrees below zero.

"It was to a family north of us, Wolf by name, that a double tragedy came. They had a sheep ranch at the head of a draw on the Walnut. Their daughter, Louise, was a lovely girl. She was engaged to a young man in the east, and he had given her a riding pony. At the first rush of the storm, without a thought of danger, she started for the stable, to see that her pony was all right. Shortly after, her father came in from the corral.

"Where's Louise?" he asked.

"Out in the stable to see about her pony," they told him.

"Why, it's awful out," he said. "I will get her."

"Neither ever came back. They found her in the garden, frozen to death. She could not stand against the storm. They found her father a mile and a half south. Evidently he had drifted with the wind, seeking his daughter. It was pioneer life. Western Kansas was taking its toll.

"During 1879 there was a small herd of perhaps thirty buffalo that used the north part of what is now Finney county and the south part of Scott county for a grazing ground and watered at Alkali Lake. That fall George Goddard, George Recker and a Schofield boy whose father had settled on the South Fork, decided to go on a buffalo hunt. They found the herd south of the sand hills.

"Goddard did not join in the race. The Schofield boy had a green horse which would not run into the buffalo, so he was soon out of it. The success of the hunt depended on Recker. He was riding a cow pony named Calico. To the old cow pony, buffalo were the same as cattle, and soon he was right among the flying herd. Buffalo to the right of him, buffalo to the left of him and buffalo in front of him. Recker could almost reach out and touch them on either side. He carried a Henry rifle that was considerably out of repair and needed fixing after each shot. He fired twice, killing one buffalo and badly wounding another. He was busy getting the old gun ready to shoot again when Calico, who had been running free, there being no hold on his bridle, stepped in a hole. Recker was thrown far beyond the horse, where he lay unconscious for two hours before he again realized he was still in this world of woe. By that time the flying herd was miles away and Mr. Recker was not able to continue the hunt. On their way back next day they came by my place on the Middle Fork of the Pawnee. Recker had on a hat, but his head was wrapped in a bandage and his face was badly scratched. James Chapel and myself were batching at the time, and they gave us some of the buffalo meat."

Soon after J. A. Goodman arrived in 1885, Garfield county was organized and the county seat fight commenced. He says: "I plunged into the thickest of the fight. Fought, bled and lived to see my taxes increase.

"Planted five crops of wheat, only one of which ever came up. Gave up trying to raise wheat and started in on a new deal. Thought that the cow, the sow and the hen would be a sure way to make a living, but the hen went to setting, the sow went to eating chickens and the cow went to sucking herself. Abandoned that idea and like John the Baptist, lived on locusts and wild honey and my raiment was camel's hair. Then about that time, along came a prairie fire and killed all the locusts and singed off the camel's hair. Things began to look desperate and I made up my mind to leave the country. Made an invoice of my finances and didn't have the price of a box of axle grease, so had to stay, and here I am, and what for is one of the unexplained mysteries.

"Now as to telling all I know about the old timers, God forbid. A great deal of it would never get through the mail and would be unfit to print. It would make many volumes. A great many of the old timers have crossed the river Styx (some were probably drowned in midstream). I do not wish to libel the living nor malign the dead."

The Southwestern Land District

OCTOBER 1, 1883, the United States Land Office was opened for business in Garden City. The territory served by this office was known as the "Southwestern Land District" and was described as follows:

"Commencing at the southeast corner of township 35 south, range 31 west of the sixth principal meridian on the south boundary of the state of Kansas; thence north on said western boundary to the fourth standard parallel south; thence east along said parallel to the southeast

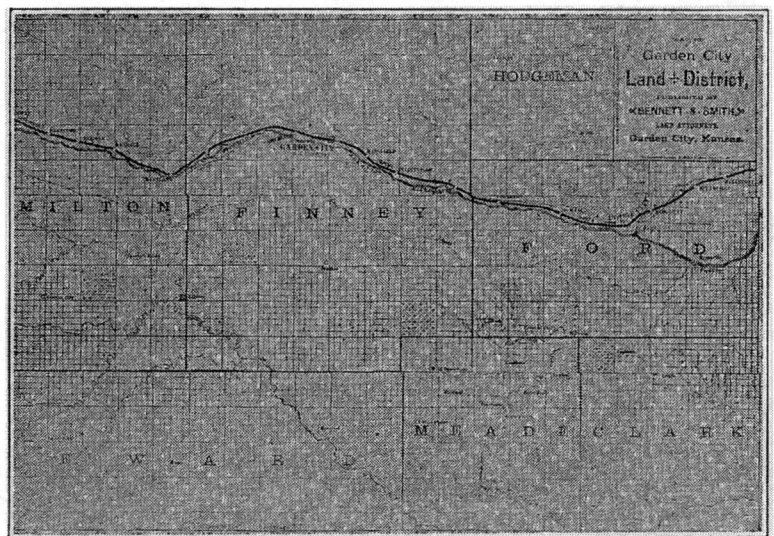

corner of township 21, south, range 31 west, and thence south to the place of beginning, in the state of Kansas."

The cash receipts of the office from October 1, 1883, to June 30, 1884, were $23,609.25; for the fiscal year ending June 30, 1885, $120,161.25; for the year ending June 30, 1886, $385,348.86; for the year ending June 30, 1887, $993,772.47; for the year ending June 30, 1888, $1,458,-333.00; for the year ending June 30, 1889, $628,515.73.

Receipts continued to decline after 1889, and the office was discontinued January 25, 1894.

The fees paid for homestead and timber claims, each $14; for pre-emptions $2 each. The first homestead entry for land in Finney county (including Garfield township) was made by George W. Close, being homestead entry No. 3497, made at Larned, January 30, 1878, for W. ½, N.W. ¼, Sec. 12, T. 24 S., R. 33 W. The entry was cancelled April 21, 1882. The land was proved up by Henry M. Wheeler April 29, 1884.

The first timber culture entry made in Finney county was No. 1646, made March 19, 1878, at the Land Office at Larned, for S.W. ¼, Sec. 24, T. 24 S., R. 32 W., by Thaxton W. Carlton. The entry was cancelled by relinquishment August 21, 1884.

The names of the registers and receivers and the periods of their service at the Garden City Office are:

Register	Receiver
H. P. Myton	A. J. Hoisington
Oct. 1, 1883—Oct. 17, 1885	Oct. 1, 1883—Aug. 31, 1885
C. F. M. Niles	Samuel Thanhauser
Jan. 8, 1886—Nov. 11, 1889	Sept. 1, 1885—July 30, 1889
Daniel M. Frost	James Taylor
Nov. 12, 1889—Jan. 25, 1894	July 31, 1889—Feb. 1, 1894

Finney County

FINNEY county was created by an act of Legislature in 1883, and was named in honor of Lieutenant Governor Finney of Woodson county. Early in 1884 efforts to complete the organization of the county began. The law required that before a county could be organized there must be more than 1,500 inhabitants and more than 250 actual householders.

State of Kansas,
County of Shawnee:

John J. Munger, being first duly sworn, states that he was on the 16th day of Sept., 1884, duly appointed by the governor of Kansas as census taker for the county of Finney. That he thereupon qualified by taking an oath to faithfully discharge the duties of that office, and proceeded to take the census of said Finney county by ascertaining the number of bona fide inhabitants, together with their names and ages, also the number of actual householders residing in said county of Finney, as well as the number of acres of cultivated land therein, all of which is embraced in the foregoing schedule and return is true; that there are 1,500 and 69 (1,569) bona fide inhabitants in said Finney county; that there are three hundred and seventy-three (373) actual householders residing therein and that there are twenty-nine hundred and five (2,905) acres of cultivated land in said Finney county.

John J. Munger.

Subscribed and sworn to before me this 1st day of October, 1884. C. J. Brown,
Clerk of the Supreme Court,
State of Kansas.

The Governor's proclamation, organizing the county of Finney and the temporary location of the county seat:

PROCLAMATION

State of Kansas, Executive Department,
Topeka, Kansas, Oct. 1, 1884.

Whereas a memorial signed by two hundred and fifty householders, residents of Finney county, Kansas, and legal electors of the state of Kansas, whose signature to said memorial have been duly attested by the affidavits of these householders thereof, showing that said county had more than 1,500 inhabitants and that more than 250 of said inhabitants are actual householders and praying for the organization of said Finney county, said affiants alleging that they had reason to and did believe said memorial to be true,

And whereas John J. Munger, a bona fide resident of said Finney county, was duly appointed and commissioned as census taker and was duly qualified as such officer, and it appears from an actual enumeration by census returns, duly made, certified and sworn to by said census taker according to law, and there are 1,500 and 69 bona fide inhabitants in said county and that 373 of them are actual householders.

Now, therefore know ye that I, G. W. Glick, governor of the state of Kansas, by authority of law vested in me have appointed and commissioned H. M. Wheeler, A. B. Kramer and John Speer as county commissioners and H. E. Wentworth as county clerk for said county of Finney and do hereby designate and declare the town of Garden City to be the temporary county seat of said county.

In testimony whereof I have hereunto subscribed my name and affixed the great seal of the state. Done at the city of Topeka, Kansas, the day and year first written above.

G. W. Glick, Governor

The boundaries of the county were defined as follows:

"Commencing at a point where the south line of township 30 crosses the east line of range 37, thence running east on said line of range 29, thence running north on said range line to the south line of township 20, thence running west to the east line of range 37, thence south to the place of beginning."

At the time of its organization Finney was the largest county in the state. It included the former unorganized counties of Sequoyah and Arapaho (now Haskell) and parts of Kearny, Grant, Lane, Gray and Meade, and was forty-eight miles east and west by sixty miles north and south. At that time the unorganized counties of Hamilton, Scott, Seward and Wichita were also attached to Finney county for judicial purposes. Those counties with Finney covered the entire area of Southwestern Kansas.

The first meeting of the board of county commissioners of Finney county was held in the Metropolitan Hotel in Garden City October 2, 1884, John Speer acting as chairman. At that meeting by virtue of authority vested in them by law, the said board issued a proclamation for an election of county and township officers and for the location of a county seat, to be held November 4, 1884.

At the first election on November 4, 1884, these were the results: On presidential electors, Republican 222 and Democratic 163 votes, total 385. The following county officers were elected: Representative, C. J. Jones; county clerk, A. H. Burtis; county treasurer, George H. DeWaters; sheriff, James R. Fulton; register of deeds, Captain John J. Munger; county attorney, W. R. Hopkins; probate judge, H. M. Wheeler; clerk of the district court, E. G. Bates; superintendent of public instruction, Albert Hurst; coroner, H. S. Lowrance; county commissioners, First District, David Fay; Second District, D. R. Menke; Third District, W. P. Loucks. The vote on county seat was, Garden City 264, Sherlock 61, Lakin 20, Pierceville 5, Deerfield 1, Bullard's Ranch 1.

Garden City was declared the permanent county seat of Finney county with judiciary power over all the unorganized counties of southwestern Kansas. This made it very convenient for the citizens of this region as the United States Land Office was already located here, since May, 1883, necessitating the homesteaders to come to this point. The Land Office was continued here until February, 1894, at which time it was consolidated with the Larned office and both were removed to Dodge City, Kansas.

At an early meeting of the board of county commissioners, it was agreed that they levy a tax on the property situated within the boundaries of the original Sequoyah county, to pay the indebtedness contracted by said Sequoyah county as an organized township attached to Ford county for judicial purposes. A motion was also made that all steps necessary be taken to secure books belonging to old Sequoyah township, now a part of Finney county. The salary of the Probate Judge was fixed at $150 per annum, and that of the County Attorney, County Treasurer and County Clerk at $400 per annum.

In June, 1885, petitions signed by citizens of Wichita, Seward, Scott and Hamilton counties, attached to Finney for judicial purposes, were presented to the board of commissioners, requesting that they be organized as municipal townships. On motion it was ordered that the county of Hamilton be organized as a municipal township and Syracuse was named as the place of transacting public business. Scott county was also ordered organized and Scott Center designated as the place of transacting public business. Seward was ordered organized, with Sunset City as the place of transacting public business. And Wichita was ordered organized with Leoti named as the place of transacting public business. Other voting precincts were established in each township, and an election was called by the sheriff of Finney county to be held on the 30th day of June, 1885. These counties remained municipal townships of Finney county until 1887.

In 1885 the two southeast corner townships were taken off Finney and added to Meade county.

The county line question was made a direct issue in the election of November 6, 1885. C. J. Jones, representing those opposed to changing the county lines, was elected. As soon as the legislature convened, an immense lobby from various quarters made its appearance to assist the county "divisionists" members in cutting up of counties in order to make more county seats. The ablest speakers and best parliamentarians on the floor of the house as well as the speaker of the house, were all advocates of the bill to re-establish the old county lines. In addition to these, all the clerks and employees of the House, even down to the doorkeepers and a great many of the shrewdest lobbyists in the state formed the opposition that Mr. Jones had to contend with. He considered it a base betrayal of the confidence of his constituents to sit idly by and see the county lines changed, so fought alone.

But by and by reinforcements commenced to drop in to assist Mr. Jones. W. R. Hopkins, Mr. House and Mr. Cook came from Finney county, and others from Hamilton. For three long weeks the battle raged fiercely and not a move was made by the friends of the bill but was checkmated by Mr. Jones and his adjutants. At times Mr. Jones would go a little further than discretion demanded, but yet all had to admire his courage. Finally the bill was made a special order for February 12th. Then there was mounting in hot haste and couriers were sent flying hither and thither to summon aid for the final charge. The friends of the bill counted on 85 votes and they believed that Mr. Jones and his friends would be crushed under the avalanche that was sure to come. The hour for the final struggle at length arrived and the friends of the bill moved bravely to the assault, and for a time it looked as if the enemies of the bill would be utterly routed, but the "gentleman" from Finney leaped to the bench and fought nobly. The fight raged on, the victory now seeming to favor this side and now that, but after two hours the victory rested with Mr. Jones and his friends. The results were hailed with shouts of applause, and cigars were distributed freely. It was one of the most stubborn fights that ever took place in a legislative body.

Ed Lauk received the following telegram at Garden City Friday night, February 12th, from the Hon. C. J. Jones:

"The bill was killed in the house two to one. Thank God, and the House and the State of Kansas.

"C. J. Jones"

The next year H. P. Myton was elected as Representative and the county line fight was renewed in the legislature of 1887. Finney county was cut down to the original lines of old Sequoyah county, and Gray, Haskell and Kearny were organized as separate counties.

In 1892 the Supreme Court decided that Garfield county was illegally organized, it having less than 432 square miles as required by law. In 1893 it was annexed to Finney county. Thus, Finney county as it has stood since that time is twenty-four miles from east to west and thirty-six miles from north to south, and with the addition of Garfield township, which is eighteen by twenty-four miles, has an area of 1,296 square miles.

The population of old Sequoyah county in 1880 was 568. Six years later the Finney county census for the year 1886 showed 14,662 people. In 1890, the census report was only 3,350, and in 1900 it was still less, being 3,214. Since 1900 each decade shows a gradual gain in population and the census of 1930 found 11,006 living in the county.

Finney county is divided into seven townships, Garden City, Pierceville, Pleasant Valley, Ivanhoe, Terry, and Sherlock named for Thos. Sherlock.

The prevailing climate is pleasant without extremes. The weather records do not show any fundamental change in climate in the half century since settlement began in this region. There is no more rainfall, no less wind, and it is neither hotter nor colder, on the average, than it was fifty years ago. There has been a change, but it is not of climate. It is one of surface conditions. The hot winds which used to sweep over the prairie with such devastating power have been conquered by the breaking up of the prairie, causing more of the rainfall to go into the soil, and by irrigation of crops. The planting of thousands of acres of alfalfa and other cultivated crops and the planting of many trees, break and cool the surface winds. The average rainfall for the 18-year period from 1908 to 1925 inclusive was 18.23 inches, and 76 per cent occurred during the growing season, from April 1 to October 1.

The most fatal storm in the history of Finney county was the blizzard of 1886. During that storm of snow and zero weather, more than fifty people and cattle by the tens of thousands were frozen to death in Western Kansas. The pioneers have never forgotten that storm and the suffering it brought, and many have written their personal experience to be preserved in history.

Below is a letter written by John Speer, of Sherlock, January 12, 1886, to "The Topeka Commonwealth":

"Sherlock, January 12, 1886. We have had the most terrible storm I have ever witnessed. Perhaps my own experience will give a fair idea of its destructive character. The last of December was a beautiful day, clear, bright and warm, and New Year's Day was quite comfortable; but about eight o'clock the wind shifted to the northwest and struck all this region furiously, accompanied with snow which fairly darkened the whole atmosphere, the snow being very fine. The temperature was exceedingly cold, but I had no means of ascertaining the degrees. It became so dark that objects could be seen only at a very short distance. At my own place we have a very warm, dry dugout barn, in which we shelter the horses; but the range cattle dropped down on us, and, climbing upon the barn roof in their famished state, crushed it in, and the horses narrowly escaped destruction. We then got them under the shelter of the dwelling house as a partial protection. This storm commenced on the night of January 1, and by Tuesday had so subsided as to make travel quite reasonable, and Wednesday cleared off, a beautiful day; but about eight o'clock that night the wind almost instantly shifted from the south to the northwest, and thenceforward for about thirty-six hours such a storm howled over this region as the oldest inhabitant, or any other man, never witnessed. Prominent objects could not be seen ten feet distant.

"We did our best for the protection of the horses by placing the plow team of my brother on the south side of the house, which is "L" shape, and the best possible protection from the northwest wind. Another horse we left under the protection of the partial roof of the demolished dugout barn, and the donkey was tied on the south side of a sod structure. By morning, no human could stem the fury of the storm. The horse had almost perished, and their lives could only be saved by taking them into the house. The donkey was alive, but died before the storm abated. One horse was ten feet under a snow drift, into which I excavated a hole much like bricklayers call a "manhole" and through that reached the animal, beating back and tramping the snow until I made a space about four by eight feet, and there fed and watered him for three days until he died. As soon as I could get out I found my nearest neighbor, Mr. Stillwagon, was digging the dead animals out of a barn, having lost four horses and nearly his whole herd of cattle had gone to the winds. Mr. Tracy, four miles off, lost a span of mules. Nearly all of Captain Ballinger's cattle were lost. Mr. McKeever said of 180 head he had found less than seventy alive. A negro on Captain Ballinger's ranch is reported badly frozen; two men are reported frozen to death near Syracuse, and others are reported frozen and as having perished in every direction.

"Frequently snowdrifts are six feet in depth. The drifts are so compact that teams can travel over them, and it is where the snow is not drifted deep that it is most difficult to get through. In many places the range cattle cross the railroad fences on the snow and wander along the track, and many are dead and dying. A gentlemen told me that within two miles west of Sherlock he counted seventy head of dead cattle along the outside of the railroad fence, and another told me he was sure there were 400 within a space of twenty acres, dead under the banks of the Arkansas.

"I think at this writing (Tuesday noon) no trains have gone west since the last storm, though one train of two passenger coaches and two cabooses has passed east—probably from Coolidge, notwithstanding the almost super-human energy of the officers of the Santa Fe company. At the earliest possible moment additional gangs of hands were at work clearing the tracks. The snow plow was of little use, owing to the compact character of the drifts. On Thursday I counted seventy-five hands with shovels who had been organized at Garden City, and had progressed west about twelve miles. Their feet were wrapped with gunny sacks and burlap, and they were bravely stemming the storm. The snow was cast out in large blocks, some digging and some throwing it out with their hands. I hear there is danger of a coal famine, but there is great confidence that all that is possible will be done by the railroad managers. Today is moderate, the sky clear and the sun bright.

"I can scarcely illustrate the severity of the storm better than by telling you that I counted a dozen antelope within twenty rods of my house, and yesterday three came into my dooryard, within fifteen feet of my front door. When antelope get so benumbed by cold and starvation as to almost invade the houses, the imagination will pretty accurately convey to all acquainted with their wild shy habits the degree of suffering which all flesh is subject to in this exposure.

"This is a poor letter, but it is the best I can do in a snow bank."

In reminiscence of that storm, I. L. Diesem wrote recently: "No one knew how much snow fell during that period of thirty-four hours, because it drifted in great piles. We lived on the farm at that time, in Diesem's addition to Garden City, and a drift formed in the yard between the house and stable 15 feet deep.

"Before 9 p.m. on the evening of the storm cattle drifted in from the Upton Ranch at Scott City, and were at our stacks of feed, tearing it down and eating it. We got the dogs out and drove them away, but a light was put in the window for us to see to return by. Without the light to guide us back to the house, we would have drifted with the storm. We saved our stock by the feed and care we gave them. When the storm subsided, we had two buckets of coal left. We would have burned the fence posts around the yard if it had become necessary.

"I. R. Holmes was mayor of Garden City at that time. He had committees out in every direction with blankets and food, as soon as the storm broke."

The pioneer constructed but a makeshift upon his claim. A shack of cheapest material, poorly put together, housed many of the homesteaders and much of the suffering from the storm was due to this fact. Those living in dugouts were secure and comfortable, provided they had sufficient food and fuel.

One of the saddest cases resulting from the storm in Finney county, was that of George Beck. He was living on a homestead east of Garden City. During the day when he was away from his shanty, some one stole a part of his roof and all his coal. When he reached home at dark, he discovered his loss but decided to stay the night, and that evening the storm came. He was in this shanty until the second day when the storm broke, and he made his way on frozen feet to a neighbor two miles away. The following account, telling of his condition, was taken from a Garden City newspaper:

"George Beck, who has been lying at the Ohio House for three weeks with frozen feet, was compelled to have them amputated. After deliberate consultation, Drs. Lowrance, Niles and Sabine decided upon this course to save his life. The right foot was taken off just above the ankle, and the left a little below the knee. He was put under the influence of ether and stood the operation well. Since which he has been getting along as well as could be expected, but the prospect of recovery is only moderately encouraging.

"The poor man was overcome with grief when told that he would have to lose his legs. Having lost one hand, and now to lose both legs was more than he could bear, and he gave vent to his feelings by sorrowful weeping. He is a poor man and has a wife and two children in Peoria, Illinois."

Mr. Beck recovered and in June, the next summer, a fund of $100 was raised among the people of Garden City for the purpose of starting him in business. A small building was erected and he was placed there in charge of a fruit stand. This gave him a chance to support himself and family. Until this time he had been kept by the city and county since he had been frozen.

In March, 1886, after the blizzard, C. J. (Buffalo) Jones, in his itinerary, says:

"As I drove over the prairies from Kansas into Texas I saw thousands upon thousands of carcasses of domestic cattle which had drifted before the chilling, freezing 'norther'. Every one of them had died with his tail to the blizzard, never having stopped except at its last breath, then fell dead in its tracks. When I reached the habitat of the buffalo, not one of their carcasses was visible except those which had been slain by the hunters. Every animal I came across was as nimble and wiry as a fox. I commenced to ponder upon the contrast between the white man's domestic cattle and those of the red man's cattle (buffalo)."

Various blizzards have taken their toll during the winters since 1886, but it is claimed by those who have lived in this region, that the one which occurred here March 26, 1931, was the worst since 1886. It was on the same order, but did not last so long and it was not as cold. Many birds and rabbits were killed, and it has been estimated that fifty per cent of the cattle in Finney county were lost. Bruce Josserand says in writing of the storm:

"Temperatures were zero and below and brought intense suffering to the live stock. Stray cattle rounded into the stock yards today by O. E. Josserand and Elmer Williams had apparently drifted for many miles. All of them were frozen, bare of hair from the hocks to the body, between their hind and front legs. They were bloody and lacerated. One or two had their hind legs frozen stiff to the hocks."

COURT HOUSES OF FINNEY COUNTY

THE first meeting of the board of commissioners of Finney county was held in the Metropolitan Hotel October 2, 1884, in Garden City. John Speer acting as chairman. Meetings were held there regularly until January

1, 1885, when a small frame building was rented for court-house purposes. It was located in block 37 on the east side of Main street. The county officers furnished their own rooms, but were allowed $5.00 per month for rent, fuel and lights. The Dickerson theatre is built on the site of the first court house.

During the summer of 1885 there was much talk of building a court house. At a meeting of the board of commissioners August 3, 1885, the following rooms were offered for court-house purposes: John Stevens made offer of rooms to be used as a court house at a rental of $420 for one year, or three. J. V. Carter offered rooms at $20 per month, for one year or three. C. J. Jones made offer of four rooms in his stone building, and he also offered to build a court house. His proposition to build a court house was accepted, and reads as follows:
"To the Honorable Board of County Commissioners, Greetings:

"For the purpose of security and safe keeping of our public records for the county of Finney, state of Kansas, I hereby make the following proposition to your honorable board, to-wit:

"I will build a stone building to be completed on or before October 25, 1885, on block A, Jones addition to Garden City, 40x40 feet, of good stone walls not less than eighteen inches in thickness, thirteen feet ceiling, iron or tin roof, with four rooms, two vaults which are to be fire proof. The two south rooms to be separated by folding doors, so as to be used for a court room if desired. Said building to be completed in a good substantial workmanlike manner, as per diagram herewith attached and marked exhibit A. All of said building to be used as county buildings for a period of two years without cost or compensation to anyone except myself.

"Signed, C. J. Jones.

"P.S.—The third year's rent will not exceed twenty

dollars per month. If the Judge of the District Court and the honorable board prefer, will furnish a suitable hall in my stone building for the purpose of holding court, free of charge for the same term as stipulated above.

"C. J. Jones."

The site was the block on the corner of Eighth and St. John, commonly known as "Court House Square". Mr. Jones gave bond of $5,000 to have the building completed as specified, and the commissioners signed an agree-

The first Finney County Courthouse. It was built in C. J. (Buffalo) Jones Park, Garden City, 1885.

ment to keep the records in said building for a period of two years, from November 14, 1885. Work began on the new court house at once.

The corner stone of the court house and the new three-story hotel now known as the Buffalo block, between Grant avenue and Laurel street on Main street, were laid September 10, 1885, in the presence of a multitude of people. Mr. Jones secured reduced rates, and the early morning train from the east brought in two special coaches full to overflowing. One coach came from Topeka, the other from Wichita and Wellington. There was also a large turnout of the people of Finney and surrounding counties.

After the train arrived from the west, the Garden City cornet band marched up the street to the new hotel, followed by people in buggies, on foot, and on horse back. Every vehicle in town was in use. Col. D. A. Mims mounted the walls, which were just being started, as master of ceremonies. He introduced Elder A. C. McKeever, who addressed the people for a few minutes, giving a brief historical sketch of Garden City from its infancy up to that time, and a prospective view of the great future before us. After that, loud cries for "Jones" brought C. J. to the front. Mr. Jones disclaimed all the honor of the present glory of Garden City, and said without the aid of his enterprising neighbors, he could have done nothing toward the developing of this grand city of the plains.

The cavity of the corner stone was then filled with various articles including a copy of the city papers, report of the state board of agriculture, 1883-1884, Kansas Horticultural report, 1884, the circular advertising the event, the banner which C. J. Jones carried at the Chicago convention, cards of all who handed them in, nickels, dimes, quarters, half dollars and dollars donated by the crowd. There was perhaps as much as $25 in cash in small mites placed in the two stones. The masons then placed the stone in position. Rev. McKeever moved that the hotel be christened "The Buffalo House" in honor of the familiar title of its builder. The motion carried with a whoop, and the ceremonies wound up with three rousing cheers for C. J. Jones.

The crowd advanced to the court house. There, speeches were made by Hon. John Speer, A. J. Abbott, A. J. Landis of Sterling, and I. R. Holmes. Time and space forbids our giving a synopsis of any of the speeches, but they all contained words of wisdom and encouragement. Mr. Landis was the gentleman who started the irrigation canals here, and one remark he made deserves a place here because of the emphatic truth it contained. He said that he had always told his friends, and believed yet that the time would come when Western Kansas would be the most valuable portion of the state.

The cavity of the court house stone was filled similarly to the former one and then the sale of lots began. (Public auction of lots in Jones' Addition to Garden City.) In the vicinity of the court house lots sold from $175 to $200. The aggregate of sales was $24,000. The sale proceeded until four o'clock, when Mr. Jones invited all to board his two coaches at the depot and take a free ride to Hartland and return. The coaches were filled, and the sales there amounted to $7,000, making a total for the day of $31,000.

The proceeds from this lot sale went to build the new stone court house. Terms of sale, one-fourth cash, balance on six, twelve and eighteen months' time, at 10% interest.

The court house, when completed, had four rooms below and upstairs was two office rooms and a large courtroom. The whole was fitted up in the best manner. The total cost of the building was about $6,000. Two iron cells were ordered placed in the county jail in an upper room in the court house February 25, 1886, at a cost of $3,464. These were the first in the county. The Jones court house was used until February, 1902. It was necessary during most of that time to use a courtroom outside of the building on account of room.

In the summer of 1901 the county decided by its commissioners, E. L. Hall, J. V. Killion and G. L. Holmes, to secure better quarters so they could all be in the same building and have better vaults for fire protection for records. The Jones court house was abandoned, except as a jail for which purpose it was used many years.

"Garden City, Kansas, July 3, 1901.
"Whereas the county of Finney is owner of special warranty deed from George W. Finnup, donated for the purpose of use by Finney county, of said real estate and building thereon, to-wit: Lot 12, block 36, original town of Garden City, and whereas Finney county has no permanent court house or county building other than the jail building, suitable for needs of said county; Finney county has accepted the donation of said George Finnup and it is deemed by said board of county commissioners to be to the best interests of the people of the county, and a saving of expense." Commissioners Journal A.

They purchased from George W. Warden lot 11, and the building thereon for $900. Also the four remaining lots south of the building were purchased at a low price and made into a park.

C. A. Schneider was the county clerk. He planned with ability the arrangement of the remodeling the court house. It had five large brick vaults and a good heating plant built in the rear, and at that time a heating plant was a luxury. The court house was 50x100 feet, two stories high, built out of stone. Fred Pyle, the leading contractor at that time, secured the job of remodeling the building for $4,303, and did the work in good shape. The county had less than $10,000 invested in the court house and eight lots. This court house was used from February, 1902, until April, 1929, over twenty-seven years.

A movement for a new court house began in 1928. W. G. Hopkins, who was county clerk at that time, and the county commissioners, R. J. Ackley, J. W. King and W. L. Thomas, deserve much credit for the building, which now stands as the "pride of Finney county" on the original court house site in the C. J. (Buffalo) Jones Park.

Petitions were circulated by members of the American Legion, and the names of fifty-one per cent of the voters were secured as favoring a new building, only five or six in the county expressed themselves as being opposed. An election was held on location, and it was voted back to the Jones Park by a large majority.

The corner stone was laid November 29, 1928, under the direction of Grand Lodge A.F. & A.M. of the state of Kansas. The first number on the program was a quartet, composed of Mr. and Mrs. W. A. Maltbie, Mrs. C. A. Carter and L. W. Cooley. This was followed by a prayer by Rev. H. O. Judd. The box was then deposited in the stone and a list of the contents of the box read. It contained a list of the members of the Tyrian lodge 246, a list of officers of the state Grand Lodge, the names of the county commissioners, and the history of the county since its organization written by George W. Finnup, a picture of the old jail, a list of the school children of Garden City, a list of the members of the band, a copy of the Garden City Herald, The Telegram and Opportunity, The Western Kansas Magazine. Judge H. E. Walters of Syracuse delivered the address of the day.

The cost of the building complete was about $186,323.21. The main contract was let to the Bailey-Burns Construction Company of Norman, Oklahoma, for $122,400; Carter Bros. Hardware for plumbing, $13,995; Eggen Electric Co., $4,844.21; special sound-proof ceiling, $975.00; furniture $16,998; architects were Rutledge and Hertz of Hutchinson, Kansas, $7,000; installing water system, $2,500; decorating $2,830. The building is 76x107 feet, and four stories high. It is of steel and solid cement construction faced with Bedford, Indiana, stone.

THE BEEF BUSINESS IN FINNEY COUNTY

The second chapter of the cattle industry began after the blizzard of 1886 under a new system and on a much smaller scale.

During the boom years the overwhelming number of homesteaders completely routed the open range cattlemen. But in 1888 the hot winds began again and crops were a complete failure, and people began leaving. In 1889-90 the crop conditions were no better, and unseasonable years prevailed all through the nineties. A great exodus of settlers took place in those first years of drouth. Soon all that remained upon many homesteads to remind one that it had once known home life were slight depressions or piles of sod marking the spots where the settlers' dugouts and shanties had stood.

The majority of those who did remain in the country suffered from poverty, but they had grit and determination and managed to stay on. But they gave up the idea of extensive farming and went back to stock raising and began to make use of all the deserted lands around them. Every farmer became a breeder, and every heifer calf was kept. The beginning of many herds was the family milk cow. Those who had money bought blooded stock, and there was a general grading up of stock cattle.

Practically all the land deserted by the homesteaders had been mortgaged to various loan companies, and it was not long until these companies held titles. Owing to drouthy years, however, they could not sell it, and there were no crops on it from which to collect rentals, so they let much of it go back to the county. Gradually the men who had stayed on the job and were making use of the unoccupied lands began buying it up by quarters and sections often as low as a dollar per acre, or bought it in for taxes. The cheap land induced big ranchers from other parts to move their interests here. This new crop of cattlemen in a few years had control of large land holdings, but this time by purchase and ownership.

The big pastures were cleared of the boom towns. Even the population of Garden City dwindled to a few hundred, and once more it became only a cow town.

The Windsor Hotel with its 125 rooms, built to accommodate eastern speculators, now became headquarters for heads of wealthy cattle firms. Its spacious corridors and spindled patios were constantly thronged with booted and spurred cowmen. Cattle deals amounting to millions of dollars have been transacted over the long table in the great inner court.

Bands of cowboys cantered in from surrounding ranches and enlivened the town with their pranks. They were always well armed with guns while on the range. But they were law-abiding citizens and respected the ordinances of Garden City, which prohibited the carrying of fire-arms in town. As soon as they arrived, they would usually go straight to Carter Brothers Hardware store, strip off guns and belts, and hand them over the counter, to be stacked away in a drawer. They would then clatter up and down the plank side-walks in their high-heeled boots and jangling spurs, stopping at the various places of business, or would be the center of an admiring crowd as they exhibited their skill with saddle ropes at which they were all artists.

During the days of '86 Garden City had supported sixteen "drug stores" where liquor was sold openly. Several of them quit business in the next few years, but those that remained seemed to prosper. According to the State Prohibition law, which had been in effect since May 1, 1881, whiskey could be sold only for medicinal purposes. Each applicant was required to fill out a blank, stating what he needed it for. They nearly always said, "for Consumption".

The cowboys usually managed for one reason or another to consume a satisfactory amount of whiskey while in town. By the time they were ready to go back to the range they were pretty well "lit up". They would call for their pistols, and there is no record that they ever shot up the town, but they did ride out shooting and yelling like wild Comanches. Sometimes in farewell they would rope a section of the high plank sidewalk, hitch it to the pommel of a saddle and go hurtling across the prairie.

To list the men in the cattle business during the thirty years following 1886 would include the greater per cent of those living in the county. Farmers, merchants, and professional men were all more or less interested in the business, besides a number of exclusive dealers. There is a large volume filed away in the Finney county court house which contains the names of cattle owners and the

Chuck Wagon of the George Heckel cattle outfit, 1881. Camped on the Heckel Ranch, southeast of Garden City.

brands they used to distinguish their cattle, horses and sheep. Many of the ranches had descriptive names registered in this volume. Broadacres, W. R. Jacques, all of Sec. 5-24-33. Herman Ranch, 800 acres, one mile west of Ravanna. Lone Elm, S.W. 26-25-32. Graceland Meadows, section 14-24-33. Ivanhoe Valley Ranch, section 7-26-31. Many of the ranches were named after their brand. Some of the well-known ranches were: The Bullard Ranch, operated by the Bullard cattle company. They owned every other section between Holcomb and Pierceville. They put down the first two wells in the sand hills south of Garden City. The Cowgill Ranch, southwest of Garden

City, also covered many sections. It was owned by James Cowgill of Kansas City. Later the Guthrie Ranch owners bought up many sections south of the river. Prominent among the ranchers at Pierceville were A. H. Warner and the Orf brothers. Straud Renick and Edward Bowles ranged long-horn cattle from Pierceville to Charleston on the south side of the river from 1886 and through the nineties.

The Pawnee valley in Garfield township was almost entirely a big pasture. Straud Renick and John Quincy Grub were herding two hundred cattle on the Pawnee about the summer of 1900. Mr. Renick tells of an unusual experience:

"It was almost dark and we were hunting a place to camp. We were driving the cattle along when we heard something coming with a rush and roar. Looking toward the northwest we saw a dazzling, terrifying light which seemed to be coming directly toward us, and it looked like it was going to drop right among the cattle. As it neared the earth it made a popping, cracking noise and the cattle all started running. By golly, we were pretty badly scared. We recognized this heavenly visitor as a meteor, and while we were pretty sure where it came from, we hadn't the least idea where it was likely to land. But we went after the cattle and managed to head them into a corral. The brilliant light disappeared almost as quickly as it had appeared, but it left a column of smoke hanging in the heavens like a pall for several minutes."

Finney county is not the cattle country that it was, but there are still a number of its citizens in the beef business. There are over twenty ranches of 1,000 acres and a few over 5,000. One of the largest ranches still in this region is the Cowgill Ranch southwest of Garden City. It was owned by Judge James Cowgill for many years, who was mayor of Kansas City at the time of his death. It is still in the Cowgill family, being now the property of Mrs. Effie L. Spratt, Mrs. Cora F. McWilliams, and Mae C. Tait, his daughters.

Other large ranchers are: J. W. Jones, W. E. Hicks and Son, E. A. Stone, J. D. Cathcart, O. J. Brown, K. M. Winters, Chas. L. Brown, the Concannon brothers, Fred J. Reed, Chester and Oliver G. Reeve, C. E. Adams, J. W. King and Son; J. F. Douglas, George O. and John Long, J. H. Burnside, A. M. Lawrence, John T. Reed, Frank Reed, Sr., D. H. Holden, E. B. Phelps, R. E. Beach, C. H. Norris, Beecher F. Breyfogle, John Landgraf and Sons, the Greathouse family, Wm. C. Erkie, Alex Legleiter. These ranchers in nearly every instance diversify in crop growing, and farm a large acreage aside from their grass-land, and grow nearly all their own feed. According to the assessor's rolls, there were 19,835 beef cattle in Finney county March 1, 1929.

While Finney county is one of the largest shippers of cattle in Kansas only a few breeders are registered with the state board of agriculture. The only breeder of Aberdeen Angus cattle listed is B. F. Breyfogle, of Imperial, and the only Hereford breeders listed are Kinney and Byler, of Kalvesta.

G. W. O'Neil, north of Cimarron in Finney county, R. F. Plummer and Bryan Thomsen of Deerfield, are breeders of shorthorn cattle.

Jersey breeders are: Rose O. Craytor, of Holcomb, W. E. Hamill, Kalvesta, and E. A. Wingett, Garden City.

Dewitt Craft of Garden City is the only Holstein breeder listed, and Peter Blotcher the only breeder of Red Polled cattle.

The beef cattle in this county are all high grade. Nearly every stockman has at the head of his herd from one to twenty or more registered sires.

OFFICIAL ROSTER OF FINNEY COUNTY

REPRESENTATIVES
C. J. Jones, 1884, 1885, 1888
H. P. Myton, 1886
W. R. Hopkins, 1890, 1892, 1894
A. H. Burtis, 1896
H. F. Mason, 1898, 1900
W. M. Kinnison, 1902, 1904, 1906
Richard J. Hopkins, 1908
J. C. Tyler, 1910, 1912
Albert Hoskinson, 1914
Chas. D. Gorham, 1916, 1918
Clifford R. Hope, 1920, 1922, 1924
I. J. Carter, 1926, 1928
Ellsworth Sherman, 1930

CLERKS OF THE DISTRICT COURT
E. G. Bates, 1884, 1885
O. A. Harding, 1886, 1888
Mode M. Pierce, 1890, 1892
D. W. Pitts, 1894, 1896
J. W. Working, 1898, 1900
G. L. Neal, 1902
Robt. J. McClurkin, 1904
M. A. Easley, 1906, 1908
W. E. Covert, 1910, 1912, 1914
Helen M. Stowell, 1916, 1918
Nellie Glenn, 1920
G. Mae Purdy, 1922, 1924
Ruth S. Ruckel, 1926, 1928, 1930

COUNTY ATTORNEYS
W. R. Hopkins, 1884, 1885, 1886
H. F. Mason, 1888, 1890
G. L. Miller, 1892, 1898, 1900
B. F. Stocks, 1894, 1896
Albert Hoskinson, 1902, 1904
Edgar Roberts, 1906, 1908
Fred J. Evans, 1910, 1912, 1914
Abram Schulman, 1916
W. C. Pearce, 1918, 1920, 1930
Ray H. Calihan, 1922, 1924
A. M. Fleming, 1926, 1928

PROBATE JUDGES
H. M. Wheeler, 1884
J. W. Gregory, 1885, 1886
J. W. Weeks, 1888, 1890
John M. Wilson, 1892
J. S. Griggs, 1894, 1896
J. E. Dawson, 1898, 1900
W. S. Johnson, 1902, 1904, 1906, 1908, 1910, 1912
Jas. McCarty, appointed 1913
W. J. Johnson, 1914, 1916
C. L. Downs, 1918, 1920, 1922
Albert Hurst, 1924, 1926, 1928, 1930
Edgar Foster appointed March, 1931, to fill vacancy caused by death of A. Hurst

SHERIFFS
James R. Fulton, 1884
W. D. Fulton, 1885
E. G. O'Brien, 1887
John M. Lingenfelter, 1889
W. T. Eggen, 1891, 1893
F. G. Bills, 1895, 1897
A. R. Jessup, 1899, 1902
I. W. Bogart, 1904, 1906
O. P. Reeve, 1908, 1910
Chas. Kite, 1912
Oll Brown, 1914, 1916, 1922, 1924
Lee Richardson, 1918, 1920
Ben L. Strawn, 1926, 1928
R. S. Terwilliger, 1930

SURVEYORS
O. P. Reeve, 1884
J. S. Humphrey, 1885
I. M. Taylor, 1887
Thos. E. Weeks, 1889, 1891
N. C. Keyes, 1893
George H. Reeve, 1895
David Weeks, 1897, 1899
H. C. Diesem, 1902
Dennis D. Doty, 1904
C. B. Eamen, 1906, 1908, 1910, 1912, 1914, 1916, 1918

COUNTY COMMISSIONERS OF 1ST DISTRICT

David Fay, 1884
G. W. Wright, 1885
E. W. Van Brunt, 1887
R. M. Lawrence, 1890
H. L. Wolf, 1893, 1896
G. L. Holmes, 1899, 1902, 1906, 1910
I. J. Carter, 1914
S. A. Oxley, 1918
J. W. King, 1922, 1926, 1930

COMMISSIONERS OF THE 2ND DISTRICT

D. R. Menke, 1884
B. F. Smith, 1885
B. P. Knaus, 1887
C. H. Godfrey, 1888
E. L. Hall, 1891, 1894, 1897, 1900
O. P. Schults, 1904
W. T. Eggen, 1908
John Slattery, 1912, resigned 7-24-1913
A. R. Towles, appointed 1913, elected 1914, 1916, 1920
R. J. Ackley, 1924, 1928

COMMISSIONERS OF THE 3RD DISTRICT

W. P. Loucks, 1884
J. H. Waterman, 1885, 1886
John Speer, 4-25-1887, apptd.
Page W. Conyers, 1889
Chas. McFadden, 1892
J. V. Killion, 1895, 1898, 1912, resigned 3-16-1914
C. V. Chalfont, 1901, 1904, 1908
D. P. Cathcart, 1916, 1920, 1924, apptd. 3-16-1914
I. N. Blanton, appointed February 10, 1927
W. L. Thomas, 1928

COUNTY CLERKS

A. H. Burtis, 1884, 1885
O. V. Folsom, 1887, 1889
T. C. Laughlin, 1891, 1893
W. D. Fulton, 1895, 1897
C. A. Schneider, 1899
W. McD. Rowan, 1902, 1904, 1906, 1908
Guy B. Norris, 1910, 1912, 1914, 1916
F. H. Laberteaux, 1918, 1920
W. G. Hopkins, 1922, 1924, 1926
A. G. Gardner, 1928, 1930

COUNTY TREASURERS

George H. DeWaters, 1884
D. R. Menke, 1885, 1887
Levi Wilkinson, 1889, 1891
J. C. Kitchen, 1893
H. V. Lawrence, 1895, 1897, 1904
Wm. Ford, 1899, 1902
A. C. Wheeler, 1906, 1908, 1910
Sidney E. Carlton, 1912, 1914
L. G. Perry, 1916, 1918
Mrs. L. G. Perry (wife), 1920
H. P. Nichols, 1922
L. M. Bland, 1924, 1926
Mrs. Katherine Dumond, died before taking office, Mrs. L. M. Bland, apptd., 1928, 1930

REGISTER OF DEEDS

J. J. Munger, 1884, 1885
J. C. Kitchen, 1887, 1889
H. P. Myton, 1891, 1893
W. McD. Rowan, 1895
D. A. Mims, 1897, 1899, Anna Mims, apptd., 1901, wife resigned, D. F. Mims, 1901, son appointed.
George H. Reeves, 1902, 1904
Joseph, Bevan, 1906, 1908, 1910
Mrs. G. L. Miller, 1912, 1914
Mrs. Eugene S. Weeks, 1916, 1918
Anah M. Vincent, 1920
Mrs. Florence Gingrich, 1922, 1924, 1926
Norma B. Beckett, 1928, 1930

SUPERINTENDENTS OF PUBLIC INSTRUCTION

Albert Hurst, 1884, 1885, 1892
Anna S. Wood, 1886, 1888
Mary E. Hopper, 1890
Ollie B. Mullins, 1894, 1896
J. E. Van Schoiack, 1898

E. J. Covert, 1900, 1902
H. P. Nichols, 1904
Freda D. Molz, 1906, 1908
Lewis Keeler, 1910, 1912
Emma F. Wilson, 1914, 1916, 1918, 1920
Jennie E. Barker, 1922, 1924, 1926, 1928, 1930

CORONERS
H. S. Lowrance, 1884, 1885, 1887, 1889
A. R. Clark, 1891, 1920, both inclusive.
Arthur Leslie, 1922
Chas. Rewerts, 1924, 1926
C. A. Wiley, 1928, 1930

THE SCHOOLS OF FINNEY COUNTY

By Albert Hurst, County Superintendent of Schools, January 1, 1885:

"To give a complete history of the schools of the county is an easy task, as the county has only been organized one year.

"The first district in the county was formed November 24, 1884. We now have ten districts with schools in each, requiring fourteen teachers. These districts are mostly along the railroad, as there were but few settled any distance from the railroad previous to the spring of 1885. Since that time they have been settling in all parts of the county and petitions are coming in from every quarter, asking for the formation of new districts.

"The population of school children in the county July 31, 1884, was 200; July 31, 1885, it was 600; December 1, 1885, it had reached 800. This great influx of children must be accompanied with the advantages of school, and I am glad to see the interest the citizens are taking in preparing accommodations for them. No sooner is there a settlement made than the cry goes out for a school. I will venture to say that one year hence we will have 50 districts in the county."

The following is the list of schools as reported by Mrs. Jennie E. Barker, county superintendent, in 1930: Valentine, District 4, Eminence, Pierceville, Lake Valley, Prairie Hope, Solid Rock, Lincoln, Silverdale, Knauston, Prairie Lea, Angleview, White Mound, Mennonite, Garfield, Liberty, Kalvesta, Gingrich Hill, New Loyal, Plynell, Alamo, North Star, Essex, Pleasant Valley, Ravanna, New Moon, Veteran, Skyline, Pawnee Valley, Mansfield, Quivera, English Hill, Pershing, New Hope, West Point, Bowman Ridge, Grand View, Prairie Lawn, Holcomb, Friend and Garden City. Seventy teachers were employed in the rural and consolidated schools, and fifty-four in Garden City.

Soil, Surface and Agriculture

THE surface of the different sections of the county varies and may be classified first, as flat; second, rolling or undulating; and third, level prairie upland. The approximate altitude is 2830 feet.

There is a wide variety in soil types in this county. It ranges from a silt to fine sand. The valley of the Arkansas river is filled with sandy alluvium. Much of the county is covered by tetiary deposits of sand and gravel and in the northeastern part of the county along the headwaters of Pawnee creek, soft magnesia limestone is exposed in large quantities.

Extending across the middle of the county is one great valley or basin with the Arkansas river winding for twenty-five miles in a southeasterly direction through its center. This long stretch of bottom land, varying from one to several miles in width, appears to be nearly flat, yet it has excellent drainage. However, the graduation of the surface as it rises to form the side of the valley is so gradual as to be almost imperceptable. The top of the south side of the valley is not uniform in height, but breaks into waves, dipping here and rising there like the crestlines of motionless waves, and beautiful views of the valley can be obtained from the high points. The soil of these low hills along the south side of the valley is sandy, but it grows good grass. The hills have a width of four to eight miles and follow the river. They are not used much for agricultural purposes, but furnish good grazing and are largely divided into big stock ranches. The land laying beyond the sand hills to the south boundary line of Finney county is level prairie upland and the soil is a sandy loam. It is well adapted for growing wheat, corn and other grain.

North of the Arkansas Valley the land is level prairie. It is intersected and watered by an excellent system of irrigation ditches, and is farmed extensively to alfalfa, sugar beets, wheat, corn, milo and kafir. The soil in the Arkansas river valley is good, being a porus, sandy loam, varying in depths to twelve feet. With ordinary rains or when irrigated, it is capable of producing almost anything that grows out of the ground in the temperate zone.

The general surface of Garfield township is more uneven and undulating. The Pawnee, with its many spring branches, forms a complete drainage system entirely within the township. The narrow valleys along the creek produce abundant crops of all kinds. The broken uplands along the Pawnee are covered with buffalo grass and provide range and pasture for many thousand head of cattle and sheep. Many acres of the level upland prairie in Garfield are being plowed up every year and converted into grain fields since power farming is possible. The soil of this region is quite largely a sandy loam, with gravel in some places, and an out-cropping of soft magnesia limestone along the creeks.

The first sod was turned in Finney county in 1878. It is now 1931. There are a number of people still living here who can tell the story of those fifty-three years of agriculture, a story of failures and conquests. They tell of the droughts and the terrible blizzards, yet they now rejoice that the failures have been in a large measure overcome due to better farming and to irrigation. The breaking up of the prairies has caused more of the rain to go into the soil, which in turn has modified the reflection of heat, thus lessening the tendency to hot winds. Trees cover large areas which were once entirely without timber and also help to modify the climate. Perhaps the thousands of acres of alfalfa have had an influence in cooling the surface winds. The conservation of the water in the streams for irrigation purposes as well as numerous pumping plants do much to insure regular crops in this locality.

During the eighties the greater part of the available land was taken up. The seasons were very favorable to crops and the country boomed. Then came a period extending into the nineties of a series of crop failures and added to that was low prices. The years of 1891-94 marked the darkest days Western Kansas has ever known and thousands of settlers deserted their farms in this region. Since those years, however, there has been gradual and almost uninterrupted agricultural advancement.

Finney county is almost purely agricultural. The growth of the towns and development of the county have been largely the result of crop production. Finney county now produces profitably the largest variety of crops in the state and modern machinery makes it possible to farm a large acreage. One man can farm ten times as much land now as he could have in earlier days. In 1880 the farmer thought it a wonderful achievement when he could turn soil at the rate of four acres per day and could seed eight. In 1930 tractors are pulling three grain drills and sowing one hundred acres in a day. In 1879 there were 2905 acres in cultivation in this county. In 1930 there were 500,000 acres in cultivation, and each year in the past decade has shown an increased acreage.

Finney county made some records in 1930 that prove the possibilities of this rich agricultural section. A total of 1,102 cars were shipped from Garden City and elevators at other points in the county shipped a large number of cars.

Finney ships more alfalfa hay, seed and meal than any other county in Kansas. It has held this record for a number of years.

Having the only sugar factory in the state, Garden City naturally leads in sugar shipments. Finney county far surpasses all others in the state in the production of sugar beets.

Finney county leads all others of the state in grow-

Farm Views in Finney and Kearny Counties

ing and shipping of grain seed, and there is a constantly growing demand for grain seed raised under conditions as they exist here. Many carloads of alfalfa seed were shipped in 1930. Sweet clover, black amber and orange cane seed, corn, wheat and many varieties of sorghum grains to be planted in other places are shipped annually. E. G. Finnup has operated the leading grain seed house in the state for many years. He ships small quantities to individuals or carload lots to seed houses in many parts of the United States and to foreign countries.

The old-time cowmen are turning to farm work or diversifying. They have found that raising crops as well as cattle is the best way for a man to succeed, and they have found that good farming pays. Wheat, corn, alfalfa, sweet clover, sugar beets and many varieties of sorghum crops are grown extensively. There has been no total crop failure for many years.

There are many highly developed farms in this region, but few will compare with the Kinney-Byler ranches on the Pawnee in Garfield township. The big ranch is divided into two units, one of 1500 acres and the other of 3500 acres. On the lower place Leonard Byler is in charge of the big irrigated farm and lives in a fine nine-room house, modern in every convenience. At the east side is located the lower dam across the Pawnee which backs water up 2½ miles following the creek channel. The big barn on the place is 40x100 feet, with a roof 45 feet from the floor affording immense storage. It is equipped with an alfalfa meal mill which has a daily capacity of 20 tons. There are three hundred acres of alfalfa on the farm and a diversity of other crops. The ranch has about 4,000 acres of pasture and several hundred head of high-grade and registered cattle.

WHEAT

Wheat ranks first in importance among crops grown in Finney county. The majority of the pioneers who came here expected to be wheat farmers. The first piece of wheat planted with a drill in Sequoyah county was put in by C. J. Jones, August 7, 1879. A number of others in the county planted wheat that fall. N. J. Collins planted 100 acres north of Pierceville which was a very large acreage at that time. However, that crop surrendered to dry air and hot winds. Not an acre of it came up to be harvested. In the years that have followed 1879 wheat has been planted every season, although many times the yield has been cut down by drouth or hail.

This climate is practically the same as that of the great wheat-growing area of Russia, and many acres in Finney county have been planted with high-grade Russian seed wheat. Improved methods of planting and summer fallowing have been consistently a part of the wheat growers' program. In 1929 about 125,000 acres were planted with an estimated yield of 1,624,000 bushels. The acreage in 1930 was 153,000. Many farmers plant a thousand acres or more of wheat. Ellsworth Sherman topped the list in 1930 with 5500 acres. Edd Shimplin of Holcomb had 1500; Towles Brothers 1050; Fred Winters 1150; Bryan McDaniel 1105; F. J. Heibert 1120; O. P. Hughes 1600; Loyd Hitt and J. T. Lear each had 1000 acres; J. P. Hardy 1220; C. W. Maxfield 1400; Leagett and Wheeler 1040; P. C. Pitson 1100; Eugene Sims 1140; Ed Boots 1100.

The first threshing machine ever owned in the county was ordered and shipped here by A. H. Burtis. It was a Nichols and Shepard vibrator, manufactured at Battle Creek, Michigan, and arrived at Garden City January 1, 1882. Mr. Burtis also bought the first McCormick twine binder the same year.

The first combine to be used in Finney county was owned by Bruce Josserand and used north of Pierceville in 1918. Sam Allen had the first caterpillar tractor in Finney county.

The first tractor, a J. I. Case steam engine, was shipped to the county by a Mr. Pickerin in 1889. E. F. Smith and his sons, Wm. R. and James H., unloaded it at Garden City, where it attracted considerable attention. They used it to pull a gang plow on land about 20 miles northwest of Garden City. It was a big engine, and Mr. Smith had to spend most of his time in driving the water wagon

The first tractor to be used in Finney County, 1889

while the boys kept the tractor and plow going. It was used only one season. No tractors appeared on the tax rolls of Finney county until March 1, 1915, when two were reported. The records show twenty-five in 1916; seventy-eight in 1924; and two hundred sixty-five in 1928. Fifteen harvester threshers were reported in 1924, and seventy-one in 1928.

ALFALFA

Alfalfa is one of the most valuable crops grown in Finney county, and leads the state in the yield per acre and produces better quality hay than more humid parts of the United States. Garden City has two of the largest alfalfa meal mills in the United States, and it is the largest seed market.

The history of the alfalfa industry really begins with that of irrigation in this region in 1880, although since then many acres have been planted and grown successfully without irrigation.

D. R. Menke planted the first alfalfa seed in Finney county. While he was postmaster he sent to Washington, D.C., for sample packages of alfalfa seed and sowed it on his homestead in 1879. However, that was a very dry year and his patch of alfalfa soon died out. The next year the Garden City Ditch was made, and Squire Worrell obtained some seed from Colorado and planted seven acres. Under the irrigation system he cut four crops in 1881. In 1882 he obtained three crops yielding four tons per acre. On his last crop he obtained one hundred and two bushels of seed which he sold at $12.50 per bushel. John Simon planted a few acres in 1881 on his farm southeast of Garden City, sec. 20-24-32. T. J. Renick sent to California for seed and planted it in 1882, and other farmers living along the Garden City Ditch began planting in 1882.

The soil is rich enough that few farmers use fertilizer. As the big ditches were built through the country the alfalfa acreage increased. The statistical reports of 1907 show 4,982 acres of alfalfa in the county. In 1915 there were 13,923 acres, yielding 45,250 tons of hay and part of the crop was allowed to seed or is used for pasture.

The sugar company follows a plan of rotating alfalfa with beets, but the majority of the farmers allow their alfalfa fields to stand many years before rotating to other crops. In the spring of 1930 a five-acre field was plowed up west of Garden City which had been planted in the eighties, and until recently the crop showed no signs of dying out. For forty-five years the field produced good crops under irrigation.

Alfalfa seed yields run from 3 to 12 bushels per acre, and the alfalfa may be harvested for hay two or three times before it goes to seed. According to W. G. Hopkins of the Co-Operative Equity Exchange, the average value of a car of alfalfa seed is between six and seven thousand dollars, against the $900 value of a carload of wheat at the 1930 prices.

The following were a few of the alfalfa seed shippers in 1930: John Domingo, 10,000 lbs; Pirl Beach, 6,000 lbs.; C. J. Blackwood, 8,000 lbs.; Chas. Smith, 5,000 lbs.; R. I. Goss, 4,000 lbs.; C. B. Oldfield and J. W. Fine, each 6,000 lbs.; J. P. Nolan, 5,000 lbs.; Mrs. Belle Woodard, 6,000 lbs.; Mrs. T. J. Dyke, 3,000 lbs. The total shipment at the end of the season was 13 cars, bringing more than $80,000 to the local growers.

SUGAR BEETS

The sugar beet industry is an important one in Finney county, which holds the record for the largest acreage and production of any county in the state of Kansas. About 1900 the farmers and land owners of this county were awakened to the possibilities of sugar beet culture in this region, a few beets were grown to test their adaptability here. The results were most satisfactory and the citizens at once exerted every effort to secure a sugar factory. This was accomplished in 1905, and now for twenty-five years the sugar beet industry has thrived without a crop failure.

The first "100" tons of sugar beets raised in the Garden City district were raised by S. Carpenter at the request of those who were trying to get a sugar factory at Garden City. Mr. Carpenter's first crop was grown in 1904 and the beets were shipped to the factory at Rocky Ford. His 1905 crop was shipped to Holly, and the 1906 crop was made into sugar in the factory in Garden City which had just been completed.

Sugar beets are one of the surest crops the farmer can grow. A rotation with alfalfa is responsible for many of the best yields. Old alfalfa ground that is properly cultivated and irrigated will produce yields of 20 tons of beets to the acre, while ground that has not been rotated for a number of years may not yield half as large a tonnage. Sweet clover is also used in the rotation plan with beets.

The 1930 beet crop averaged 12 tons per acre, but many fields returned a yield of 15 to 20 tons. The price received was $6.00 per ton. W. H. Herr had 91 acres in beets in 1930, from which he sold 1,070 tons net weight. His average was 11.6 tons an acre. His total receipts from his beet crop amounted to $6,420. Probably the largest returns per acre from beets was received by Chas. Bentrup, who had 41 acres that made an average of 18.6 tons an acre, after tare had been deducted. The beets and value of the tops amounted to $121.60 an acre. J. W. Huser's crop averaged 17 tons per acre on his farm, sec. 8-24-35. A. J. Kettler in 9-24-35 had 50 acres that averaged 12 tons per acre. Joe Zubeck had ten acres of beets that averaged 18 tons an acre and ten that averaged 15 tons per acre. Sugar beets usually do not weigh over two pounds, but many grow much larger. Mrs. A. J. Caraveau exhibited one in 1930 weighing 11 pounds and 14 ounces. According to the 1915 crop report there were 4,481 acres with a yield of 40,344 tons. In 1928 reports showed 4,867 acres with a 46,237-ton yield.

VEGETABLES AND GARDENING

The subject of gardening is well worthy of special mention. There are a number in Finney county who have made money for years on their gardens. These gardens or truck patches range in size from five to forty acres and are irrigated either with pumping plants or from ditches. All the vegetables such as beets, melons, cucumbers, peas, beans, potatoes, onions, etc., do well and the local markets are always supplied with the best vegetables. Several years ago there was an unusual interest manifested in the growing of truck crops for commercial purposes. This resulted in a truck-growers' association. The Garden City associa-

Top, Bartell's Vineyard. Center and lower,
Onion Fields on Farm of I. L. Diesem.

tion in 1922 had forty members with 2,000 acres in sweet potatoes, Irish potatoes, onions, tomatoes, melons and other varieties. Among other things this association was reported to have shipped 60 cars of onions and 120 cars of sweet potatoes during the season of 1922.

J. T. Pearce was the pioneer sweet-potato raiser of

Finney county, and he always insisted that it was one of the best crops for the valley. He said: "As a money-making crop I raised sweet potatoes for 35 years. Let me say that if raising sweet potatoes in this country does not pay it will not pay in any country, for this is emphatically the home of the sweet potato. I have never made a single failure. I take it the average yield, one year with another, would not be far short of 200 bushels to the acre, which on a low estimate would bring $100.

Records show that in 1928 there were 9,380 bushels of Irish potatoes raised from 67 acres and 10,790 bushels of sweet potatoes from 83 acres.

Watermelon, muskmelon, squash and cucumber seed have been raised successfully in Finney county for many years. It is said that the best seeds of the kind are grown

Threshing Melons, Kearny County

in this locality. In 1905 John Ballinger had to say of seed growing: "I have had some experience in raising watermelon, muskmelon, squash and cucumber seed, all of which did well and proved a profitable crop. Two hundred pounds of seed and in some instances 400 pounds can be raised to the acre. All honor to King Alfalfa and his Ambassador the sugar beet, but you can do away with both of them and still our people can get rich raising melon and squash seed."

DAIRYING

The dairy business is one of the most dependable as well as profitable businesses of the Finney county farmer. Many have depended on cows for a living since the date of their arrival in this region. There were years when they only received five or six cents a pound for butter and times when they were paid fifty cents or more. They have sold raw milk to local dairies and for the manufacturing of cheese. They find a ready market for cream and their cream checks come in regularly.

H. P. Hood of Emporia said many years ago: "When the first travellers crossed the plains they found the buffalo cow and the prairie hen, which indicated that it would be a dairy and poultry country," and so it has proven that this is so without doubt. The cow has become of as much importance as a source of revenue as any other feature of the farm.

In 1905 R. J. Churchill stated: "From the farmer who milks a few cows to pay a grocery bill to the specialist who erects commodious barns and milks his cows by machinery, dairying in Finney county is now and has been from the earliest settlement a paying proposition. Cheap feed, good markets and a land blessed with abundant sunshine makes the conditions ideal."

SWEET CLOVER

Sweet clover has overcome the handicap of being classed as a despised weed and has won the hearts of the Kansas farmers. A few years ago it was common to hear sweet clover and cockleburs referred to as of equal value. After many experiments they have found that sweet clover is the best combination for pasture and soil improvement of any crop available to Kansas farmers.

The first sweet clover in Finney county appeared along the river, growing on the overflows. It was considered a pest and owners of the land made efforts to dig it out to keep it from spreading. In 1910 D. R. Menke found his prairie hay mixed with it and he could not sell it. Stockmen would not buy it as the clover looked stemmy and lacking in foilage, and they were afraid the cattle would not eat it. E. G. Finnup and Wm. Stone were feeding cattle in lots located on the Finnup park site, and needed hay. Mr. Menke offered his hay to them at a price far below market, so they decided to try it. They began feeding it to their cattle. To their surprise they noted that the cattle began nosing out the prairie hay and greedily ate the sweet clover, and did unusually well on it. They did not advertise their discovery, and the next year they bought all the mixed hay they could get, and got it below market.

In 1911 E. G. Finnup bought a manure spreader and had the manure hauled from their feed lots to the fair grounds and fairly saturated eighty acres. The next spring the eighty acres was thickly covered with sweet clover. He let it go to seed and threshed 900 bushels. A lot of seed and no market. He tried to sell it to several big seed concerns, but they did not want it. Finally he succeeded in selling a carload to Barteldes Seed Company at Lawrence, which was the first carload of sweet clover ever produced by one person. Since that time his sales have increased every year, and he buys seed from farmers of Western Kansas and Eastern Colorado to supply seed houses of importance all over the country. In 1914 Mr. Finnup had 3,000 acres in sweet clover. Many other farmers in Finney county now have large fields of this crop. They have found it to be a soil builder and use it in crop rotation, especially with sugar beets. They have found it to be a great pasture, forage and seed plant. It is also a great bee plant, the honey is clear and of the highest flavor. Sweet clover will thrive on any type of soil and under almost any climatic conditions, yet it is very easy to get rid of, as it is biennial and only needs to be kept from seeding. The roots decay rapidly and are soft, giving no trouble in plowing.

CORN—MILO—KAFIR

Corn, milo and kafir are important crops in Finney county, until recently the combined value of these was equal to that of wheat. The acreage and yield of the years given here are not exceptional, but give some idea of the magnitude of these crops.

1915—Kafir, acres planted 4,481. Yield 134,430 bushels.

Milo, acres planted 10,544. Yield 305,776 bushels.

1924—Kafir, acres planted 22,962. Yield 507,012 bushels.

Milo, acres planted 26,535. Yield 742,980 bushels.

1930—There was 300,000 bushels of corn raised in Finney county and a much greater amount of milo, kafir, and sorghum crops.

BEES AND HONEY

The thousands of acres of alfalfa and sweet clover of this county when in bloom furnish the bees with unlimited supplies of their raw material, and the honey is clear and of the highest flavor.

The first bees brought to Finney county were by A. H. Burtis in the spring of 1882. He procured them in Ohio and had them shipped by express, and when they arrived here they cost him $20 per colony. Since that time the industry has steadily grown until now there are hundreds of colonies of bees located in different parts of the county in apiaries ranging from a few colonies to several hundred. The agricultural report of 1928 gave 6,690 pounds of honey and beeswax.

RANK IN VALUE OF CROPS RAISED IN FINNEY COUNTY IN 1928

1. Sorghum crops (including milo, kafir, feterita, cane, etc., used for fodder and seed) $955,977.28
2. Wheat 869,844.27
3. Alfalfa (hay and seed) 521,122.00
4. Corn 511,487.60
5. Sugar beets 277,422.00
6. Barley 245,565.00

(Since 1928 the value of wheat has far exceeded that of any other crop. Corn, too, has probably advanced in rank, though complete figures for years later than 1928 were not available when this was written.)

This record was made from the Assessor's Statistical Rolls.

Year	Crop	acres harvested	yield per acre
1885	Wheat	97;	20 bu.
	Corn	138;	30 bu.
1886	Wheat	97;	20 bu.
	Corn	138;	30 bu.
1888	Wheat	559;	8 bu.
	Corn	2,570;	13 bu.
1889	Wheat	434;	25 bu.
	Corn	7,536;	30 bu.
1890	Wheat	1,090;	18 bu.
	Corn	2,423;	20 bu.
1891	Wheat	9,072;	14 bu.
	Corn	2,719;	14 bu.
1892	Wheat	7,805;	18 bu.
	Corn	2,947;	18 bu.
1893	Wheat	16,937;	F
	Corn	1,281;	5 bu.
1894	Wheat	26,607;	10 bu.
	Corn	1,571;	5 bu.
1895	Wheat	26,607;	3 bu.
	Corn	2,058;	10 bu.

1896—Wheat, acres harvested   9,394; yield per acre, 3 bu.
      Corn   "   "   1,329;   "   "   "   13 bu.
1897—Wheat   "   "   8,195;   "   "   "   3 bu.
      Corn   "   "   876;   "   "   "   12 bu.
1898—Wheat   "   "   3,921;   "   "   "   4 bu.
      Corn   "   "   425;   "   "   "   18 bu.
1899—Wheat   "   "   1,625;   "   "   "   4 bu.
      Corn   "   "   331;   "   "   "   21 bu.
1900—Wheat   "   "   409;   "   "   "   10 bu.
      Corn   "   "   1,213;   "   "   "   15 bu.
1901—Wheat   "   "   1,616;   "   "   "   7 bu.
      Corn   "   "   1,287;   "   "   "   6 bu.
1902—Wheat   "   "   2,372;   "   "   "   4 bu.
      Corn   "   "   1,055;   "   "   "   9 bu.
1903—Wheat   "   "   2,964;   "   "   "   18 bu.
      Corn   "   "   881;   "   "   "   25 bu.
1904—Wheat   "   "   5,851;   "   "   "   5 bu.
      Corn   "   "   759;   "   "   "   10 bu.
1905—Wheat   "   "   6,842;   "   "   "   17 bu.
      Corn   "   "   1,574;   "   "   "   23 bu.
1906—Wheat   "   "   12,294;   "   "   "   9 bu.
      Corn   "   "   1,744;   "   "   "   22 bu.
1907—Wheat   "   "   18,692;   "   "   "   7 bu.
      Corn   "   "   6,452;   "   "   "   20 bu.
1908—Wheat   "   "   26,842;   "   "   "   6 bu.
      Corn   "   "   9,633;   "   "   "   14 bu.
1909—Wheat   "   "   24,455;   "   "   "   10 bu.
      Corn   "   "   9,328;   "   "   "   16 bu.

	Acres			Yield
Year	Seeded	Abandoned	Harvested	Average
1910—Wheat	.....	.....	11,681	9 bu.
Corn	10,659	.....	.....	13 bu.
1911—Wheat	14,654	8,792	5,862	5 bu.
Corn	10,039	.....	.....	10 bu.
1912—Wheat	10,310	2,990	7,320	10 bu.
Corn	4,307	.....	.....	18 bu.

Year		Acres Seeded	Abandoned	Harvested	Yield Average
1913—	Wheat	11,254	4,051	7,203	8 bu.
	Corn	4,786	.....	.....	5 bu.
1914—	Wheat	19,291	.....	19,291	18 bu.
	Corn	3,328	.....	.....	15 bu.
1915—	Wheat	16,269	1,302	14,967	16 bu.
	Corn	4,931	.....	.....	30 bu.
1916—	Wheat	30,642	2,758	20,884	16 bu.
	Corn	7,333	.....	.....	7 bu.
1917—	Wheat	45,351	40,362	4,989	9 bu.
	Corn	15,301	.....	.....	10 bu.
1918—	Wheat	34,795	22,965	11,830	12 bu.
	Corn	13,876	.....	.....	10 bu.
1919—	Wheat	39,179	.....	39,179	16 bu.
	Corn	6,309	.....	.....	17 bu.
1920—	Wheat	45,466	8,639	36,827	21 bu.
	Corn	5,990	.....	.....	23 bu.
1921—	Wheat	46,644	5,877	40,769	12 bu.
	Corn	8,944	.....	.....	21 bu.
1922—	Wheat	65,376	7,845	57,531	12 bu.
	Corn	11,746	.....	.....	11 bu.
1923—	Wheat	68,645	62,467	6,178	F
	Corn	20,177	.....	.....	25 bu.
1924—	Wheat	49,107	982	48,125	18 bu.
	Corn	14,802	.....	.....	16 bu.
1925—	Wheat	76,530	7,500	69,030	7 bu.
	Corn	14,086	.....	.....	15 bu.
1926—	Wheat	87,204	17,441	69,763	14 bu.
	Corn	13,793	.....	.....	8 bu.
1927—	Wheat	108,156	38,936	69,220	4 bu.
	Corn	22,410	.....	.....	16 bu.
1928—	Wheat	98,021	39,208	58,813	17 bu.
	Corn	31,730	.....	.....	26 bu.
1929—	Wheat	113,620	3,409	110,211	16 bu.
	Corn	28,416	.....	.....	16 bu.
1930—	Wheat	153,000	.....	.....	.....

These records were obtained from the Assessor's Statistical Rolls.

Year	Milk Cows	Other Cattle	Sheep	Horses	Hogs
1885	944	6,745	17,199	625	167
1886	944	6,745	17,199	625	167
1887	....	.....	....	....	....
1888	1,484	2,230	1,601	1,393	450
1889	1,950	3,544	2,616	1,853	559
1890	1,826	3,091	2,723	1,238	1,308
1891	1,696	4,979	2,651	1,079	1,874
1892	1,597	5,471	3,410	1,126	929
1893	1,554	4,464	5,677	1,776	724
1894	1,690	4,433	3,923	3,106	917
1895	1,690	4,433	3,923	3,106	917
1896	1,775	7,482	2,585	3,119	1,890
1897	1,838	9,803	3,505	3,337	1,711
1898	1,616	17,696	5,752	2,607	1,513
1899	1,566	18,829	6,889	3,044	2,442
1900	1,325	24,259	2,800	2,739	629
1901	2,100	21,543	5,195	3,410	1,761
1902	1,491	22,726	4,891	3,242	731
1903	1,250	24,267	9,382	3,630	554
1904	1,481	24,535	10,251	4,196	1,050
1905	1,719	25,305	8,930	3,805	928
1906	1,454	17,197	2,580	3,496	648
1907	1,684	15,402	2,714	4,176	841
1908	2,095	11,683	1,742	4,492	1,488
1909	2,605	11,018	2,798	4,432	1,146
1910	2,773	15,322	1,691	5,596	1,164
1911	4,324	12,243	4,175	5,072	1,298
1912	4,585	9,456	3,118	5,035	1,041
1913	4,518	15,048	9,766	4,973	1,322
1914	5,062	14,420	1,856	4,932	1,806
1915	6,807	17,972	2,653	5,167	2,919
1916	9,330	30,814	3,629	5,827	4,824

Year	Milk Cows	Other Cattle	Sheep	Horses	Hogs
1917	2,484	28,012	1,466	5,986	5,591
1918	3,365	27,577	506	6,671	4,357
1919	3,112	37,593	390	7,193	2,951
1920	1,552	29,605	629	6,760	1,756
1921	2,701	27,919	568	7,335	3,005
1922	2,991	28,451	1,031	7,419	4,294
1923	2,367	27,576	243	7,514	5,794
1924	2,395	30,160	234	6,968	3,983
1925	1,858	19,950	247	6,700	2,451
1926	2,080	18,097	200	6,495	1,888
1927	2,759	15,099	1,850	5,919	3,169
1928	2,997	17,282	4,466	5,588	4,731
1929	3,164	19,835	1,088	5,551	5,330

ROADS AND BRIDGES

For several years after the settlement of Southwest Kansas there were no surveyed highways in this region. Only dim, cross-country trails led to the different towns and to the homes of the settlers which were scattered over the prairie. And it was still longer before any bridges were built.

Finney county was organized October 1, 1884, and early in January, 1885, road viewers began to be appointed and roads located and vacated. Road petition No. 1 was signed by J. W. Gregory and others and was granted July 6, 1885, and declared to be a public highway, all parties interested having given right of way. It began at the southeast corner of the northeast quarter of section 18, twp. 24, range 32, terminating in the southeast corner of the northeast quarter of section 17, twp. 24, range 32.

A bridge! A bridge! My kingdom for a bridge! was the sentiment of the people voiced by the Garden City Sentinel, in the fall of 1884. The region south of the Arkansas river was being settled and new towns were to be built, but the river lay between them and the towns along the Santa Fe railroad from which they were obliged to haul all their supplies and building material.

There was no public money as yet available for bridge purposes, and there was much discussion as to ways and means of river crossings. A meeting of the citizens of Garden City was called January 17, 1885. A committee was appointed to raise a loan of $1,000 asked by E. Johns of the Kansas Lumber Company, who would build a bridge under the name of "Garden City Bridge Company," incorporators, H. Emerson, E. Johns, Chas. Perry, Jos. Johns and L. N. Akers, all of Burrton, Kansas. The bridge was finished in April, 1885. This was a narrow, wooden structure with a low railing and spanned the river near the southeast corner of Finnup park. A toll was charged and H. W. Crow and family lived in the toll house on the north side of the river and operated the bridge.

Bridge toll rates, as published in the Garden City Sentinel, were: Two-horse wagon, round trip, 50c, one way, 25c; each additional horse, 10c. One or two horse, single seat buggy, 40c; one way, 25c. Two horse, double seat buggy, 40c, one way 30c. Horse and rider, round trip, 20c, one way, 15c. Sheep, per head, ½ cent. Hogs, per head, 1 cent. Horses and cattle, 5c.

E. J. Pyle operated the "River-Side Wagon Yard", located just north and west of the toll bridge, for the benefit of the travellers. Mrs. Ida Pyle Maltbie has written some recollections of that "first tourist camp.".

"Our family came to Garden City in the fall of 1885, moving from Butler county, Kansas. The family consisted of my father, the late E. J. Pyle, and mother who passed away in 1902, my sister, now Mrs. Frank Dunn, and Mrs. C. E. Hopper, brother Charles, now of Topeka, and myself.

"We lived for a time south of the railroad. My father owned and operated what must have been the first tourist camp in Garden City. But it was established for the benefit of weary pilgrims who came across the wide prairie with their families and all their earthly possessions stored in a covered wagon drawn by a span of horses or mules, and sometimes by a team of oxen. This camp was called "The River Side Wagon Camp". It occupied a half block and was enclosed with a high board fence. Around this fence inside were small sheds where a man might drive his team and wagon and find a dry, comfortable shelter. A small house at one end of the yard served as an office. It contained among other articles of furniture, a cook stove, where the travellers might make their coffee and cook their meals. A fee was charged for shelter and for hay for the animals. The traveller and his family in many cases were forced to live in their wagon until a suitable shelter could be erected for them. The office building served also as a real estate office for father, in which business he continued until the time of his death in 1913.

"Often at night, usually along in the 'wee sma' hours of the early morning, we would be awakened by a crowd of shouting, singing, drunken cowboys, riding like Jehu down the street, and a little later would hear faintly the noise of the horses hoofs as they clattered across the wooden bridge and over into the sand hills. But often just as their horses struck the bridge, there would be a regular fusillade of shots, given as if in derision to the civilization that had come to their plains."

The toll bridge was not very satisfactory to the business interests of Garden City, as many people could not or did not want to pay the toll. Soon after the bridge was completed arguments arose over various things.

Dan Larmor, whose ranch was south of the river, had given the bridge company a right-of-way on his land with the understanding that he should have a free pass across the bridge at all times. Failing to receive the pass as agreed, he stationed himself with a good team at the foot of the bridge. Whenever anyone came up to cross the river he offered to help them across the old ford in the river free of charge. As a result the bridge had no traffic, and in a short time Mr. Larmor received a free pass over the bridge and used it continuously as long as the bridge stood.

The county tried to rent the bridge but the bridge company insisted on selling it instead. The question of buying the toll bridge or of building a new one at the foot of Main street was a big issue. The following article is from the Garden City "Irrigator":

"The question of voting bonds to buy the toll bridge was voted upon April 24, 1886, and was defeated. The vote stood 162 for and 285 against. The bridge company

First bridge across the Arkansas at Garden City, 1886

got rattled at the result and raised the toll to $1.75 for a round trip for a two-horse team. This was done Tuesday and caught about 60 teams from the southern county in town after supplies. The complaint from them was serious. A meeting of the business men was held and enough money collected to pay the toll of teams in town, but to attempt to pay the toll of all teams until a free bridge is completed will be impossible."

Garden City township voted on the question of issuing bonds for the purpose of building a bridge over the river at the foot of Main street, in June, 1886. A canvas of the votes was made, resulting in 276 in favor and 40 against. This settled the free bridge question. The Kansas Lumber Company received enough in tolls and from the sale of the old material in the toll bridge to pay the original cost.

An election was held April 12, 1887, in accordance to an act of legislature of the state of Kansas, authorizing Garden City township to vote bonds to the amount of $10,000 to build a road through the sand hills. The vote was 294 in favor and 13 against.

The bridge problem at Pierceville was first solved by the Bartons whose ranch was south of the river at that place. On July 30, 1885, they put into operation a ferry boat on the Arkansas river, of 4,000 pounds capacity, and no fee was charged for crossing on it. "Ho! Bring the ferry over!" rang out many times during the next year, for the people south began using an excellent pass which had been made through the sand hills to Pierceville.

Bridge bonds were voted by Pierceville township April 26, 1886. The vote was 307 in favor and 143 opposed. The contract for its construction was let to W. H. Hobson of St. Joseph, Mo. On August 11, 1886, the town celebrated the opening of their first bridge.

The first wagon bridge across the river at Holcomb was built in 1886. A new bridge of steel and concrete construction was completed over the river south of Holcomb during the summer of 1930.

In July, 1919, bonds were voted to build the present bridge at Garden City across the Arkansas river on the Great Plains highway. It was not to exceed $50,000 and to be of steel and concrete construction.

The county now has an excellent system of graded roads and is crossed by three national highways. In 1920 it was paved entirely across from east to west, and in 1921 the road south for a distance of six miles was paved across the sand hills. The county has built many small bridges over the creeks in Garfield township and over the great irrigation canals in all parts of the county.

FINNEY COUNTY NEWSPAPERS

By Hamer Norris

THE newspapers have played an important and far-reaching part in the development and settlement of Finney county and all southwest Kansas. They came with the pioneer and covered wagon, and in many instances preceeded the church and the school. They were loyal to their communities and local institutions, and although at times they battled for mere existence they ever remained optimistic, visioning a brighter future, bidding all to hope for better days. Blizzards and drought might come and cause loss, hot winds might parch and blister, yet they continued to point out the silver lining to the clouds; they recorded the joys and sorrows of the pioneers; they stood rejoicing beside the cradle, they stood at the altar of the bride and mingled their tears with the bereaved at the open grave; they helped the merchants fight their battles and loyally stood by their party convictions, and were ever steadfast in support of all that was moral and right. Fortunately nearly all the history they wrote has been preserved by the State Historical Society, and here almost a complete story of Finney county can be found, and what a story, well worth reading and remembering.

During the so-called boom days, when the country was being homesteaded, and claims were being proved up in the land office, every little hamlet boasted its newspaper, kept alive and nourished by land-office patronage and nothing else, changing their political coat with the changes in the political complexion of the national administration and fading away just as soon as the land office milk ceased to flow.

Down to 1912 there were published in Garden City three outstanding newspapers, The Herald, The Sentinel and The Cultivator, all the others ceasing to exist after short and checkered careers; and of these three The Herald alone survived up to 1928 when it was purchased by The Telegram Company. The three papers mentioned above represented something solid and permanent, but two of them failed because hard times came and there was nothing to support them in the way of business.

These three newspapers and their editors deserve a little more than a passing notice for they represented the best that there was in the community, and were guided and controlled by editors of the old school who were fearless in expression, true to their convictions and loyal to the town and its interests.

The first of these, The Cultivator, devoted to farming and stock-raising, was guided and controlled by Judge L. D. Bailey, who came to Garden City with John Speer, Jake Shoop and other hardy pioneers who had gone through the bloody border warfare and the sacking of Lawrence. Judge Bailey was an educated and brilliant man and made his paper a power in the early days, and from the columns of which the farmer and stockman drew knowledge and inspiration.

The Sentinel was under the editorial management of several men of whom two at least were men of considerable ability. One of these, Col. C. J. Coutant, was a brilliant writer and left his name impressed upon the community and in the history of The Sentinel. He was followed later by Judge J. W. Gregory, a rather able and forceful man, but lacking the financial resources to make his paper what he wished.

The Herald, the sole survivor for many years of this triumvirate, withstood the tempests of adversity for several years, but finally went into the hands of a receiver, from which it was taken by S. G. and Hamer Norris in 1901, and was published by them until it was sold to the Kelleys after the death of the senior partner. At the time of this sale it was the oldest paper in southwest Kansas with the exception of one, the Dodge City Globe, which was several years its senior. S. G. Norris, the head of the firm, was a man of great industry, tireless energy, indomitable courage and possessed a brain that could plan and achieve the tasks that confronted him, a man born to take the hard knocks of the pioneer editor, and everywhere he was recognized as an artist in job printing.

Of all the other early-day newspapers in Garden City, some established for political reasons, others to promote the interests of irrigation, reciprocity, farming and even communism, lived and died natural deaths, except The Prolocutor, an anarchist sheet, which was wrecked and thrown into the street because of slanderous utterances.

In 1912 Henry J. Allen established the Daily Telegram and during its life was edited by Paul Rankin, Ralph Faxon and Lester Combs, all men of ability and influence.

In this year of 1931 the newspaper field is occupied by The Garden City Daily Telegram and The Garden City daily and weekly News, both progressive in business and successfully conducted. Their history is still to be written, but when it is, it is to be hoped that they preserved the traditions and character of their pioneer predecessors, and always maintained the position of the greatest power for good in the city.

NEWSPAPERS WHICH HAVE BEEN DISCONTINUED

GARDEN CITY

Garden City Paper. April 3, 1879, to October 30, 1879.

Baim and Himrod, editors. "Garden City is to have a newspaper. It will be five-column folio. Himrod and Baim, both long-legged printers, will be publishers. Kirk Himrod is well known to the people of this section. Amos Baim, better known as "Bonaparte", comes from the job department of the Rice County Bulletin. Both are first-class printers."—From a Dodge City Exchange.

Irrigator. June 29, 1882, to 1887. O. H. Knight and W. E. Carr, editors. They sold to Myton and Bennett in 1884, who operated it until 1885, when Layne and Naugle became proprietors.

Herald. March 17, 1883-1884; 1887.

Sentinel. July 30, 1884, to 1900. Joe H. Borders, editor, sold to E. L. Stephenson in 1886. It was called Sentinel and Cultivator, July, 1887, to August, 1888.

Cultivator and Herdsman; Kansas Cultivator, May to September of 1884; May, 1886, to 1887. Judge L. D. Bailey. He was a man of great ability and his papers were devoted to the interests of the farmers and stock raisers of Southwest Kansas.

Optic. November 13, 1880. N. C. Jones, editor.

Bundle of Sticks. February 15, 1885, to September 15, 1885. This was a paper devoted to the interests of "Odd Fellows". Joe H. Borders and D. B. Long, proprietors.

Sentinel (d) January 5, 1886, to 1888. Col. C. G. Coutant, an experienced journalist, was the editor and proprietor. Published every morning.

Finney County Democrat. February 5, 1887, to 1891.

Imprint. April 20, 1889, to 1912. D. A. Mims and E. N. Keep, editors.

Herald. April 23, 1886, to 1890. Wallace and Painter, publishers. (Nov., 1888, to April, 1890, not published.)

Taxpayer. March 7, 1891, to April 25, 1891.

Lookout. August 1, 1891, 1892.

Tribune. November 10, 1892, to 1894. R. E. Stotts.

Irrigation Champion. September 1, 1894, to Feb. 15, 1895.

Reflector. July 13, 1905, to 1917.

Reflector (d) September 26, 1906, to 1907.

Telegram (Evening). December 10, 1906, to 1912.
Proculator, January 13, 1910, to 1911.
Arkansas Valley Journal. August 23, 1912, to 1914.
The Bugle. April 2, 1886. Walter W. Davis, editor and proprietor.

RAVANNA

Chieftain. April 22, 1886, to 1894. M. L. Hart, editor.
Kansas Sod House, also the Ravanna Leader. May 6, 1886, to 1887. Ferris and Enos, publishers; later these papers were bought by Thomas and Company.
Enquirer. December 9, 1887, to 1888.
Record. July 15, 1887, to 1889. Enos and Davis, editors.

TERRY

Enterprise. July 9, 1886, to 1887. W. E. Cautant, editor.
The Terry Eye. February 17, 1887, to 1889. B. L. Stephenson, editor.

EMINENCE

Garfield County Call. July 1, 1887, to 1893.

ESSEX

Sunbeam. June 10, 1887, to November 25, 1887.

HATFIELD

News. August 18, 1887, to 1889.

LOYAL

Garfield County Journal. July 1, 1887, to 1889. G. L. Sigman, M. L. Hart, and Mrs. C. F. Hoadley each took a turn as publisher.

PIERCEVILLE

The Courier. May 14, 1886, to 1887. H. B. Brown, editor.

KALVESTA

The Herald. 1886 to 1887. Mr. Bond from Hodgeman county was editor.

At the present time Finney county has only two publishing companies, and both are in Garden City:

Busenbark and Stowell, Editors and Publishers. Established November 12, 1929. *the Garden City Daily News* (evenings except Thursday and Sunday); *The Garden City News* (Thursday); *Opportunity* (monthly).

The Garden City Publishing Company. *The Garden City Daily Telegram* (every day except Sunday).

Lost Towns of Finney County

A MAJORITY of the pioneers who came into this region were ambitious to have a part in the building of a town. In this day the big dream of the farmer is of possible oil discoveries on his holdings; but in the early days of settlement the dream of the land owners was of a city, preferably a county seat, being located on his quarter section. History proves that some of them realized this ambition to the extent of a townsite, but in most cases they were disappointed in seeing a flourishing city develop. Many speculators came into the country and took up land with no other thought than to sell it off in town lots.

Finney county has had its share of mushroom towns, which appeared for a brief time but are now only a memory. A few evidences of some of those towns still remain upon the prairie, but the ruins are slowly decaying. Others experienced a sudden end and were hauled away to build up a more successful rival. Some of them still hold a place on the map, but no longer have a post office, and all that is left is a school house or gasoline station. Many sites of the boom towns have been plowed under and lay buried beneath a field of wheat or other crops.

BUFFALO CENTER

Buffalo Center was the first attempt to establish a town in Garfield township, which was then Buffalo county. A. D. Wettick of Cimarron, having visions of the county being organized, decided to start a town and make it the county seat. He put up a sod store building on the southeast quarter of section 36-21-29, and stocked it with goods in 1878 from his store at Cimarron. He had a man in charge who also handed mail out to the few settlers and cattle men whenever it was brought up from

Cimmaron by freighters. The country was practically unsettled, but strangers were beginning to come in, and they were welcomed first and then allowed to prove their worth afterwards. One day a bunch of men were loafing around the store waiting for the mail to be brought in when a couple of young fellows rode up to the store on horseback. But in reply to the customary "Howdy, stranger," they whipped out guns and ordered the store keeper and the patrons to line up against the wall. They took what they wanted from their victims and some merchandise from the store. Seemingly satisfied one held the gun while the other mounted his horse, and then the other held his gun while his partner backed out and got on his horse. They made a successful get-away, and soon vanished from sight among the Pawnee brakes.

Mr. Wettick failed to find well water near his store at Buffalo Center and the location was early abandoned.

TERRYTON

Terryton the town and Terry the township were named for a real estate speculator from New York, Porter D. Terry. He had some money and great visions for the future of his town, which he founded during the boom of 1885-86. It was the half-way station on the stage line between Garden City and Scott City. There was a stage barn where they kept eight horses for change on the route. Four stages came in every day. The Cannon Ball, with Hank and Bronks as drivers, put them through from Scott to Garden in five hours.

The town was located in the southeast corner of section 25-21-23. Young and Jeffrys were in the grocery business; George W. Morse advertised provisions, glassware, and flour; Mr. Terry operated a real estate and livestock exchange; J. M. Dunn had a general store. There was a comfortable hotel, drug store, livery stable and bus station. A newspaper was published by W. E. Coutant called

"The Enterprise" during 1886-87. During 1888-89 it was called "The Eye", with B. L. Stephenson editor. The townsite was on the line of several projected railroads and had great expectations on that score. There was also a good lumber yard.

The "Old Kentucky Home" where they all went to Sunday School and where church services were held, was a half-mile north of Terryton. The Old Kentucky Home was named by its first owner, a son of George Wilson, who came there from Kentucky. Mr. Terry bought the Wilsons out and then sold the place to Dr. L. H. Johnson, an eastern speculator. He and his wife bought several sections in that neighborhood about 1895, but Dr. Johnson was blind and they did nothing to develop the land.

J. J. Glascock and family located one mile west of Terryton in 1886. Mrs. Glascock tells an incident of pioneer life which caused her great agony: "Terryton had one of the best ball teams in the country, and every Saturday afternoon there would be a big ball game, and nearly everybody in that trade territory made it a point to be there. One Saturday afternoon in August the men went to the ball game. I took the baby, Clarence, 22 months old, and went to spend the afternoon with Miss Rosa Wilson. A little later he ran out of the house and fell into the well, which was 44 feet deep. I ran all the way to town, waving my white apron, while Rosa stayed by the well and talked to the baby, telling him they were coming to get him out. He was standing in one corner holding to the two-foot curbing. His leg was broken and he was holding his chin up to keep the water out of his mouth. I have always thought it a miracle that he did not give up and drown. They got him out just in time, and it is lucky that we had a doctor in the neighborhood. Dr. Miller, his wife and four daughters lived west of us on section 26."

For three or four years Terryton flourished, but the

drouth which drove the homesteaders from the country also blighted the hopes of Mr. Terry and the town has long passed into oblivion. The following was copied from the Hatfield News, which was published in a rival town:

"For Sale. A one-horse railroad boom, broken in the middle and without head or tail. It might be repaired to suit emergencies, as its constitution and plan were constructed with that end in view. A quit-claim deed will be given. Will be sold very low, as I wish to (or rather the people wish me to) give place to a more able man, and hie myself back to Yankee-dom where my real estate interests are. Porter D. Terry."

WHITSON AND HATFIELD

Those interested in preserving the history of southwestern Kansas are indebted to John H. Whitson of Rowley, Massachusetts, for the story of Whitson and Hatfield. Mr. Whitson came to Sequoyah county in 1884, and with his father, Aaron F. Whitson, and his sister Barbara, homesteaded three quarter sections in section 20-22-33, northwest of Garden City. He is now a well-known author, having had a number of books published, and is listed in "Who's Who in America". In his novel, "The Rainbow Chasers", published in 1904, he calls Garden City the Golden City and portrays the boom days of 1886.

Mr. Whitson tells a story on himself that in some way got started as to his singular literary activity while he was living on his Sequoyah county ranch: "Robertus C. Love, then a Garden City editor, later and at the time of his death connected with the St. Louis Globe-Democrat, wrote to me from St. Louis saying he was getting out a book that would deal with characters of the old days on the plains; and that he would like me to furnish him for inclusion in it the story of how I used to write my stories in some kind of a house built on an old windmill. I had to tell him that some one had hoaxed him. I knew my stories might have been rather windy, as they were fiction emanating from a wind-driven country, but I had written them in an ordinary room, in an ordinary house, on an ordinary ranch.

"A man we became well acquainted with was John W. Gregory, who became editor of the Garden City Sentinel, was probate judge, and later laid out the town of Hatfield, adjoining our quarter sections on the northwest. I helped in the surveying of Hatfield, carrying the surveyors' chain. We had at our place a post office named Whitson which served the settlers of that part of the country. It was probably the smallest post office in the United States as it occupied only a portion of my mother's kitchen, with a few pigeonhole boxes for letters, and some drawers for stamps and records. In 1886 the post office was moved to Hatfield which started out with a fireworks of advertising and collapsed. It was 15 miles northwest of Garden City on the proposed line of the Denver, Garden City and Southeast railroad, and on the line of the Cannon Ball Stage and U.S. mail route to Leoti. At its best it had a store, operated by Thompson and Crawford, a claim house occupied by Rev. Godley, a local minister, a town hall, the Antelope hotel of eleven rooms, a few other houses; and a little later having the most magnificent sod house that was perhaps ever built.

"This sod house was erected by C. G. Coutant, who succeeded Gregory of the Garden City Sentinel, coming out from New York where he had held positions on New York City papers. His house of sod, cut from the plains, was a large square structure, two stories high, with four rooms on each floor. It had a shingle roof, board floors and was ceiled; the inner walls smoothed down with coats of plaster and whiting; with carpets on the floors, good furniture, a fine piano, book cases, etc. It made a good, comfortable home of which he had a right to be proud. He drove out to this home each day from Garden City, lashing a span of fiery ponies that took him over the trail at a great rate."

The Hatfield News was published from 1887 to 1889, the issues ceasing with the death of the editor. The fall of Hatfield was due in part, no doubt, to the uprising of Terry on the northeast.

J. N. Reeves and family lived four miles east of Hatfield. Mrs. Reeves taught school in all the adjoining districts, teaching a term in later years among the deserted ruins of Hatfield. Mr. Reeves was a member of the board of education while his wife taught. Several children came from without the district, but within the district the school consisted only of the Reeves children.

ESSEX

The following description was taken from the 'Sunbeam", a newspaper which was published at Essex in 1887 by W. F. Ellsworth.

"Essex is situated in the Pawnee valley, one of the most beautiful and fertile regions in the state. It is on the proposed line of the Kansas Air Line Railroad, which will connect the main line of the D. M. & A. running southwest into the coal fields of Colorado, giving us direct communications north, south and southwest. Essex is 22 miles from Garden City. 15 miles from Ravanna. 14 miles from Pierceville. 8½ from Eminence. It is surrounded by the most fertile soil of Kansas, which is being rapidly improved. Water is first class, found at a depth of 15 to 50 feet in the valley. The best of soft magnesia limestone building rock is found within ½ mile of town. Essex has a hotel, general store, printing office, real estate office, blacksmith shop, lumber yard, and five dwellings. It has a complete canning outfit with a 2000-can capacity, and a large sorghum mill."

James Concannon with his wife and family settled in Garfield township in 1887. He reared his family in

Essex and for many years after the boom of Western Kansas had passed, he remained as post master and operated a general store. At the same time he engaged extensively in stock raising and owned many acres of land in the Essex neighborhood. The post office was discontinued in 1914, and there is nothing left to mark the old townsite of Essex except some farm buildings.

PATTENVILLE-PANSY-LOYAL

The post office of Pattonville was established in old Buffalo county March 1, 1880, with Adam S. Van Patten as the appointed post master.

The name of the post office was changed to Pansy November 28, 1881, and David Goddard was appointed post master. According to county lines at that time, Pansy was in Gray county. The name Pansy was suggested by John H. Churchill. February 7, 1882, Martha Hoadley was appointed postmistress.

The name of the office was changed to Loyal March 3, 1882, and Mrs. Hoadley was re-appointed postmistress. After July 6 of that year the mail route from Garden City increased its trips to twice a week. Loyal was located on section 5-29-22. The Hoadley family was prominent among the early settlers of Garfield county. Their first home was a dugout, dug back in a creek bank. The rafters over the roof were covered with willows and then a layer of sod, and extended out on a level with the top of the bank. One morning while they were at breakfast a steer walked casually out on the roof after a nibble of green grass. First two front feet went crashing down through the willows, followed almost immediately by two hind ones, but the steer stayed on top, balanced across a rafter. Fortunately he was near the edge and with the help of neighbors they soon rolled him off.

H. D. Collins describes C. F. Hoadley as being a man of large stature, large hands, large feet. Rather ugly in appearance: "I never knew his height. When asked as to his height, he would reply: 'It is either six feet ten or ten feet six, I can't remember which.' He told me he had never met a man who could measure him with outstretched arms. He was a jolly good neighbor, well informed, intelligent, ranchman, cabinet maker by trade and a professional gambler. He was reputed to be one of the slickest gamblers in the west. Later in life he reformed, joined the church and was known as a kind old man."

Loyal was a popular trading point and community center for several years. It was a typical village of pioneer days, with a general store which carried many things; a blacksmith shop, where the settlers took their plows and wagons to be re-conditioned; and a schoolhouse which was also used for church and social gatherings. The Garfield County Journal came into existence at Loyal July 1, 1887, and lived until 1889. Several took a turn at editing. G. L. Sigman, M. L. Hart and Mrs. C. F. Hoadley, who many times got out the weekly issues on the old hand press all by herself. They all boosted the upper Pawnee valley. It abounded in water, good soil, grasses, building material, good society and predicted that mineral material would yet be found in the valley.

The post office was discontinued September 15, 1899. There is nothing left now to mark the site of Loyal. The buildings have all been removed. When the new Loyal schoolhouse was built a new location was selected.

———o———

FELIX had a post office in 1882, receiving mail from Garden City twice weekly. It was located in Garfield township, and was in the center of the cattle range of that region and was patronized largely by cattlemen.

LORENZ was located in section 23-23-28 in the southeast corner of Garfield township. It had a post office and several places of business during the boom years of 1886-87-88. Later the name was changed to Canyon post office.

BURHAM was placed on the map in 1910 by the projected Nebraska, Kansas & Southern railroad, but neither was ever developed. GAS CITY was also allowed a place on the map for the same reason.

PASSEDENA was advertised as a thriving town, but it never existed except on paper. A site was selected and some lots staked out in section 30-21-29, then in Garfield county. This was during the boom days of 1886. Lots were sold or given to people who thought they were making a good investment, and they willingly paid a fat recording fee, but no records could ever be found. It was only a fake promotion scheme.

KNAUSTON was located in the northwest part of Finney county in 1885 by a man named Knaus from Knobnoster, Missouri. He was postmaster and operated a general store in connection. This point had a few houses and a building which was used for school and church purposes. During the blizzard of 1886 the citizens had to abandon their homes and live in the church to conserve fuel.

———o———

MASON-COWLAND-RAVANNA

C. L. Brown was one of the first to file on land in old Buffalo county, coming there in May, 1878. He says the settlers worked fast in those days. Two men, Mason and Coulson, who had also come there in the spring of '78, and himself, were driving to Larned that fall after supplies, when they met some men with wagons. After a brief conversation they found the men were headed toward Buffalo county.

When the Brown party returned home after a few days, they discovered that the men they had met on the road, under the leadership of John Bull, had settled in their neighborhood. They had already located claims, and more than that, they had staked out a townsite, and intended to make it a county seat. They were also out circulating a petition to get a post office, although it was hard to find any bona fide inhabitants.

John Bull was born in Quebec, Canada, in 1847. He came to Buffalo county, Kansas, November 16, 1878, and filed on the northwest quarter of Sec. 3, T. 22, R. 28. His first shelter was a half dugout of one room built of rock which he quarried from the Pawnee creek, and in this he put a stock of merchandise. The place was first called Mason in honor of Seamon Mason, and was the second attempt to locate a county seat in Buffalo county. A post office was established January 9, 1879, and Samuel Wood was appointed postmaster. Mr. Bull's efforts to get a water supply at this point proved unavailing, and he took another claim near a spring three miles west. This he also released a little later. In 1880 he pre-empted the southwest quarter of the same section which was the scene of his activities for several years. At this time, February 15, 1880, the name of the post office was changed to Cowland, to moderate the term "Bull town".

Cowland was advertised as a beautiful village on the Pawnee, and the Hotel Golding sheltered many weary travellers, early speculators and cattle men. That region was divided up into cattle ranges, and the name "Cowland" seemed a very appropriate one and corresponded with the character of the country and its industry. It was the address given by a number of noted cattlemen.

As the seasons became more favorable, the county began to be settled up numerously by men who wanted to farm and objections were made to the name Cowland. A town meeting was called with the idea of changing the name. James Cross suggested the name of his native town in Ohio, Ravenna, and by vote, it was selected, but in making out the official papers, the government spelled it Ravanna. This occurred September 25, 1885.

Mr. Bull became the "Merchant Prince" of Garfield

county, and continued to sell goods at Ravanna for eleven years under the name of John Bull and Co. His wife was the "Company". At one time Mr. Bull was the proprietor of the leading store, the blacksmith shop, the harness shop and the butcher shop. Later other stores were added to the town. A building for church purposes was erected, the first preacher being Elder Booth of the M.E. denomination. Mr. Bull was the first pastor of the Christian church, while the first school-teacher in the town was Miss Agnes Sinclair, whom Mr. Bull hired to teach the neighborhood private school.

Schoolhouse built at Ravanna, Kansas, 1889

The story of the county seat fight between Ravanna and Eminence is told in the chapter on Garfield county history. During the time that Ravanna was the county seat the town soon reached a population of 700. The Ravanna Chieftain was established April 22, 1896, with M. L. Hart editor. He was a town booster and extolled its beauty. He talked railroads, advocated a Hook and Ladder Fire Company and a telephone line to Cimarron. Alexander and Rody became editors of the Chieftain in the fall of '87, and were active in the county seat fight. They devoted considerable space to berating the poor

Eminence fools who seemed to think there were some slight irregularities in the election recently held.

Ferris and Enos were editors and publishers of the "Kansas Sod House", which was published in Ravanna in 1887; it was later edited by Thomas & Co. The Essex Sunbeam was moved to Ravanna and was called "The Enquirer" and was published there for a year. The Ravanna Record appeared July 15, 1887, with Enos and Davis editors. They at once proceeded to show the futility of trying to disorganize the county on such a small technicality as being a few acres short of requirement. They printed some pictures showing Friedman and McCoy, Eminence butcher and hotel men, grinding cats and dogs to make hash.

In 1886 the advertisers were as follows: Bennett & Weaver, contractors; Gorden, blacksmith; Chalfont, undertaker; Murphy, physician and druggist; O. W. Crow, dentist; W. B. Jones, dentist; Johnson & Alleman, contractors; John Maehl, carpenter; John Bull, merchandise and windmills; G. L. Ensign, merchandise; W. D. Herman, real estate and law; Harper's Livery Barn; G. W. Parker, auctioneer; Golden, groceries; Goldford & Swartzman, merchandise; W. E. Collins, stage driver to Garden City; A. R. Wise, pianos and organs; Bank of Ravanna, J. F. Crocker, cashier; and Wm. Speck's Hotel was completed the summer of '86.

July the Fourth of 1886 was a big day. People came in on horseback and in farm wagons for miles to celebrate. The biggest attraction was Lee Price who did some fancy tight-rope walking. The rope was stretched from the tops of two story buildings, across Main Street.

A $10,000 court house was built at Ravanna in 1889 after bonds had been voted by the county. It was built of rock from the Pawnee quarries, two stories high and a large basement. Bonds were also voted to build a two-story school building of native white rock.

In a few years it became evident that the region was, after all, better adapted for raising cattle than grain. In order to build up the industry Mr. Bull conceived the idea of establishing a cheese factory. This inspired the settlers to engage in the dairy business. His cheese products won prizes at state fairs and were shipped to many cities. This industry was a big thing for the early settlers of Garfield county. Mr. Bull left Ravanna about 1890 and became widely known as a minister of the gospel. He died at his home in Cimarron, Kansas, in 1930.

Ravanna lost the county seat in 1889. Following that was a series of bad seasons, and most of the settlers left the county which was disorganized in 1893, and the town was abandoned. All that remains of Ravanna is the school house, some farm buildings, and the crumbling ruins of the court house. There is not even a post office to make it an official point on the map.

Towns of Finney County

HORACE GREELEY said: "It takes three log houses to make a city in Kansas, but they begin calling it a city as soon as they have staked out the lots." That was certainly true of Southwest Kansas. Much of its history dates from those first two or three houses which in this region were necessarily of frame or sod construction, instead of logs. In them were housed the pioneer merchants of Dodge City, Scott City, Garden City and others which were not called cities.

A study of the maps published in succeeding decades of Finney county impresses one that townsite locations have been as shifting as the "sands of the desert." The location and names of the post offices have been subject to many changes. Pierceville is the only town in the county which has both its original name and location. At the present time Finney county has seven post offices. Garden City, Pierceville, Holcomb, Eminence, Imperial, Friend and Kalvesta. One rural route and four star routes give daily service to all parts of the county from Garden City.

PIERCEVILLE

In 1872 Pierceville had the distinction of being farther out in the wilderness than any of the frontier towns in Southwestern Kansas. In all that vast area west of Dodge City and south of the Union Pacific railroad, and for many miles into Colorado and the territory south, there was no other established habitation of the white man. A number of incidents mark the town as a place of historical interest.

Early in the spring of 1872 the noted firm of Barton Bros. drove 3,000 head of cattle up from southern Texas over the Western Trail. They were the first to bring in a trail herd to feed on the government ranges in Western Kansas, and this was about three years before Dodge City became a center of the early cattle industry. They reached the present site of Pierceville in the fall of '72 and established ranch headquarters in dugout buildings along the Arkansas river. Their mongrel herds of long-horn cattle were grazing belly deep among the rank wild grasses of the valley when the Atchison, Topeka and Santa Fe surveyors came along driving stakes to mark their right-of-way to the state line.

Across the river in the sand hills lay the grewsome remains of a large wagon train which the Indians had attacked and destroyed several months before. So far as is known not a soul had been left alive to tell the story of their awful butchery. Strewed over the ground were the bones of man and beast, and many of the wagons had been burned. A man named Emerson salvaged the ruins. He hauled three carloads of old chains and scrap iron to Dodge, had about thirty-five good wagons left. With these he started a freight train from Dodge to Fort Elliott, Oklahoma.

The Barton Bros. ranch headquarters was chosen by the Santa Fe officials as a railroad townsite and was named in honor of Chas. W. and Carlos Pierce, members of the original Atchison, Topeka railroad company. As soon as the survey was completed gangs of construction men were put to work, and as fast as the rails were laid the work train advanced down the line. A commissariat was established at Pierceville with ex-governor Stubbs in charge, and five hundred workmen were fed and bunked in box cars. Hired hunters were also quartered there to supply meat from the herds of buffalo and antelope that ranged the plains.

A pump was put down and a windmill attached for power to supply water for the Santa Fe engines. In case of a calm spell of weather without enough wind to turn the mill, a supply of water was always kept stored in a wooden tank. About the time the railroad was completed through Pierceville, Thomas O'Loughlin, brother of John O'Loughlin of Lakin, put in a store. He kept everything to make the place a popular resort for hunters, cowboys, section crews and adventurers who happened to be in that region. He traded provisions for buffalo meat, and in turn traded it to wholesalers for provisions, clothing and ammunition. A post office was established June 10,

Original water tank at Pierceville, Kansas, on the Atchison, Topeka and Santa Fe Railroad, 1873.

1873, with George B. Clossen as postmaster. There were several dugouts in town, most of which had been built to shelter soldiers who had been stationed there.

At this time Pierceville was in a fair way to out-rival Dodge City for the title of "Cowboy Capital", for the first trail herds brought into Western Kansas came down the Arkansas river from the west. The town was ideally located. No more beautiful prairie scene could be imagined than the valley surrounding Pierceville, knee-deep with grass, the islands in the wide river bed studded with green trees, the rising uplands in the background covered with green grass and dotted with wild flowers. There was not a sign for mile after mile in any direction that man had ever inhabited that region. The river ran bank full, never having as yet been drained by irrigation canals. Trappers glided quietly along the river channel in strings of row boats, gathering many fine pelts from the beavers and other animals that lived along the banks.

For a year the town flourished, and then July 3, 1874, dawned clear and bright. As the day advanced the sun blazed down on the adobe buildings and the few citizens and a bunch of cowboys stood around in the shade, wondering if anyone would drift in from off the vast range to help them celebrate the glorious Fourth on the morrow. As if in answer to their speculations some buffalo hunters came into sight urging their horses at top speed. They soon arrived in town, bringing the news of the fight of Adobe Walls, Texas, which had happened a few days previously, and stated that a band of the defeated Indians were headed north. They were still on the war path, and were making for the settlements along the Santa Fe railroad. Mrs. Ellen O'Loughlin, wife of Thomas O'Loughlin, said in a letter written to her niece, Mrs. B. C. Hurst:

"Immediately after hearing this news my husband hitched the horses to a wagon. We loaded it with some bedding and a few clothes. We put our son and daughter in the wagon and drove to a cow camp run by Bancrofts, near Pierceville, and stayed there that night. At this camp there were fifteen men, but I was the only woman. The men did not seem to be worried about a possible attack by the Indians, and left the horses staked out around the camp all night. The next morning they went out to bring them in, but they were on the watch for Indians. Suddenly a fast-moving body of color loomed in the distance in the sand hills south of the river, and as the thing began to take shape it looked like horses galloping in the air. However, they decided it was but the heat waves rolling up from the hot sand causing a mirage, which so frequently deluded them into believing they were seeing things. But they continued to watch and on it came. Presently they had to admit that it was no optical illusion—it was Indians! A number of mounted warriors decked out in all their savage war paint!

"The men did not wait to gather in the horses but raced back to the camp. This cow camp was built of pickets chinked with mud. The men knocked the chinking out just enough to get their guns through so they could fire at the Indians. As soon as the Indians got within range, and before they got to the horses they fired at them. The Indians turned and ran toward our store south of the railroad track.

"We watched the Indians from Bancroft's cow camp. They rode around the store and dugouts several times before they went into the store. When they found that no one was there they went in, took what they wanted, and set fire to it. After this they started toward the Arkansas river.

"About this time there was the sharp blast of a whistle, and a Santa Fe train came puffing into sight. A number of the Indians mounted on fleetest ponies ran down the track to meet it, but the train never stopped. The savages continued to chase it, and the noise they made seemed like pandemonium broke loose, above the shrieks of the steam whistle. They fired at the train, and into the windows with arrows and revolvers. It is not known whether any of the crew or passengers were hurt, for none of them ever returned to tell the story."

Mr. Bancroft, who was in charge of the cow camp, had been a telegraph operator. He rode down to the railroad and hastily throwing a rope over a telegraph wire, he pulled it to the ground and sent the following message by touching the ends of the wire together:

"For God's sake, come to Pierceville. Surrounded by Indians."

He intended the message for soldiers at Fort Dodge, but the agent at Granada, Colorado, heard the message and sent cars flying to their relief. But long before any relief arrived, Pierceville lay smouldering in ruin, and the Indians were far on their way back to the Indian Territory.

It was learned afterwards that these same Indians had attacked a family named German, killing the father, mother, son, and a little child, and took captive four girls. They had them when they passed through Pierceville, but they were rescued later.

During the next four years there was no effort to re-build a town. The site was used only by roving bands of Indians or drivers of trail herds as a camping ground. But in 1878 John M. Stowe built a dwelling and Mr. Vermillion put up a store building. The post office was re-established July 24, 1878, with Richard E. Welch as pastmaster. By this time, a number of towns had been established farther west, but Pierceville had the only coal chute, and settlers came for many miles to get coal and do their trading.

In 1879 many claims were taken around Pierceville and several business enterprises were begun in town. Wm. Harvey operated a general store in the Vermillion building; R. W. Sholes had a general store; Wm. C. Newlin opened a real estate office, and John Brown was the village blacksmith. Prominent among the original '79'ers were Wm. Harvey, M. R. Logue, N. J. Collins and George Wallace.

The Barton brothers operated a ferry during those years, which made it possible for people south of the river to trade at Pierceville. They could haul a load of four tons and made trips whenever teams and wagons or horsemen appeared on the opposite bank and hailed the ferry. They used a saddle horse to pull away from the bank, by tying a rope to the saddle horn. Once out in the current, a sail was hoisted and it didn't take much paddling to get the boat across. The fall of '86 they started across with five tons of coal. There was a strong wind blowing, and in spite of its big load the boat was carried along at a rapid rate. The sail was dropped as usual when within thirty feet of the bank, but the boat failed to stop, and shot clear over the bank, wrecking it beyond repair.

N. J. (Elder) Collins was an educated and cultured man with a modest amount of wealth. He came west from New York with the ambition of establishing a great wheat ranch. During the summer of 1879 he built "The Summit", a twelve-room, three-story house above a full story basement of native rock. A spacious portico extended from each story, and he painted the building white. Standing on the hill overlooking Pierceville on the north, it towered like a castle above the plains which were so barren of comfortable dwellings or even trees. That fall Mr. Collins planted 100 acres of wheat. But there was no rain, and it never came up. The hot winds continued to blow all during the next year, and the drouth showed no signs of abating. He had a vision that it was going to take a long time to tame the wild sod, and the still wilder climatic conditions. His ambition to be a farmer left him and he was overcome with a desire to again occupy the pulpit. Abandoning the Summit, he moved to Dodge City and devoted the rest of his life in preaching the word of God.

For the next few years the big house stood empty, and served only as a land mark for people travelling through the country. Reports were circulated that the house was haunted. Its flapping shutters and swinging doors appeared to be moved by unseen hands. Even those in dire need of shelter shunned the place. But during the boom of 1886 the problem of housing the boomers became so acute that some one conceived the idea of making it into an apartment house. Four families of newcomers, who knew nothing of the ghostly rumors connected with the place, were comfortably and happily sheltered there. The boom of '86 didn't last long, however, and the boomers left the country faster than they had come in. Once more The Summit was deserted and left to the bats and the owls. One nice Sunday afternoon the Wallace boys and some other young people strolled over to the old house and were resting and happily chatting on the front porch, but they were well aware of the ghostly reputation of the place. There wasn't a breeze stirring, nothing to break the quiet calm except the sound of their voices as they jokingly related how different ones had heard "things" when they visited the house. One of the boys jumped up and said he was going to investigate, but before he took a step they heard distinctly a "dull thud" within as though a heavy body had fallen, and that was instantly followed by a terrible crash that rocked the house on its stone foundation. The party on the porch jumped to the ground and started running, and they never stopped or even looked back until they reached Pierceville. They thought the spooks were after them sure, but later they discovered that one of the tall chimneys had fallen. During succeeding years the house gradually fell to pieces and the material was hauled away to put in smaller buildings.

In the spring of 1879 Mr. and Mrs. George Wallace and children, Blanche, Charles, Guy and Ernest, came to Pierceville to try their luck in the new country. They found that cattle were dying in the valley from Texas fever, and they were advised to take their three milk cows farther north. They located on a branch of the Pawnee. Mr. Wallace left his family in care of his father-in-law,

Capt. C. M. Gilbert, and went to Pierceville to seek employment.

The Santa Fe at this time had a wooden tank which was supplied by water from a windmill. Shortly after this, coal chutes were built and a pumping system installed to pump water into the tank by horse power. Both were crude affairs, but answered the purpose at that time. Mr. Wallace was employed as foreman of the coal chutes, and also operated the pumping plant. There was no railroad station agent here at that time and each railroad crew had one member who was a telegraph operator, and in this way received orders by attaching their telegraph instruments to a wire.

After frost that fall the family moved into town and began the usual life of the pioneer family, made more picturesque, perhaps, by the daily visits of bands of cowboys from south of the river. They never ceased to thrill the children with their well-trained ponies and colorful garb. Each little boy's heart yearned for a pair of boots and a broad-brimmed hat.

In 1886 a plat was made of the town and many lots were sold or given to people to induce them to build in the town. The population reached 400. At this time a bridge was built across the Arkansas river and a road opened south. The Pierceville Courier, a weekly newspaper, was managed by H. B. Brown; M. R. Logue was acting postmaster; G. L. Ensign, surveyor; G. W. Wright, real estate; David A. Armstrong, painter; Orr & Stapelton, lumber; J. R. Drillinger, restaurant and rooms; John Clark was section foreman, and his wife operated a hotel; J. A. Hurd was in the harness business; Cory & Newman, hardware; Don Proseaux, doctor and druggist; Mr. Grub, carpenter; D. McDonnel, blacksmith; A. S. Van Patten, who came from New York in 1879 and engaged in ranching, also operated the Laclede hotel.

An election was held in Pierceville township August

28, 1888, to vote on purchasing ten acres of land in the northeast corner of section 13, T. 25, R. 31, to be used as a cemetery. The agreed price was $250.

A. H. Warner married Miss Jennie Logue in 1886, and engaged in mercantile business in Pierceville. Later he was justice of peace and postmaster. When drouth set in, nearly all of the citizens deserted the town, but Mr. and Mrs. Warner stayed on and made a financial success where others had given up in despair. He became interested in the cattle business and made several trips to Texas with neighboring ranchers to buy and drive up cattle. During his absence his wife would manage the store, handle the business of the post office and care for their little family. She would cut out their little garments on the store counters and sew the seams between waiting on customers. For many years Mr. Warner was active in the banking business in Garden City. Mrs. Warner is one of the few remaining '79'ers who are still living in Finney county.

The following is the list of postmasters and the date of their appointments: George B. Closson, June 10, 1873; Charles Stewart, June 1, 1874; the office was discontinued July 1, 1874, and re-established July 24, 1878. Richard E. Welch, July 24, 1878; Joseph R. Culbertson, Oct. 11, 1878; John B. Prescott, Oct. 23, 1878; Mrs. Sarah Cash, July 24, 1879; Annah B. Prescott, April 29, 1880; Henry D. Everett, Oct. 4, 1880; William Harvey, June 16, 1881; Jacob Wiehler, Dec. 22, 1886; William Harvey, June 10, 1887; George W. Wallace, April 26, 1889; William P. Booker, August 25, 1893; Simon Orf, June 10, 1895; Clarence A. Warner, April 16, 1904; Clarence M. Douglas, April 23, 1908; Emma R. Meader, June 12, 1920; Truman G. Armstrong (acting) May 10, 1930, and still serving.

A steel and concrete bridge has replaced the old wooden structure over the Arkansas river. New and modern school buildings have been built in recent years. The district grade school is of brick and has two rooms and a large basement auditorium. It was voted July 12, 1919, that bonds be issued to build a rural high school, not to exceed $17,000, and a good fire-proof building was erected. Three teachers are employed in the high school and two in the grades.

Pierceville has never had a church building, but regular services have always been held in the school house. For many years George R. Hedges has been in the grocery business; The Knox Mercantile Company has a general store. Fred Borger has an up-to-date blacksmith shop. Mr. Williamson, C. O. Webb, and Ned Norris have garages and machine shops. The population of Pierceville in 1930 was 166.

After the burning of Pierceville, 1874, the post office was discontinued, and the postmaster, Charles Stewart, was obliged to change his occupation. He roamed over the prairie gathering bones, and dealing in buffalo hides, and lived a wild and lonely life. He began to show signs of insanity, and the few settlers scattered over this region called him a lunatic and were afraid of him. On March 30, 1875, he was taken up by James Watt, who swore he was incapable of managing his own affairs. An inquiry was held before Herman J. Fringer, Probate Judge of Ford county, and twelve jurors, and they found that Charles Stewart was of unsound mind. David Morrow was appointed as guardian on April 1, 1875, but he was unable to constrain Stewart on account of his violent manner, and asked that he be confined in some jail. By order of the court he was confined in the Barton county jail for a few days, and then Charles Bassett, sheriff of Ford county, was instructed to deliver Stewart to the superintendent of the insane asylum. Among the inventory of the effects of Charles Stewart were listed: one lot of bones at Aubrey, Kansas; one lot of bones at Pierceville, Kansas, about a carload; one lot of buffalo hides valued at $27.35.

SHERLOCK, NOW HOLCOMB

Sherlock was located by the officials of the Atchison, Topeka and Santa Fe railroad company in 1872. It was named in honor of Thos. Sherlock, Sr., a director of the Santa Fe.

In 1878 the town consisted of a siding, section house and water tank. It was only a flag station, but mail was thrown off there for Garden City, which the railroad company refused to recognize as a station. H. Porter had a horse ranch south of the river with headquarters in a dugout near the section house, and section crews worked in and out of Sherlock, but there were no permanent residents there until early in the spring of 1879. During that spring a number of people came from the east to take up the government land or to buy from the railroad company. A. F. Lee and family from New York were among the first to settle at Sherlock. Mrs. Lee is still living and is ninety-four years of age, but she remembers well the day they landed. There was nothing there but a section house, and they and some other families lived in it until lumber was shipped in to build some kind of a shelter on their claims. James Mangan and family, W. R. Hopkins and family, and John Calhoun and family were among the earliest settlers.

By May, 1879, Spencer and Company were operating a store; J. E. Woods and Company had shipped in lumber to start a yard; Thos. Julian had a restaurant and bakery; J. H. Holmes ran the section boarding house; George Igou was doing a land-agent business, and by July the town had a saloon, called the "Hoo Doo Shop".

Sherlock flourished but a few months. Garden City was putting out every effort to be the city in the valley. They offered to move the Sherlock citizens, building and all, free of charge, if they would locate in Garden City, and most of them took advantage of the offer.

The seasons which followed were hot, dry and windy, and Sherlock and the country which had been so recently taken up was deserted of all except the cowboys and a few determined settlers. Mrs. Lee says she used to sit up in her little house, two miles north of Sherlock, for days without seeing signs of life except the trains coming in and leaving the station; or the range stock and wild animals running down to the river to quench their thirst. The grass was dry and brown and crumpled beneath her feet when she walked across the prairie. Mr. Lee had a team of oxen and "Buffalo Jones" secured him jobs of plowing the required acreage on tree claims. The money from this plowing kept them in food, and they managed to remain on their homestead.

The Porter horse ranch was bought out by Fred Harvey in 1881, and Major Falls had charge of the cattle which were driven down from Wallace, Kansas. S. H. Corbett was a cowboy on the X Y ranch. The headquarters were at Lakin but Mr. Corbett says the boys always liked to eat at the section boarding house at Sherlock because they put out good meals. They sank barrels in the river and kept them stocked with fish for table use, and they always had fresh river trout, bass and catfish to serve their guests.

One of the oldest names in the annals of Finney county is that of James Mangan, and he told me a few experiences of early days in his charming Irish brogue: "I came to Sherlock the 10th of March, 1879. The first mornin' I went out an' looked around, an' I thought it was the purtiest sight I ever seen. An' after livin' here all this time, I still think so yet.

"I filed on land two and a half miles northeast of Sherlock, and built a little frame house on top the sod, for the last words of me wife had been when I left New York, 'Jim, don't make it a dugout, for I don't want to go under the ground as long as I'm a livin'.' An' then purty soon after I got the house built, me wife and childers came out. For two years it was purty hard. Nothin' to do, an' nothin' to do with. There wasn't any fences, an' we couldn't keep any hosses or cows without keepin' thim fastened up, or they would drift off with the range stuff and be lost. There wasn't much of any way to get around, an' that mostly a foot, so we didn't go much.

"There was nothin' ever came here in the way of money, but the soldiers' pension checks. For two years we lived here without a cint—didn't even buy a postage stamp in all that time, but the people had enough to eat, and seemed to have a good time. There was always plenty of fresh beef. The prairie was covered with cattle, an' whin the neighborhood run out of meat, somebody would go out huntin' an' bring in a cow about the same as they would a jackrabbit, an' then passed the meat around, but they never wasted none. On Sunday, the neighborhood for eight or ten miles around would gather in some settler's house, and the wimmen folks would set inside the dugouts and the men would sit around on the wagons outside, all a visitin' while the childers played.

"But times got so bad I decided to go to Leadville, Colo., to work in the mines, but I didn't like it there abit, an' wanted all the time to get back to me wife an' childers in Kansas. They asked me five cints a mile to ride back in an old wagon, an' if I paid that, I would have to go hungry, so I started walkin'. After about fifty miles I came to a railroad camp, building the Denver, Rio Grande, a narrow-gauge mountain railroad. I asked for something to eat, but the boss said, 'No one eats but the ones who work'. 'Well,' says I, 'I'll try, but don't abuse me.'

"He said he had heard lots of men say that, an' he looked at me funny, but he put me to work with a gang. Sometime along in the afternoon he came ridin' along on a mule an' seen I was about all in, an' he told me to go lay down in the shade of a tree. The next day he told me I was to take charge of the supply wagons. They used mule teams, sometimes four, sometimes six, an' I didn't know a thing about mules, an' had niver harnessed a team in me life. But the young man who had been drivin' stayed four days an' showed me how to act. I had good luck an' the corral bosses took charge of the mules at each end, an' the wagons were loaded an' unloaded for me. It rained every day for 24 days that August, an' snow in the mountains every day. When I went to the commissary to get money to sent to me wife, they wouldn't give me none, for fear I would leave, an' I didn't get any money until November 1st. Then the boss offered me a better job an' said I had saved the company thousands of dollars, for there was niver a cint's worth missin'. But I wanted to get back to Kansas, an' I have niver wanted to leave since.

"After that I worked out of Sherlock on the section for five years, at $1.15 a day. I turned every cint over to me wife, an' during that time she paid up some back debts, provided for a family of eight an' saved a couple of hundred dollars. She was a wonderful woman. She was hardly ever gone except on sick calls, but one time she went visitin' an' was gone ten days, an' that was the longest time I ever passed in me life. I was thinkin' nights and watchin' days, a hopin' she would be a comin' back. An' whin she did come back, she shure did laugh at me a teasin'. 'An' what did you think about me all them months you was away workin'?' she said.

"She was a wonderful woman. There were no doctors in the country, an' 'twas me wife they always came for. She would be gone two or three days at a time waitin' on sick folks, an' washin' an' cookin' an' never chargin' a cint. An' of all the babies that came, she never lost a one, neither mither nor childer.

"Then one time when I got home, I didn't see her about, an' I asked one of me boys, 'Where's mither?' an' he said, 'She's in there sick.' I hurried in a worryin' an' seen her a layin' there in bed, an' I could hardly ask her how she was.

" 'Why, I'm a feelin' fine,' an' she laughed at me, an' lifted the blanket to give me a peep. 'He's your own wee bit of a son,' she laughed.

" 'Why in the wor-rl didn't you get somebody to help you?' I asked.

" 'Well,' she said, 'do you think I'm a coyote to go runnin' over the prairie at a time like this? What kind of a reputation as a doctor do you think I'd be havin' if I couldn't take care of me own family.' An' she laughed.

"The first seasons were dry. Big, black clouds, with thunder an' lightnin' an' sand a blowin' would come up suddenly any time of the year, but it never rained. The winter weather was usually mild, but I remember one bad snow storm that came an' stayed about a week. Cattle drifted down from the north. A bunch of cattlemen got together and sanded the river, an' in one afternoon I seen them drivin' cattle across, 'tis said, 80,000 head. I was workin' on the railroad. People began comin' in about 1885 an' they're a comin' yet. I wouldn't trade this country for the whole East, unless I could sell it.

"There are some things that better not be told, but 'tis wonderful about the people out here. Accordin' to me judgment, they are the best on airth. Some days when there's a big celebration, I think it must be in the air or somethin', but I get so happy I could jest lay down an' roll, to see everybody laughin' an' happy an' not disputin'."

Beginning with 1884 Sherlock began to show signs of the general prosperity over the country. A post office was established December 6, 1883, with John W. Gregory as the first postmaster. According to the "Irrigator" of January 3, 1884, "It will be kept at present in the section house and will be a great convenience to the people in that part of the county."

In the Sherlock items in the Irrigator of March 6, 1886, "The new station building on the railroad is completed, a new store building is to be erected. The contract is let for the new bridge across the Arkansas and various lines of business will open soon." James A. Barkley was appointed postmaster April 26, 1886. The post office was discontinued at Sherlock, March 27, 1890, and mail for that office was sent to Garden City.

For the next twenty years, Sherlock had no post office, but in 1910 the office was re-established, and the name was changed to Holcomb, in honor of D. C. Holcomb, who was very active in developing that part of Finney county. The town was platted and a great many lots sold. The following are the names of the postmasters who have served and their date of appointment: Abram W. Edmiston, March 2, 1910; Charles McConnell, April 19, 1912; Ernest McConnell, January 29, 1913; Warren F. Carpenter, February 14, 1914; Miss Florence Carpenter, August 23, 1915; Miss Francis R. Harrison, February 27, 1917; Mrs. Vernie Harwood, February 5, 1919; Alfred Towles (acting) April 1, 1920; Mrs. Gertrude Towles, April 16, 1920; Lenora Brown (acting), November 22, 1929; David H. Clare, March 4, 1931, still serving.

Sherlock built its first schoolhouse in 1883 on the same site as the present buildings. There were about eighteen or twenty families in the neighborhood and they all donated some money to buy the lumber and did the carpenter work themselves. It had but one room but it was large enough to be used for church and Sunday school as well as day school, which was financed by subscriptions. In 1885 or soon after Finney county was organized and school districts began to be formed, Sherlock built the first district schoolhouse in the county. It was a large frame building, and every cent of the indebtedness was paid before the first school was held. The town has always had good schools and now Holcomb is famed as having the largest consolidated school in the state. It is composed of six districts and contains 125 square miles.

The school plant at Holcomb has an ultimate capacity of 1,200. The plant now consists of seven buildings, besides an athletic field and a first-class farm of twelve acres, equipped with an irrigation plant, possessing a fine orchard, alfalfa field, and plats for agriculture experiments.

The main building houses the intermediate department and the junior and senior high schools. It contains seventeen classrooms, including shop, agriculture, household science and art, music and drawing department, a commodious study hall, three offices, four dressing rooms, two of which are equipped with shower baths and a large combined auditorium and gymnasium. The primary department is located in a pleasant six-room modern building near by.

The teacherage, the home of the lady teachers, is a modern twenty-room building, with sleeping rooms, living rooms and kitchen. This is under the care of a matron. Of the other three buildings on the grounds, one is the home of the superintendent, one of the agriculture instructor, and the other for the janitor. In addition to these there is a brick garage large enough to hold sixteen auto busses.

FRIEND

The Friend post office was first established in Scott county two miles north of its present location. W. E. Stover was postmaster from 1899 to 1910, but resigned when it was moved to the new townsite of McCue.

Friend is now located in Sec. 2, twp. 21, range 33, twenty-two miles north of Garden City, on the Garden City, Gulf and Northern railroad. A town company was organized and a plat made in 1910. It was named McCue in honor of B. F. McCue, the president of the company which promoted the building of the railroad. The Friend post office was moved to the new town of McCue, but the government refused to change the name of the post office, so the town was called Friend.

In 1920 the Friend school district consolidated with three others, and the school buildings were all centered at Friend. It was not long until a cyclone destroyed all the buildings, and they were replaced by a modern structure in 1922. About one hundred students are enrolled annually in the four grades, and four teachers are employed. Two busses are used to convey the pupils to and from school.

Mrs. H. L. Miller is postmistress. The office occupies a space in the I.G.A. grocery store of which her husband is manager. N. W. Shinnerer owns and operates the Square Deal general store. Jim Scott has a first-class blacksmith shop. The George B. Gano Grain Company has a large elevator which makes it a loading point for wheat growers.

W. E. Stover is one of the earliest settlers in that part of the county. He recalls that it used to take him a day to drive in to Garden City when he drove an ox team hitched to a wagon. He would spend the night at the Windsor Hotel, and take the next day to drive back home. He now drives the distance in an automobile in less than an hour.

W. S. Ruth is another pioneer in the Friend community. He located 22 miles north of Garden City in 1886. He helped make the sod road across the sand hills south of Garden City in 1887, and hauled freight from Garden to Scott City before the railroad got to Scott City.

G. W. Armentrout and family have lived in the vicinity of Friend for many years. He is a successful farmer and has been a factor in school affairs.

IMPERIAL

The history of that interesting locality known as Imperial can largely be told in the story of Daniel S. Carl, who has lived there since March, 1887. The post office of Imperial has been housed in the Carl home since 1889.

When Mr. Carl came to Finney county he found a settler on almost every quarter, therefore from necessity, rather than choice, he filed upon the hill which was later to become locally famous as Imperial. He pre-empted the northeast quarter of section 4, and as soon as he could lay up a soddy he was joined by his wife and two sons,

Imperial, the home of D. S. Carl, 1888-96.

Harry and Forest, and baby daughter Opal. Later he homesteaded the northwest quarter of section 3, twp. 21, range 30.

Great were the toils and privations they endured—the father working at anything and everything honorable to maintain his family, which was increased in a few years by the advent of twin daughters, Cecil and Ethel and another son, Plum. They and the Chalfont family, neighbors for a time, were the only people who had the nerve and foresight to remain in that region and face the continued drought and hardships.

In 1886 C. V. Chalfont moved to Garfield county and lived near Imperial for many years. He built one of the best sets of farm improvements in this region, and was one of the first farmers to really make a success of diversified farming.

During the summer of 1887 the Imperial neighborhood sought a place to hold meetings and Sunday School. They decided to use the new stable built by Mr. Carl. It was built of sod, 16 feet wide and 40 feet long, covered over with boards. It was roomy and seemed adapted for that purpose. All the people in the neighborhood, without regard to religious belief, met here for union service under the leadership of the pioneer pastor, Rev. Turney.

Mr. Carl and his wife helped to organize school district No. 4, Imperial school and alter, commonly known as Carl's district. When nearly all the settlers left that section Mr. Carl and his wife had to serve together on the school board in order to comply with the law and keep up the school. Until 1917 this district made use of a makeshift schoolhouse and the Carl home had to serve as the place of public meetings. But after many years Mrs. Carl's ambition to have a good schoolhouse was realized. It was built on her tree claim and offers a convenient and comfortable place for church and public gatherings for that neighborhood. The Carl soddy has long been replaced by a large frame structure, which provides shelter and hospitality to all who desire to enter its portals and still houses the post office, so long looked after by Mrs. Carl. She died a few years ago and her husband now hands out mail to his friends and neighbors from behind the old sign "Imperial" which still hangs above the door.

CUYLER-EMINENCE

The post office of Cuyler was established May 7, 1883, and Nancy J. Van Patten was appointed postmistress. In 1886 the office was moved about two miles east on the Pawnee. It was located on Smith and Quick's school land, in sec. 16, T. 22 S., R. 29 W. This was very near the center of Garfield county. The site had been selected for a county seat location by a committee appointed for that purpose, and the new town was named Creola. However, when the petition was sent in asking to have the name changed from Cuyler to Creola, they were informed there was already a town in the state by that name. Lyman Naugle then suggested the name Eminence, and the name was changed to that June 3, 1887.

C. J. Jones and other Garden City men were interested in the townsite and put up some two- and three-story buildings. Frederick Finnup owned the building which was afterwards used for the Garfield county court house. The Garfield Call was published at Eminence, beginning July 1, 1887, and existed six years. The county seat fight was bitter and the editor boosted Eminence and berated Ravanna. The account of the county seat fight is given in the chapter on Garfield county history. Town boomers and the settlers in the west part of the county worked desperately to hold the county seat to the center.

Eminence still has a post office which is served by a star route out of Garden City and still holds a place on the map, but the office is kept in a farm house. There is nothing left of the town and all evidences of the platted townsite have been erased from the face of the earth.

KALVESTA

The original town of Kalvesta was established in 1886 and was located two miles east and one and one-half mile north of where it now stands. Kal, beautiful; vesta, pure; the beautiful and pure of the prairie. The Hodgeman County Herald moved to Kalvesta September 17, 1886, and began at once to advocate the formation of a new county out of the west half of Hodgeman and part of what is now Garfield township, making Kalvesta the county seat. It claimed Kalvesta was designated to be one of the best cities of the west. Don't leave Kansas until you have seen this "Goddess of the West". Mr. Bond was the editor and he talked railroads and encouraged various big enterprises for the city. Lots could be bought on

Broadway for two hundred dollars. The town had several stores, two blacksmith shops, lumber yard, coal yard, drug store, livery stable and the printing office which edited the Kalvesta Herald. Daily mail was carried to Kalvesta and the people would stand in line to wait their turn for mail. By 1889 or after a year or two of continued drouth, people deserted the country, and there was no one left to support the "Goddess of the West".

The present town of Kalvesta is located in sec. 10, T. 23 S., R. 27 W., on U.S. Highway 50 north. G. S. Norton is postmaster and operates a general store. Kalvesta has a number of business places, good school and a fine Sunday school and church services. It is a good trading point with a large trade territory.

One of the early-day families was the Maurice Taylors, who arrived in 1885. The father and mother are dead, but nearly all of the children still live in the neighborhood. S. H. DeArmond and family also came to that neighborhood in 1885, coming to Dodge City from Ohio. At Dodge they bought an ox team and drove the distance to their claim. The parents are dead, but all the children still live in the neighborhood of Kalvesta, and Mrs. Jim Sweet, a daughter still lives on the homestead.

LAKIN

So far as is known, John O'Loughlin was the first settler in Southwest Kansas. He came to Lakin in February, 1873, and established a store in a dug-out. There was no money in the country at that time, and the young, pioneer merchant traded provisions for buffalo meat, and later, for buffalo bones. These in turn he traded to wholesalers for provisions, clothing, ammunition, etc. One item he carried in stock was ox shoes. Located as it was, on the Santa Fe Trail he did considerable business with the freighters of those days, and would take their worn-out oxen and horses and trade them teams that he had kept and fed until they were in condition to again take up the long overland trek across the western part of the continent. One of Mr. O'Loughlin's early-day employes was D. H. Browne, who for many years after that was cashier of the Kearny County Bank.

On February 5, 1885, John O'Loughlin married Miss Mary Farrell. Their children are: Mrs. D. C. Hurst, W. D.

John O'Loughlin established a store at Lakin, Kansas, in February, 1873. This was the first settlement in Southwest Kansas.

O'Loughlin, Mrs. F. F. Thomas, all of Lakin; J. C. O'Loughlin, Garden City; Jennie R. O'Loughlin, Lakin; Helen O'Loughlin, Tana, Illinois; and T. J. O'Loughlin, Mineral Wells, Texas.

In 1873 there was nothing but a telegraph office on the Santa Fe railroad that had been completed a few months previous to the coming of Mr. O'Loughlin. The first regular station agent and telegraph operator in Lakin was A. B. Boylan, who came in 1875. John O'Loughlin was the first merchant and was also appointed postmaster when the office was established in the fall of 1873.

Mrs. A. B. Boylan succeeded Mr. O'Loughlin as postmistress of Lakin. For more than three years she was the only married white woman in that region. Mrs. Harry Tate, a daughter of Mrs. Boylan, is still living at Lakin. Mrs. D. H. Browne of Lakin is a daughter of Joseph Dillion, who established the first newspaper at Lakin. Other prominent pioneers are Francis L. Pierce, William Russel, J. H. Waterman and C. A. Loucks.

Lakin was platted in 1882, and was named in honor of a director of the Santa Fe railroad. J. H. Waterman was agent for the townsite company. A man by the name of Potter started the first Santa Fe eating house at Lakin, but he sold out to Fred Harvey about 1880. The town was included in the territory of Finney county in 1884 and until 1887, when Kearny was organized as a county. The Kearny County Advocate was established as a weekly newspaper in Lakin in May, 1885, by F. R. French. The Pioneer Democrat was established in November, 1885, by G. K. Estes. Mrs. A. M. Loucks located on a homestead near Deerfield in 1879, and in November of that year, went to Lakin and started a hotel. The bank of Lakin was established February 8, 1886, with I. R. Holmes, president; John O'Loughlin, vice-president; R. M. Spivey, cashier; and Sam H. Carr, assistant cashier.

In 1886 George H. Tate had a shoe store; J. B. Harbolt and A. W. Smith were among the carpenters of the town; William Shakespear was a clerk in one of the stores; S. V. Goeden and Richardson & Judd were operating cigar and confectionary stores; V. D. Bond was the proprietor of a hotel; W. J. Price was one of the real estate agents.

The story of the little clump of elm trees, located

about four blocks west of Main Street, close to the railroad on an avenue known years ago, as Railroad Avenue, is told by Carrie E. Davies:

"These beautiful ornamental trees had their beginning in the year 1879, and were the first to be planted in Lakin. A short time before this date I had moved from the East to Lakin and had taken up my residence on a claim just west of where Mr. and Mrs. Chas. Smith now live. The country looked very barren and cold to me, since there were no trees, except a few along the river. I sent to Florence, Kansas, and bought one dozen and a half trees. But a smile flitted over the faces of my neighbors when I told them of my plans for a beautiful shady yard. They had lived there longer than I, and they knew the trees would not live in such an arid country, without artificially supplying water. I was disappointed, but I gave heed to their advice; and when Mr. Fisher, the manager of the Harvey Eating House, offered to relieve me of my trees by purchasing them, I sold them.

"Mr. Fisher had the trees planted around a fountain in the front yard of his busy eating place, and passengers admired his yard of trees very much as they would an oasis in a desert. The water supply was sufficient to keep the elms alive, but the cottonwoods, like many of our dear old settlers, faded away and died. Those little trees, now grown to be beautiful large ones, are the only things in the town that mark the year 1879."

FORT HAYES—FORT DODGE TRAIL

Before the railroads crossed the state there were several transportation highways. One that was important but not widely known was the Fort Hays-Fort Dodge Trail.

Fort Hays was established by the government in 1860, and in 1864 they established another at Fort Dodge on the Arkansas river. All supplies for Fort Dodge were shipped to Fort Hays over the Union Pacific Railroad, and then hauled overland through a country infested with Indians. In 1867 the government officially established the Fort Hays-Fort Dodge Trail, beginning in Ellis county, it crossed Rush, Ness and Hodgeman counties, terminating at Fort Dodge.

John O'Loughlin joined General Sheridan's forces at the close of the Civil War, and in travelling over the trail had great difficulty in crossing Pawnee creek on account of the steepness of the banks. Recognizing the possibilities of trade on such a highway he decided in 1868 to settle there and build a bridge and store. He constructed the bridge of logs, cut from trees growing along the stream. He charged toll: one dollar for each government team and fifty cents for all others. He also built a house of logs and made a stockade by setting the poles in the ground on end. He dug a well in this enclosure so in case of an Indian attack he would not be without water. Mr. O'Loughlin was the first white settler in Hodgeman county.

The O'Loughlin Trading Post, as it was then called, did a thriving business with government troops, freighters, buffalo hunters, cowboys, and with Indians, in spite of the fact that the main purpose of the trail was to subdue and control them. Famous chiefs including Little Robe, Black Kettle, Satanta, Dull Knife, and Little Raven, led their warriors along the white man's road. Mr. O'Loughlin tried to supply the needs of all classes. Besides the staple groceries and dry goods, he sold feed, rifles, ammunition, saddles, spurs, boots and other things that were necessary on the frontier.

There was never a dull day on this highway. General Sheridan was stationed at Fort Hays, and used it as a base in his operations against the Indians. He followed this trail many times in order to protect people and supplies. General Custer with troops of the United States Cavalry, camped near O'Loughlin's Trading Post in

November, 1868. The names of President Hayes, Colonel Dodge, General Hancock, Colonel Lewis, Amos Chapman, Wild Bill Hickok, Jesse James, and many others are recorded as having made use of the crossing. In one instance, the government sent a large supply train, consisting of thirty wagons each pulled by six or eight mule teams to the wagon.

When the Santa Fe Railroad was built into Dodge City in 1872, Mr. O'Loughlin anticipated a big falling off in his trade. He sold his interests to George Duncan, and after that for many years the place was called Duncan's Crossing. The old trail is now but an incident of history, and the log bridge was replaced by a modern bridge in 1923. A monument in memory of the pioneers and for the soldiers who made it safe for their coming, has been erected by the settlers of Hodgeman county at the historical Duncan's Crossing.

The First Settlers in Lane County
By John O. Loyd

I CAME to Kansas with my parents in 1878, and we landed in the little town of Alamota, in Lane county. We stayed with Mr. Herring and his three sons.

My father pre-empted on the flats between Alamota and Dighton, and with the help of my uncle, he dug a well and built a house. Sometimes I went out with father while he worked on the house, and we saw wild horses, antelope, buffalo, coyotes and swifts in the country.

Father and my uncle went away out on the prairie to gather bones to sell. They got lost and for three days they were without water. Our horses died one after another, and we got discouraged and were going to leave the country. But about that time father got acquainted with the Brown boys on Hackberry, and he went there and filed on a homestead called "Wild Horse Johnson Place", and we lived on this place a number of years. Some of the others in that neighborhood were: Mr. Dow, who had a drug store; Mr. Ketch was the first assessor, I think about 1882; other families were Cronius, Gollodays and Broadericks. Mrs. E. W. Collins was the first baby born in the neighborhood, as I remember.

Father went to work on what is now Fort Dodge. Later he worked for H. B. Bell in a livery stable at Dodge City. I stayed with mother while he worked away and we managed to hold the claim while he was gone. Texas cattle were driven up over a trail that passed our claim, and they watered at our place. They gave me the calves that were too young to go with the trail herd. In this way I got a start with stock, and soon had quite a herd of my own.

After we took this claim, our neighbors were the Newbys, Dan Pergren, John Brown, Tom Brown, Henry

Offerle, Steve Smith, John McKinley, E. E. Miller, Chas. Wolfe and his father, mother and sister.

Mr. Wolfe and daughter and the Newby boy all froze to death in the blizzard of 1883. I almost froze to death too, while trying to feed my cattle. We started back toward home about noon, but the storm was so bad we could not see where we were going and got lost. We travelled miles before I came to a place I knew. Three times I fell from my pony, too numb with cold to hold on, but each time I managed to get back on the horse. Finally I got to the creek and followed it to the house. My hands and one ear were frozen, and the bit was frozen in the horses' mouth. Its mouth was so sore for weeks that we had to feed it gruel.

In 1878 the Indians made a raid through this county, and took a white woman, and they also killed a man named Armstrong in the southwest corner of Ness county. We went through the prairie fire of 1893. We lost our home, feed and everything we had. The fire went as far as Great Bend.

I went through all the hardships of pioneer days and have seen the county grow and improve; homes have been built; good roads and better times have come. I still live close to father's original homestead, which has been my stamping ground for more than fifty years.

Early Incidents at Medicine Lodge
Told by BARNEY O'CONNOR

BARNEY O'CONNOR came to Finney county in 1884, and proved up a claim north of Lakin. He engaged in farming and cattle raising, and during that time, he also conducted a business of shipping horses from Mexico to Dodge City and other points. For four years he served as undersheriff of Finney county, and for three years was Deputy United States Marshal. Mr. O'Connor came to Southwest Kansas in the days when settlements were small and many miles apart, and he had many thrilling experiences.

In 1874 he rode the pony express from Medicine Lodge to Wichita. He started out early one morning on a regular trip, but had travelled only a few miles when he came in sight of a large band of Indians camped on Sand Creek. He turned back at once to warn the settlement at Medicine Lodge.

"What brought you back to town?" they asked him.

"Indians," he answered.

O'Connor was a tall slender lad of seventeen, and the men were inclined to joke him about seeing Indians. "Why, Skinney, you are not scared are you? It would be about as easy to shoot a well-rope as to try to hit you."

"Well, you better go tell Captain Ricker, anyway," advised O'Connor. He had started out before breakfast, so he left the men and went into a restaurant. The bugle sounded before he was through eating, and in a very short time he was called to lead Captain Ricker and his company of thirty-five soldiers to the place where he had seen the Indians.

"When I yell, it's everybody for himself," said Sergeant John Mosely, and about that time they came in sight of the Indians. They charged down upon them, and the Indians fearing a large detachment of soldiers were after them, deserted their morning meal, tepees, and everything but their ponies on which they fled across the prairie. The soldiers fired after them and killed seven bucks, and captured one big, fat squaw. O'Connor stood around while the soldiers scalped the dead Indians, and then they voted on whether to kill the squaw. They decided to put her on a horse, and ordered her to travel. She lost no time in making a get-a-way, and soon vanished from sight.

That night a big celebration took place in Medicine Lodge. Two of the soldiers played "The Buffalo Girl" and other popular tunes of that time on fiddles, and a gay dance took place in the street. The girls all danced bare-footed.

Mr. O'Connor was at Medicine Lodge when the famous bank robbery happened there April 30, 1884. He arrived in Medicine Lodge that morning from El Paso, Texas, with seventeen carloads of Mexican horses, twenty-four horses to a car. Most of them were wild, but he had six carloads of saddle horses that were broken, to be delivered at Dodge City.

The first thing he wanted to do that day was to see his friend, E. W. Payne, the president of the Medicine Valley Bank, and he waited in a saloon across the street until time for the bank to open. About 9 o'clock he stepped out in the street just as the robbers rode up to the rear of the bank and stopped their horses at an old corn crib. They were Henry Brown, chief of police of Caldwell, Kansas; Ben Wheeler, assistant chief of police; and John Wesley and Billy Smith, cowboys. Smith held the horses while the other three entered the bank. They ordered E. W. Payne and George Geppert, the cashier to put up their hands. Geppert obeyed, but Payne reached for his six-shooter which lay on his desk. Henry Brown then shot Payne through the body and at the same time, Geppert sank at his window with two bullets through him from the guns of Wheeler and Wesley. The shots alarmed the town and the bandits made a hasty retreat to their horses without a cent of the bank's money.

O'Connor ran into a livery stable that was on the corner across from the bank, and saddled the first horse he came to. He started at once with Vernon Lytle, Alex McKinney and C. J. Talliafarro after the bandits, who had headed their horses for the canyons west of town.

Medicine Lodge bank bandits: John Wesley, Henry N. Brown, William Smith, Ben Wheeler

They kept exchanging shots with the robbers all the time, and all were experts with guns, but not a shot took effect on either side. It was raining steadily and Talliafarro soon gave up the chase. The other three kept on and about eight miles west of Medicine Lodge they cornered the robbers in a canyon at a point where they could not force their horses up the steep banks. They dismounted and laid down on the ground, but continued firing at their pursuers. They held this stand until the water from the rain on the hills, began pouring down on them through the bed of the usually dry canyon. The water kept rising around them until just their heads were showing, and they were forced to surrender.

About this time Tom Doran, Lee Bradley, Roe Clark, Wayne McKinney, George Friedly and John Fleming came up. The bandits objected to being taken back to

Tom Doran, Barney O'Connor, Alex McKinney, Vernon Lytle, Lee Bradley, Wayne McKinney, Roe Clark, George Firedly, and John Fleming, who captured the Medicine Lodge bank bandits.

Medicine Lodge, for fear of being hung. Their captors assured them they would be protected and turned over to the sheriff, regardless of the demands of any mob. They started toward town, and about half way they met C. T. Riggs, who was sheriff, leading a big posse of men. The sheriff at once took charge of the robbers and they were escorted by the whole crowd back to Medicine Lodge, where they were locked in the jail.

The news of the attempted robbery and the shooting of the bankers travelled swiftly, and by evening the town was thronged with men from all the surrounding counties. About dusk, a howling mob formed in front of the jail and demanded the prisoners, threatening to tear the jail down if the sheriff did not give them the keys. Barney O'Connor happened to be standing near the sheriff, and he was given the keys.

As soon as the door was opened, Henry Brown made a dash for liberty, but a load of buckshot from the gun of Bill Kelley hit him in the back and he died in a few minutes. Ben Wheeler also made a break to get away, but was shot and badly wounded. The other two were taken out of the jail, and with Wheeler, led to a big elm tree, standing in the river bottom east of town, and hung. Wesley and Smith never flinched, and their only request was to have their belongings sent home to their mothers in Texas. They were drawn up at the same time. Wheeler begged them to let him live until morning, but they hung him in the same tree.

Seven men lay dead in Medicine Lodge that night. Two bankers, four bandits and a citizen who dropped dead from heart failure during the excitement. The four bandits were buried in one grave. Henry Brown had only been married a short time, and it is claimed that his bride drove a horse and buggy from Caldwell, and had some one to help her dig up Brown's body. She propped it up in the buggy seat by her side, and in this way, took it back to her home.

Garden City

THE founders of Garden City and the first to make settlement on homesteads in Finney county, were the Fulton brothers. They had ranged over this region for several years, following the business of hunting buffalo

Mr. and Mrs. William D. Fulton

and wild horses before they ever thought of starting a town. William D. Fulton was born 1826 in Ohio. He died at the age of eighty-four years in Garden City, Kansas. James R. Fulton was born in 1829 in Ohio, and died suddenly at his home in Garden City in 1885.

In February, 1878, James R. Fulton, William D. Fulton and his son, L. W. Fulton, arrived at the present site of Garden City, bringing with them Chas. Van Trump, the county surveyor from Dodge City. Mr. Van Trump had previously surveyed as far as the Point of Rocks, nine miles east of Garden City. From there he started to find the center of old Sequoyah county. They drove up in their wagons and pitched camp not far from where the city pumping plant is now located. They were anxious to locate in the exact center of the county, and were afraid they had gone too far west. But when the engineer found the county lines, they discovered their camp was not one hundred yards from the center, east and west.

After completing the survey they went to Larned, Kansas, where the United States Land Office was then located, and on March 16, 1878, William D. Fulton filed on the southeast quarter section 18-24-32, and James R. Fulton filed on the southwest quarter of the same section. The other two quarters in the section were to have been taken by Chas. Van Trump and John A. Stevens, but by mistake their filings were both put on the northeast quarter. Van Trump did not discover the mistake until in the summer, and by that time, Stevens had built a house on the northwest quarter, and held it. A young man at Larned, seeing that the northwest quarter was still vacant, placed a timber claim filing on it, and Van Trump lost out in the townsite deal. Late in 1879, C. J. Jones found the young man who had filed on the northwest quarter and bought his relinquishment for $90 and a gold watch. In this way Mr. Jones became the owner of the northwest quarter of section 18, which is now Jones Addition of the town of Garden City.

The original townsite of Garden City was laid out on the south half of section 18 by engineer Chas. Van Trump. The land was a loose, sandy loam, and covered with sage brush and soap weeds, but there were no trees. Main street ran directly north and south, dividing Wm.

D. and James R. Fulton's claims. As soon as they could get building material, they erected two frame houses. Wm. D. Fulton building on his land, on the east side of Main street, a house one story and a half high, with two rooms on the ground and two rooms above. This was called the Occidental Hotel. Wm. D. Fulton was proprietor. He often joked that it should have been called

John A. Stevens

the Accidental Hotel, because it was an accident if you got anything to eat. James R. Fulton built a house of two rooms on his land, which joined Main street on the west. This house was sold to D. R. Menke in August, 1878, for a cash consideration and a one-sixteenth interest in the original townsite was given him to establish a store in the building. No other houses were built in Garden City until November, 1878, when James R. Fulton and Mr.

L. T. Walker each put up a building. The Fultons tried to get others to settle here, but only a few came, and at the end of the first year there were only four buildings.

These first settlers lived a life of thrilling adventure, yet there were many lonely hours. Mrs. E. L. Wirt, daughter of Wm. D. Fulton, recalls that first year:

"There was not a sign of civilization on either side of the railroad. Just mile after mile of barren prairie. Frequently we would catch sight of a herd of wild horses or buffalo, and at night the antelope would come close to feed. The only sound was the howling of the coyotes and the fierce wind. I have seen Indians scouting along the river banks, hunting a place to cross, and one night a band passed not far from our house.

"Storms were not uncommon, and while they raged we would be buried deep in the darkness on a bleak prairie. The wind with sand beat against the house like a heavy hail, until every part seemed to groan and surge like a tempest-tossed wreck on the sea. Then my father would get up and change the props on the house to keep it from blowing away. Sometimes he would have to put a rope around his waist and tie it on the inside of the house, and then we would all hang onto the rope and pull him safely back.

"There were no side tracks, no depot, and the nearest post office was at Dodge City. The trains did not stop at Garden City, and there was only one way to get our letters mailed. I would fasten them to the end of a stick, and when the train came through I would hold them up so one of the train men could reach it and he would snatch them off and mail them for us."

The cattlemen did not want to see the settlers come in, and did a great many things to discourage them. But the Fultons were not bluffed by the rough manner and shooting around of the cowboys. Shortly after they arrived a cattleman came to the camp and said it was impossible to raise corn here and offered $50 a bushel for all they would grow. He urged them to leave, but they decided to stay anyway. And that summer of 1878, all crops planted produced bountifully, and there was an abundance of vegetables. The name of "Garden City" was suggested because of the fine garden in the Fulton yard.

The Occidental Hotel, operated by the Fultons, was visited by a tramp one day. He inquired of Mrs. Fulton:

Mr. and Mrs. David R. Menke

"What do you call this place?"

"It has been called Fulton by the railroad men," she answered, "but we are still debating on a permanent name, and I have been selected to decide on something appropriate."

"Why don't you call it Garden City?" said the tramp, glancing out over her lovely garden. The name came into instant favor and has since been retained.

Mr. and Mrs. D. R. Menke and three children, Olivia, Harry and George, arrived from Farmington, Illinois, and established a residence in Garden City August 20, 1878. Garden City was not recognized by the Santa Fe railroad as a station, but the conductor was kind enough to slow the train down and let them off about a half mile up the track, and they walked back to the little village of fifteen people. There were five in the Wm. D. Fulton family, and two in the James R. Fulton family. Five in the family of Rev. Michael Turner lived on a claim just east of Finnup park. John A. Stevens and Emanuel Schnars, young men who had been with the Fultons for several years in the business of hunting wild horses and buffalo, and a hired man who worked for the Fultons that summer.

Mr. Menke states: "I would have been here sooner, if it hadn't been that the Indians were on the war path, and soldiers were stationed along the line warning people to stay out until the trouble was settled." Very soon after his arrival, Mr. Menke opened the first store in Garden City. He was not a man of wealth, but had ambition, and realized the opportunities of a new country. He had been a cigar salesman before coming to Kansas, and used to go into the stores back east to sell the merchants, along with Mr. Heinz of pickle fame. Mr. Heinz at that time was peddling his wares from a basket on his arm. Those tempting bottles still lingered in the memory of Mr. Menke and he determined to place on the shelves of his own store in Garden City, a high-grade line of canned and bottled goods. He also added a shipment of boots and shoes to the general stock. After arranging his merchandise to his own satisfaction, and he had artistic ability, he stepped back to admire the effect. It was a keen little store, and he knew it. He then went outside to look around, and for the first time it came over him that no one lived in the whole surrounding country to buy his fancy groceries and boots. The few living in Garden City could afford only flour, dried beans, coffee and work shoes.

Money was pretty scarce among the settlers, and times were hard. Mr. Menke could not sell his canned goods, so he served them on his own table, not because he could afford to eat such food, but the family had to be fed, and they ate what could not be sold. His boots did not sell very fast either, but one day some cowboys were driving cattle along the river trail and they stopped at the store. One of the boys took a fancy to a pair of the boots, and gave Mr. Menke a ten-dollar bill to pay for them. Mr. Menke did not have the change. He stepped across to the Occidental Hotel to see if W. D. Fulton could change it. Uncle Billy could not. He went around to the other men of the settlement, and tried to raise the amount, but there was not enough cash among the bunch to change a ten-dollar bill, and they were grieved because Mr. Menke would have to miss a sale. However, when the cowboys learned of their predicament, they handed over the exact price asked for the boots.

Mrs. E. L. Wirt recalls the first death in Garden City. She says: "The first to die in Garden City was a man named Brown. He was travelling through the country with his wife and baby, and died in his wagon of a fever after being sick only a short time. My father made his coffin out of rough pine boards and we blacked it with shoe polish. He was the first to be buried on the hill, near where the cemetery is now located."

About the first of October, 1878, Joseph W. Weeks, N. F. Weeks, W. L. Williams, W. B. Wheeler, and D. W. Smith made actual settlement on land near Garden City.

Joseph W. Weeks enlisted in the Union army, August 4, 1862, in Company K, 18th Iowa Infantry. He took part in a number of engagements and was wounded in the battle of Prairie Grove, Arkansas. After his return from the battlefield he lived in Iowa until 1878. Leaving his family with his parents in Iowa he started in company with his younger brother, N. F. Weeks, in a covered wagon for Kansas. They arrived at Garden City May 5, 1878, and soon afterward both filed on homesteads north of town. In the early fall the family of J. W. Weeks came to Sterling, Kansas, by train, and he met them there at the home of his wife's father, J. W. Smith. They continued the journey in the covered wagon which Mr. Weeks had left at Sterling. The wagon contained the family and all their possessions. When they arrived at Garden City the town consisted of three houses. The children of J. W. and Elizabeth Weeks were: Elmer A., David F., Olive E., Eugene S. and Charles L. The first-named four made the trip to Garden City in the covered wagon. The Weeks brothers employed themselves the first years in picking up buffalo bones and in catching up wild horses.

D. R. Menke was appointed as the first postmaster of Garden City October 8, 1878. After the post office was established, he thought the mail should be thrown off at Garden City, so he stopped the trains about a dozen times, but the railroad reported him to the post office department. He received a notice to quit flagging the trains, and to go to Sherlock for his mail pouches, and he did so for the next five or six months. About all the men in town were sworn in as carriers and each took his turn, without pay, in going for the mail, which was carried daily. Mr. Menke usually gave the carrier an order for the mail, but one time he forgot it. He says:

"The carriers were all known to the acting postmaster at Sherlock, and I thought he would let them have it without an order, but he refused, and the carrier, N. F. Weeks, came back without it. There was a very bitter feeling between the people of Garden City and Sherlock at that time, and Weeks and I went back for the mail with the expectation of having a scrap. I was mad enough to do the scrapping myself, but I changed my mind when I saw the big, six-foot postmaster for the first time. But we had no trouble in getting the mail after that."

C. J. Jones came to Garden City for an antelope hunt, about the middle of January, 1879, from Sterling, Kansas. Before returning to his home, the Fulton brothers arranged with him for his services to assist in the promotion

C. J. (Buffalo) Jones

of Garden City, and especially in trying to influence the Santa Fe railroad to put in a switch and station.

Parties interested in the Atchison, Topeka & Santa Fe Railroad had organized the Arkansas Valley Town Company for the purpose of promoting townsites along the line of the railroad. This company had located Sherlock on section 7-24-33, about six miles west of the Fulton settlement, and planned to make it the principal town and county seat of the new county to be organized. Considerable rivalry arose, not all good natured. The Fultons realized the effort and sacrifice it would require if they succeeded in planting a town between the sites first selected by the railroad. They were fortunate in securing the service of C. J. Jones. He went with whole soul into the work of laying the foundation of a city. His ear, trained to catch the first rumble of the thundering herds of buffalo, now seemed to detect as easily the rumble of the wagons of approaching settlers. He met them far out on the prairie and guided them into Garden City. He went up and down the railroad to meet homeseekers, and would induce them to stop and look over this beautiful country.

Finally C. J. Jones made an agreement with the Santa Fe railroad early in 1879, and the Fulton location at Garden City was agreed upon as the town-to-be. It became necessary for the Fultons to immediately acquire title to their lands. To save the time and expense necessary to make commutation proof, they relinquished their filings, and title to the land was acquired by placing thereon, Land Script (additional homesteads) in the names of Edmund Guy, John Welch, John N. Baughn and A. R. Clark, each of whom were veterans of the Civil War. These four men to whom patents were issued for eighty acres each, conveyed to William D. Fulton the southeast quarter of section 18 and the southwest quarter to James R. Fulton. The Fultons in turn conveyed to the Garden City Town Company about 51 per cent and received a minority interest in the town company in consideration of the conveyance.

The townsite of Garden City was re-surveyed by the Garden City Town Company, and the streets made to run at right angles to the Santa Fe railroad tracks. The engineer completed the survey in April, 1879, and also put down side tracks that month. The frame for a station house was loaded on cars at Topeka and shipped to

WARRANTY DEED

THIS INDENTURE, Made this ___ day of _____ A.D. one Thousand Eight Hundred and Seventy ____ between The Garden City Town Company, party of the first part, and Frederick _____ of the Town of Garden City County of _____ and State of Kansas part__ of the second part:

Witnesseth, That the said party of the first part, for and in consideration of the sum of _____ ($__) Dollars, to it in hand paid by the said party of the second part, the receipt whereof is hereby acknowledged, does by these presents sell and convey unto the said part__ of the second part, all the following-described Real Estate, situate in the County of _____ and State of Kansas, to wit:

LOT No. Fifteen (15) Sixteen in Block Twenty three (23) As recorded Plat now on file in the Records office at Dodge City Kansas _____

in the Town of Garden City, as designated by the Recorded Map of said Town.

To Have and to Hold the said premises above described, with the appurtenances, unto the said part__ of the second part, his heirs and assigns forever. And the said Garden City Town Company hereby covenants that it has full power to convey the same; that the said premises are free and clear of all incumbrances; and that it will warrant and defend the same, unto the said Frederick _____ part__ of the second part, his heirs and assigns against the lawful claims of all persons whomsoever.

In Witness Whereof, The said party of the first part has hereunto set its hand and seal, the day and year above written.

ATTEST: _____ Secretary

The Garden City Town Company By Geo R Peck President

STATE OF Kansas,
COUNTY ___ } ss.

BE IT REMEMBERED, That on the ___ day of _____ A.D. Eighteen Hundred and Seventy nine before me, the undersigned, a Notary Public, in and for the County and State aforesaid, came George R Peck, as President of the Garden City Town Company who are personally known to me to be the same who executed the foregoing deed, and they duly acknowledged the execution of the same.

IN TESTIMONY WHEREOF, I have hereunto set my hand and affixed my seal of office, the day and year last above written.

Robert S Bell
Notary Public

Garden City. Carpenters came to finish the building, and by May 1, 1879, as good and substantial a depot as any on the road was completed. It was nicely painted and set up on posts about two feet above the ground. It had a front platform twelve feet wide and eighty feet long, and a platform eight feet wide on the other three sides. C. J. Jones was installed as the first station agent. He had his office well arranged and seemed to understand the business. Tom Daly who had been at Pierceville, was transferred to Garden City to take charge of the telegraph office. The first telegraph message was sent from the Garden City station May 25, 1879, by C. S. Merrill, and read: "Office O.K. at Garden City."

Only one tree was planted in Garden City in 1878, and that was in front of the hotel. Mrs. W. D. Fulton gave it four buckets of water a day to keep it growing, two in the morning and two in the evening. But about the first of April, 1879, C. J. Jones shipped a carload of trees from Sterling, Kansas, and donated them to the town to decorate the streets. The remark was made at that time, "if the desert does not bloom like the rose it will not be the fault of C. J. Jones". These were all cottonwood, but they were nice trees. They planted them all up and down Main Street, and on the side streets. Only a few of these trees survived the drouth of 1879.

The first marriage among the settlers at Garden City was that of John A. Stevens, age 29, and Sadie A. Fulton, age 18. The license was issued by N. B. Klaine, probate judge of Ford county, on February 10, 1879, and they were married by Reverend O. W. Wright, of Dodge City, pastor of the Presbyterian church, same date. The second wedding was that of Emanuel Schnars, age 32, and Belle Turner, age 18. They were married May 5, 1879, by R. G. Cook, justice of peace, at Dodge City. M. G. Smith and Miss Emma Carlton were married August 5, 1879, at the home of W. R. Stapleton. This was the first wedding to actually occur in Garden City.

The first child born in Garden City was Code Wilkinson, the daughter of Levi and Virginia Wilkinson. She was born December 1, 1879. She is now Mrs. H. B. Holcomb, of Long Beach, California.

In the spring of 1879 people began coming in to locate in Garden City and on surrounding homesteads. Prominent among them were the families of Isaac Hurst, J. M. Day, Eli Keyser, Richard D. Stuver, Nathan B. Adams, Levi Wilkinson, H. W. Crow, the Craigs, Roll Hopper, and a number of others came later in the summer. On one of his trips in April, C. J. Jones met Frederick Finnup, who had come to Kansas from Vevay, Indiana, to look for a location. He was persuaded by Mr. Jones to come on to Garden City. Mr. Finnup was at once convinced with the future growth and development of the town and country and decided to stay. He bought the first lot from the Garden City Town Company, and was issued deed No. 1, April 22, 1879. He began at once the erection of a full two-story building, the ground floor to be used as a store room, and the rooms above as a place for his family to live.

The gaining of Frederick Finnup as a citizen of the new town was of second importance to securing the railroad, because his ambitions were backed by means, which the others lacked. He began at once a building campaign which continued steadily, but in a conservative way, and added greatly to the building up of Garden City. He was ready to boost every worthy cause, and helped the settlers to stay after the drouths had made them destitute. He occupied comparatively the position of banker, and seldom turned any away who came to him for a reasonable loan. He had faith in his fellow citizens, and they in turn had respect for his good judgment. A man who has lived here many years remarked that he drew at various times from Mr. Finnup money to the amount of $14,000 and offered to give security for the amount. But Mr. Finnup knew that the man's word was as good as his note, and in a short time he received every cent of the loan. As soon as Mr. Finnup completed his first building, Mrs. Finnup and their three children, George W., Edward G., and Sallie M., came to Garden City. The sun was just coming up when they got off the train, and as she stood on the depot platform looking at the few scattered buildings, and the country so barren of trees and vegetation, she was

Building erected by Frederick Finnup in April, 1879, on lots 15 and 16, Block 23.

terribly disappointed. "Oh, Fred," she exclaimed, "Why did you bring me to such a place?" The children romped and played and the life in a new country held many thrills for them, but Mrs. Finnup, in spite of her determination to do her part in this frontier settlement, would cry day after day, while the hot winds almost rocked her rooms above the store, as she thought of her old home, with its trees and flowers.

Lumber arrived April 1, 1879, for the Landis and Hollinger Lumber Yard, and for the erection of their two-story building. They put in a large stock of goods in the store room, with Levi Wilkinson as manager. The hall above the store was used for school and church, and all community activities for the next three years. W. H. Armentrout was manager of the lumber yard.

The first issue of "The Garden City Newspaper" appeared April 3, 1879, and for genuine truthfulness and earnest co-operation for the interests of Garden City, it

Mr. and Mrs. Frederick Finnup

has never been excelled. Three months after the paper was established, the editor states, "there are now forty buildings in town." The list of advertisers were as follows:

Garden City Hotel, Wm. D. Fulton, prop.; N. F. Weeks, Blacksmith & Wagon Shop; Fulton & Stevens, Livery & Feed; N. R. Gardner, attorney at law; Charles Perrell, plasterer; Wm. Groendyke, Lumber; D. R. Menke, Groceries, Boots & Shoes; J. W. Weeks, Land

Agent, Notary Public, Surveyor; M. G. Smith, Painter; Fulton & Stevens, Hardware, Lumber, Flour & Feed; G. D. McConnell & Company, Architects & Builders; Williams & North, Contractors and Builders; W. B. Wheeler, Jeweler; Central House, L. T. Walker, prop.; J. D. Duncan, Harness; Landis & Hollinger, General Store, Lumber & Implements; Rock & Adams, Butchers; George Koons, Grocery; A. T. Levy, Livery; Lou C. Reed, Concrete Factory; R. N. Hall, Doctor; N. M. Carter, Groceries, Grain & Vegetables; Pennsylvania House, J. B. Hayward, prop.; Frederick Finnup, Lumber & General Merchandise; Jacobs & English, Druggists.

Prairie fires were terrible in 1879. The year before had been wet and a dense growth of buffalo grass covered the whole country, while on the fertile bottom lands was a grass that grew shoulder high, but this grass was brown and dead by the spring of 1879, and there were no spring rains to start it to growing. Many fires were accidently started, usually from the fires of campers. Once started, they would soon be beyond control and sweep rapidly across the prairie, the fiery tongues of flame lapping up everything in their course, and night after night the sky would be lighted by a red glare.

Adjutant General P. S. Noble was in Garden City May 22, 1879, and organized a militia company. James R. Fulton was elected captain, and J. W. Weeks lieutenant. The company had seventy-five members, nearly all of whom were frontiersmen, with considerable experience on the plains. They were all supplied with Sharp's rifles and no doubt would have given the Indians a warm reception should they have appeared with their little "tomahawks". This organization was called the Seventh Independent Militia-Cavalary Company.

On the evening of June 28, 1879, Garden City was visited by the hardest rain storm it had yet experienced. About 4 o'clock large, black clouds began to gather in the northwest and travelled southeast at a rapid rate, although the wind was squarely against them. In a few minutes the wind shifted to the northwest, and immediately the storm struck. The rain fell in torrents, flooding the streets, and it was accompanied by considerable wind. The first thing the wind took hold of was W. B. Wheeler's new building, wrestled with it a moment and then set it out in the middle of the street, right side up with care. It next tackled M. G. Smith's building and took a part of the roof off; after this it visited the lumber yards and scattered lumber promiscuously between the town and the Arkansas river. An old lady in attempting to go from one house to another, was blown a considerable distance, but was finally rescued and carried into the Pennsylvania House. The rain wet the ground to a depth of about eighteen inches.

This was the first and last rain that summer. It started the grass, but the crops were very poor. The settlers became very discouraged and some left. In order to hold them the first irrigation ditch was dug from a point on the river west of town and ran through the town. People discovered they could grow most anything by irrigating and those who remained were content. But business was pretty slow and the town did not grow any, although a few new people came in to take the place of those who left.

Dan Larmor came to Garden City in the summer of 1880, and the following November he married Miss Mary Frances Simon, whose parents lived on the land just east of Garden City. Mr. and Mrs. Larmor have lived here since that time, and on November 10, 1930, they celebrated their golden wedding anniversary. They hold this record over any other Garden City couple. The Larmor land was south of the river. They owned a mule and a horse and these were their only means of travel. Mrs. Larmor thought no more of swimming her mule across the river at flood time with a baby in her arms, and a sack of groceries tied on behind than she would now in driving an automobile across the bridge. Since those first years Mr. Larmor has developed some fine farms, and is still a Garden City booster.

Mr. and Mrs. Dan Larmor, who were married in Garden City in 1880 and have lived here since that time.

B. L. Stotts arrived in Garden City in 1880, and since that time the Stotts family has always been numbered among the most substantial citizens of the town. Mrs. Stotts and their children, Eugene, Ethel and Raymond, did not come until May 2, 1881. Mr. Stotts was on hand to welcome them at the train, but his wife was not favorably impressed when she looked over the town. The next day Mr. Stotts took her for a drive into the country to show her the J. W. Gregory farm west of

Garden City. It was well improved and he thought it might make her like the country better. But in speaking of that ride, Mrs. Stotts admitted recently:

"When Mr. Stotts took me out to see the Gregory place I wore a heavy brown veil, and all the time he was

Mr. and Mrs. B. L. Stotts

telling me what a fine country this would be, the tears were falling, unnoticed by him, beneath the veil. He also promised to give me a piano, and he did so a short time after. This was a Hale piano, and the first in Garden City."

Mr. Stotts was leading the family milk cow down Main Street one morning soon after they had arrived in Garden City, when he noticed two men coming toward him. The one in the lead was H. M. deCordova, but he was walking backward. The other man was N. J. Earp and he was following close with a drawn gun in his hand. Gonzalvo, the ten-year old son of deCordova, was playing in the street, and his black Spanish eyes snapped when he saw what was happening to his father. He ran full speed to their home. Just as the two men reached Mr. Stotts, the boy returned. He slipped up behind his father and put a gun in his hand. "Dad, here is your gun," he whispered. The situation changed instantly. N. J. Earp, the town constable, did some rapid manoeuvering, and soon had Stotts and the cow between him and Mr. deCordova, and continued to use them for a breast cover as he backed away to a safe distance.

A. H. Burtis came to Garden City March 13, 1881, for an antelope hunt with his friend, C. J. Jones. The Burtis and the Jones families had been neighbors in Illinois. Mr. Burtis thought he had arrived at the end of the world when he alighted at the Santa Fe station, but within a few days he was overtaken by the "spirit of the West", and decided that Western Kansas was the place he was going to make his home, and he has claimed this as his residence since that time. He has always taken an active part in the upbuilding of Garden City and community, and has held several public positions, including that of mayor for several years.

Mr. Burtis was married to Ella E. Worrell, daughter of Squire Worrell. To this union was born one daughter, who is now Mrs. Gertrude Cone. Mrs. Burtis died when Gertrude was eight days old.

In 1891 he was united in marriage to Miss Sadie Mack of Garden City, and their children are Preston Arthur of Garden City, Aurel and Maxine, of Chicago, and Aleyn Henry of New York. After fifty years' residence in Garden City, Mr. Burtis feels he made no mistake in coming to the frontier in an early day, and staying here after he came. His experiences in life have been many and interesting.

Mr. and Mrs. O. V. Folsom heard of the great opportunities awaiting people in Sequoyah county, so they sold their comfortable home near Osage City, Kansas, and with a few others came here to establish a new home early in 1882. Mrs. Folsom is still living, and recalls those first years:

"Before we could irrigate and we were living on our dry land, nothing growing, no near neighbors, we frequently had calls from the land agents showing their prospective buyers our beautiful country. One gentleman I remember with interest was from Michigan, and I will never forget the look of pity he gave me as he asked me: 'Mrs. Folsom, why did you ever come here?' I did not have the courage to tell him we came because we heard it was such a grand place to grow onions.

"I will never forget the sensation I received when the water from the ditch came with such force through the flood gates and watered our parched land. I have since seen both Niagara and Trenton Falls of New York, and I believe with no more feeling of pleasure and awe than when I watched the water as it poured from the flood gates at the northwest corner of our farm. Mr. Folsom was the first, I believe, to raise a crop of alfalfa in that part of the country twelve miles northwest of Garden City. From the proceeds of the first load he sold he presented me with a gold watch which he purchased from Charley Dickinson, and it is still highly treasured by me."

J. T. Pearce came to Garden City in 1882 and engaged in the sprouting and cultivation of sweet potatoes. In this business he was very successful, and because of fair dealing with his fellowmen, he was an esteemed citizen. For a long time he was a member of the city council, and was later elected justice of the peace. He was a devoted member of the Grand Army of the Republic and a licensed preacher of the Methodist church. Mr. Pearce reared his family in Garden City, and each member has been prominent in everything that has been for the betterment of the town.

Whiskey, dance houses, prize fights and plots of ground to "bury them with their boots on", have not been necessary to the success of Garden City. Her claim to prosperity and greatness has been brought about by good moral sense, wisdom and virtue of a sober, contented people; backed by agricultural conditions that are among the best in the state. But in the life of a town, as in the life of a person, things happen that are to be regretted. As time went on, Garden City, like every community, has had shootings, robberies and even murders.

The first death resulting from a shooting affair occurred here on Easter Sunday, in April, 1882. The following account was gathered from talking to P. C. Pegan, A. H. Burtis, and others who were living here at that time, and this is the way it happened:

In the early eighties, the Santa Fe had what they called "emigrant cars". These were old passenger coaches attached to freight trains. It was a slow way to travel, but the fare was very low, and the people could sleep, cook and eat in the cars.

Many of these passengers were honest, hard working people, going to new locations to build homes, or to find work. But there was always a rough element, taking advantage of this low rate to travel over the country, just to have a good time, and out looking for adventures in the "wild west". This latter class considered it great sport to look and act like "regular two-gun men" whose country they imagined they were invading. They carried firearms and used them pretty reckless, partly for devilment, shooting out of the car windows at rabbits, coyotes, antelope and birds, but some of them went farther and would see how close they would come to cattle, and even people travelling along the road, without quite hitting them. Sometimes when several were travelling together they would slip out when the train stopped at a station and make a raid on a store. For this reason, Levi Wilkinson, manager of the Landis and Hollinger store, was always on guard against these emigrant ruffians. Capt. J. R. Fulton was assisting in the store, and he always kept his Winchester loaded, ready for use when the emigrant train was due.

In April, 1882, Robert Cartney, a young Scotchman from Pleasant Valley, Pa., was a passenger on the western bound emigrant train. He was on his way to Arizona to get the body of his father, who had been killed by a cave-in while working in the copper mines. The undertaker at Pleasant Valley, who was an old friend of the Cartney family, and expected to take charge of the father's body upon its arrival at the home town, accompanied Robert to the train. He noticed that the young man was armed, and he cautioned him:

"Bobby, I lived in Leadville, Colorado, for a few years, and let me tell you something. You are going into a country where, if you take out a gun, you've got to use it. You are a hot-headed young scamp, and you better just leave those guns with me." But Bobby took the guns.

It was about noon on Easter Sunday when his train reached Garden City. Times were extremely dull here and there was no money in the country. There were several ambitious boys and girls from the best families in Garden City who desired to make a little money, and they had a habit of meeting these trains with baskets containing coffee, milk, pies, boiled eggs, etc., which they sold to the emigrants.

On this Sunday George Finnup, Eugene Stotts and Willie Jones, son of C. J., all about fifteen years of age, and some young girls, were on hand to meet the train with their baskets of food. There was a good crowd and by the time the train was ready to leave, they had about sold out, but Robert Cartney had got off the train and was scuffling with the boys, trying to get their baskets. He grabbed a pan of something belonging to George Finnup, and started for the train which was slowly moving out, and had reached the rear platform, when George picked up a hard-boiled egg and threw it after him. The egg missed its mark and struck a car wheel, but Cartney leaped to the ground and a race started. George reached Main Street about the time the train was on the west side of the present freight depot, but Cartney was a well-built athlete, and soon overtook him, and started shaking and kicking him.

Pliney C. Pegan, who operated the Metropolitan Hotel, had been watching the fracas, ran out and took hold of Cartney, saying:

"Here, fellow, we don't allow that kind of business here." He tried to hold him, but Cartney was strong, and swung around, and got loose. He started back toward the train which was still moving west, but as he ran, he began shooting back, firing three shots at Pegan, who was following. But they all missed, although the two men were not more than ten or fifteen feet apart. At this time a friend of Cartney's began shooting at Pegan from the rear platform of the train, and Pegan started for the depot to get a gun from B. B. Black, who was agent.

By this time the whole crowd was excited. Squire Worrell had just driven into town, and was standing on the opposite side of the street. He had in his pocket a new 38 Colt's revolver, which belonged to A. H. Burtis, who had just received the gun as a gift from Major Falls of the XY ranch. H. M. deCordova, a cattleman who had spent his life in the west and knew no fear, stepped up to Worrell, knowing he usually carried a gun, and said excitedly, "Give me your gun, Squire". Just as he took the gun, Cartney raised his arm to shoot again, but deCordova fired first and it struck Cartney under his uplifted arm, wounding him fatally. He was taken down to the depot and laid on the plank platform. An old French doctor, by the name of Ballou was over him examining his wound when Cartney asked:

"How am I getting along, Doc?"

"You are getting along pretty fast; you'll be in hell in about fifteen minutes," the doctor answered. And in a little while the man was dead.

While all this was taking place the passengers on the train had set the brakes and stopped the train, and a number of men got off in a rage, vowing they would burn the whole damn town, and their guns and rifles glistened in the noonday sun, as they started down the track. The townspeople scattered, and directly the barrels of Winchesters and carbines were protruding from doorways and around corners. These had been furnished to the town by the state to be used in case of Indian raids, and were kept stored in a blacksmith shop. It looked like a civil war was imminent. N. C. Jones fired some shots over the heads of the passengers to let them know they had opposition. This apparently calmed the emigrants, for they turned and went back to the train, and it immediately pulled out.

Mrs. B. L. Stotts lived near the depot and heard the shooting, and went out to see what it was all about. She was told there had been some trouble between the boys who were selling food and the emigrants. At once she was concerned about the safety of her son, Gene, who had stepped out so business like with his basket of homemade goodies to sell to the emigrants, and she ran down the street crying and calling, "Genie! Genie!!" The train was on its way and the guns of the citizens had all disappeared when Gene, who had taken refuge under the depot, which was built up on posts, came crawling out, dragging his empty basket, and yelled out, "Aw, here I am, mother."

An inquest was held over Robert Cartney, and he

was buried that evening. Mr. deCordova was cleared of any charges, the law holding that the shooting was justifiable, as it was done in self defense.

The saddest part of the incident happened when Cartney's mother, in company with the undertaker who had warned him, came to Garden City for the body. She asked to see Mr. deCordova and George Finnup, and they met her in front of Landis and Hollinger store. She was dressed in black and looked very sad when she spoke to deCordova:

"You are the man who killed Bobby," she sobbed.

He was touched deeply with regret when he saw how great was her sorrow and he answered her earnestly, "I am very sorry that I did it." Mr. deCordova lived for many years after that at Cripple Creek, Colorado, and was a highly respected citizen, but he often told his friends that he would always regret his part in the Cartney affair.

After the emigrant train left Garden City officers telegraphed to Lakin and had Cartney's partner, who had kept shooting from the rear platform, arrested. He was brought back and taken before Justice of Peace H. M. Wheeler. He was told that he had committed a terrible outrage, and that he was probably the cause of the death of his friend. A sort of trial was held, and the jury was then sent out to deliberate on what they had better do with him. They returned directly, and one of the men had a saddle rope. Their faces looked very grave, as they announced they had decided on a "neck-tie party". The man was almost scared to death, but they showed no mercy, and started to take him out. At that moment a train whistled. The Justice of Peace cleared his throat. "Men," he said, "let's give him a chance. If he can catch that train he is a free man. What do you say?" There was a shout of assent, and the man was turned loose. He bolted like a flash of lightning. Probably the foot race he made to catch the train broke the record for all time in Garden City, but he made it and got away. No doubt he thought he had narrowly escaped being the victim of real "Western justice", but the fact was that the trial and the whole proceeding was all a bluff to teach him and others like him a lesson.

Garden City, a village in the unorganized county of Sequoyah, was incorporated and became a city of the third class on January 13, 1883. An election was held January 26, 1883, at which time the following city offic-

Garden City in 1883. First building on the right was erected in 1878 by Jas. Fulton and was the D. R. Menke Store.

ers were elected: C. J. Jones, Mayor; J. A. Stevens, George W. Ricker, A. Hurst, and O. T. Knight were elected councilmen, and J. L. Dunn police judge.

There were approximately three hundred people living in Garden City. The poll books of the first election show there were thirty-four votes cast, and the names of the voters were: N. C. Jones, A. H. Burtis, J. W. Lewis, M. E. Wolf, George Edwards, M. J. Abbott, P. C. Pegan, T. A. Wright, W. H. Butts, J. L. Dunn, W. E. Carr, H. W. Crow, A. J. Shorb, L. A. Bearsley, J. E. Biggs, B. B. Black, J. D. Hose, George W. Ricker, John A. Stevens, C. J. Jones, J. S. Edwards, J. J. Erisman, Daniel Goff,

J. H. Jones, R. M. Morton, H. S. Lowrance, George H. DeWaters, Wm. D. Fulton, A. Hurst, B. L. Stotts, H. M. deCordova, H. M. Christian, B. Russell and Geo. Martin.

The first ordinance was adopted February 8, 1883. It prohibited the running at large of cattle and all live stock within the city limits. The second ordinance related to offenses against the public safety, principally to regulate the speed of trains through the city limits, and to restrain them from holding street crossings for longer than five minutes. An ordinance was passed April 30, 1883, requiring property owners to erect hitching racks in front of their premises, that growing trees might be properly protected.

George T. Inge, an ambitious young merchant, came to Garden City to establish a store in the spring of 1883. This was his first independent business, and he continued to sell goods in Garden City for the next twenty-four years. For a few years of that time, the store was conducted as Inge Brothers. Mr. Inge married Miss Sallie M. Finnup March 11, 1903, and they have one son, George.

The Kansas Lumber Company established a lumber yard in Garden City early in 1883. L. Nean Akers was the manager from September 1, 1883, until 1889. They were the first lumber company in Western Kansas to build iron sheds, and probably sold more lumber than any other one yard, their sales often amounting to $20,000 per month. In 1886 they put in a branch yard at Scott City. The lumber to start that yard was shipped to Garden City and then hauled across country in wagons. The first wagon train of lumber they sent to Scott City consisted of ninety-six loads, drawn by a continuous stream of teams. Including those ninety-six loads there were one hundred twenty-nine hauled out from the yard that day.

The first burials made at Garden City were on the private property of George E. Morgan on the brow of the hill north of town, but he objected to his land being used for this purpose. In December, 1882, Joseph W. Weeks offered to sell a tract of land to be used as a cemetery on his land north of town. This offer was accepted. February 2, 1885, an ordinance, No. 27, was passed and approved by the city making an appropriation to pay Mr. Weeks for the five acres of ground which was outside the city limits. That ordinance also provided for the survey and platting of the ground; for the sale of lots therein; and for a sexton to take care of the cemetery. In the spring of 1885 Squire Worrell agreed to furnish and plant 200 trees and guarantee them at 20 cents a piece. He also agreed to wait until the spring of 1886 for his pay.

In June 1884, Jacob V. Carter came to Garden City and engaged in the mercantile business with his brother, N. M. Carter, who had located in Garden City in 1879. The Carter Brother's Hardware Store is one of the oldest establishments in Garden City. The Carter families are distinguished as being steadily progressive, and they have prospered accordingly.

J. W. Mack came to Garden City in June, 1884, and developed a fine farm north of town. In the spring of 1886 he planted thirty acres of trees, his order amounting to $718. This included 1000 apple trees, 500 peach trees, and 100 each of plum, pear and cherry trees, and 10,000 Concord grapes. Also a variety of berries, shrubs, and ornamental trees. His son, George H. Mack, opened a grocery store in 1889, and has been in the same room in the Windsor building since that time. Working with him is his brother Robert Mack.

One of the saddest affairs that ever occurred in this section was the strange disappearance of Joseph Foy, a lad of eleven years, son of Mr. and Mrs. Martin Foy, who lived northeast of Garden City. He left his home on horseback to hunt the cows about noon on April

16, 1884, and was never seen again. The whole country was scoured over but not a trace could be found. Three days later the horse was found north of Syracuse, at a point sixty miles from his home. The horse, saddle and bridle were all right. The rope bridle rein was tied around the front leg of the horse, and proved that the boy had got off and hobbled him. Several well-beaten trails lay between the horse and his home, and since the boy was well used to prairie life it is thought impossible that he had wandered away.

On September 17, 1885, more than a year later, Dr. J. W. Holmes received a telegram announcing that a skeleton had been found thirteen miles north of there. Mr. and Mrs. Foy, accompanied by the coroner, Dr. Lowrance, and attorney W. R. Hopkins, left on the train at once for Syracuse. They learned that settlers had found the skeleton laying on the prairie. The parents recognized the boots and clothing as that worn by their son when he left home. He had a sore foot and had cut a hole in his boot on account of it; he had also tacked a piece of saddle girth on the sole, and these marks helped to identify them. The bones were gathered up and taken to Syracuse where an inquest was held, and the following verdict was reached after considerable consideration:

"We believe the skeleton before us to be that of Joseph Foy and we further find that he came to his death by means unknown to this jury." The jury was strong in the belief that there had been foul play, but there was not enough evidence on which to base a verdict of that kind. The bones were placed in a tin box and brought to Garden City and buried near the Foy home.

During the years of 1885-86-87 a rush was made for Western Kansas, and a settler came in for every quarter section. The United States Land Office was located at Garden City and this drew people to Southwest Kansas, and they came to Garden City to make filings on their land. There were also many contests to be settled, and this brought many men of the legal profession. I. R. Holmes was agent for the sale of lands of the Atchison, Topeka, and Santa Fe Railroad and the offices of himself and his excellent partner, A. C. McKeever, were located at Garden City. During the year 1885 this firm sold thousands of acres of railroad and private land.

The streets of Garden City were crowded with horses, wagons, buggies and ox teams. Long lines of people stood out in the weather waiting in turn to call for mail at the post office, and there was always a crowd in front of the United States Land Office to make filings on land. The space in front of the door would be jammed with people at closing time, and they would be there long before opening time in the morning. In order to escape the crowd during closing hours, the officials used a ladder both in entering and leaving the building, which they lowered from a rear window.

A serious incident took place in front of the United States Land Office October 24, 1885. There had been a change made in the office and the register, H. P. Myton, was very angry over the deal, and seemed to think Col. B. L. Stotts was responsible for bringing the change about. On this day Col. Stotts drove in after a trip to the country and stopped in front of the office about 2 p.m. Myton was standing in the door and as soon as he saw Stotts he drew his gun and with a curse started to push his way toward him, for as usual there was a long line of people waiting in front of the office. Instantly the crowd parted and the two men began shooting at each other down this open aisle, firing nine shots. Stotts had a small revolver and shot Myton in the breast and also shot his finger off, and then he stopped. Turning his gun up, he exclaimed, "The damn thing is empty." He stood still and faced Myton, who was swearing to kill him, and was holding him with a fatal aim, but just as he pulled the trigger, some one struck the gun. The bullet missed its mark, but it hit Stotts in the leg, just below the knee. The men were taken to their homes, and it was thought Myton would not live. Feeling ran high among the citizens of the town, and certain friends of Mr. Stotts took it upon themselves to guard him, fearing trouble in the event Myton should die. But Mr. Myton recovered quickly, while Mr. Stotts was confined for a long while with his wound, and it left him lame for the rest of his life.

Garden City grew very rapidly and soon reached a population of six thousand. About fifty large and small

Garden City in 1886. The day this picture was taken 129 loads of lumber were loaded out of the Kansas Lumber Yard, 96 of which were hauled to Scott City, Kansas.

additions were laid out to the town, and there was much speculation in buying and selling lots. The largest additions were those of C. J. Jones and John A. Stevens. Both were true pioneers of a new country and each pushed his addition and spent fortunes in building up properties far ahead of the needs of the country. There was keen rivalry between these two, and their efforts to out-do each other did much to boost the town. But in the depression which followed the boom, property values shrunk, and their holdings went into other hands for merely a small part of the original cost. The following notes from the Garden City papers of 1886 show a little of the spirit of rivalry which existed between the two men:

"Mr. Stevens bought a strip of land just west of the Buffalo Hotel, paying $1,500. He now owns the outlet to Grant Avenue, and intends to hold it to prevent any more buildings going up in that direction, and thus force the business to go to Main Street, where his property is. Signed, C. J. Jones."

The famous "Buffalo Block". It was built in Garden City by C. J. Jones in 1886, of native rock taken from the quarries at Kendall, Kan. It is widely known as "Jones' Marble Block".

"If Jones is elected, I will not build the opera house. Signed, J. A. Stevens."

"Mr. Stevens would have abandoned this months ago if he could reasonably have gotten out of it. The facts are, it looks as though the opera house has all been a myth, as he has advertised the third time for bids, and has each time cancelled them, except the last, and it will go as before, no doubt. Signed, C. J. Jones."

"Jones is going ahead with his stone block and that compels me to build. Signed, J. A. Stevens."

C. J. Jones built the "Buffalo Block" from stone quar-

Stevens Opera House and Windsor Hotel built by
John A. Stevens, 1886-87.

ried at Kendall, Kansas. Mr. Stevens built the opera house, and then went Jones one better in 1887, by building the Windsor block to a height of four stories. These were built mostly of brick that were manufactured in Garden City. The night the Stevens Opera House was formally opened a committee of Mr. Stevens' friends raised a fund, and presented him with a $65 gold-headed cane, which they bought of W. G. Dickinson, jeweler. Mrs. Stevens, beautifully dressed, entered her private box through a door which connected it with her suite of rooms in the

Stevens Opera House, 1886

Windsor Hotel. Her appearance with a group of friends always created a stir in the audiance.

Mr. Jones donated a block in his addition for court house purposes, and so did Mr. Stevens. Each was determined to hold the building to his addition. But these men, while business rivals, were not enemies. Many years after the boom of 1886, just before his death, Mr. Jones wrote affectionately of Mr. Stevens:

"John Stevens and I shared many ups and downs with a small number of sturdy pioneers. Some of our achievements will stand out as 'footprints in the sands of time'. Some of the landmarks of the town are the Stevens block, the Buffalo block, and the thousands of trees we planted, and the hundreds of miles of irrigation ditches that were built." His daughter Olive added to the letter:

"Papa is very feeble now, and can hardly stand alone, and it is only a question of time until he goes on that 'last adventure'. He has had a wonderful life and enjoyed to the full the glorious time he had. He is quite ready to go on and meet his old friends over there. His thoughts and conversation are largely of John Stevens, Frederick Finnup, the Fultons and John Biggs, and others whose lives were interwoven with his own. He said one day: 'I would like to move into the old court house (Jones Addition) and die there. I would like to lie and watch my old friends pass by, and look through the windows at the buildings we erected there. Garden City has always been home to me.'"

During the height of the boom the town had nine lumber yards. Lumber was hauled from these in all directions to build up inland towns, and to improve the homesteads over the country. Thirteen drug stores were in operation. The town had two daily newspapers. Everybody used coal oil lamps and a few were on posts up and down Main Street, as street lamps. There was no city water works, and everybody drank from wells, which were strong of alkali, as they were only put down to the shallow water. Ice was $2.50 per hundred.

Passenger trains of two and three sections came in daily, loaded with people and most of them got off at Garden City. It was a common joke that the trains might as well stop at Garden City for everybody got off here.

S. P. Reynolds of the Reynolds Land Company of Dodge City, and his father P. G. Reynolds, operated stage lines all over Southwest Kansas. From Garden City

This stage coach was owned by Harry L. Hill and William Walker and was operated by them in 1886-87. It made regular trips between Garden City and Dighton, stopping at Sutton Post Office, of which A. B. Freeman was postmaster. The picture was taken in front of the Avenue Hotel in Dighton.

to Leoti; Springfield, Fargo Springs; Hartland to Hugoton; Granada to Springfield, Colorado. Mr. Reynolds says: "I have enjoyed life during what I think has been a very interesting period. The one thought which now comes to mind is personally seeing transportation from bull trains to airplanes."

The prairie adjacent to Garden City was dotted with ever-changing groups of tents and covered wagons, the temporary homes of people waiting to file on land. There were many rooming houses and hotels, but they did not have rooms enough to accommodate all the people. The

Metropolitan Hotel, Dr. F. Hall, prop.; Kankakee House, W. O. Finch, prop.; Valley House, A. S. Van Patten, owner. The Buffalo Hotel was built by C. J. Jones in 1885, and the Windsor Hotel was built by John Stevens in 1887.

The streets were graded in February and March, 1886, and on March 12 a street sprinkler was put on the streets with J. Grantham in charge.

The Garden City Railway Company filed a charter December 2, 1885. The capital stock was $5,000. Directors were: R. A. Baird, H. P. Myton, A. C. McKeever, all of Garden City; E. J. Hudson and J. A. Hudson of Lincoln,

Main Street in Garden City in 1887

Ill. Allen Ditson, proprietor of the Larned Foundry, was awarded the contract to build a mile of street railroad and furnish two cars. Consideration $3,000. The cars were built at Larned and shipped to Garden City. The line began at the Santa Fe depot and extended north on Main street one mile. The cars were small and were pulled by a mule team.

Several manufacturing projects were in operation; the Western Planing Mills, of Hillyer and Green. This firm employed twenty-five to thirty men and turned out all kinds of wood work; the Carriage and Wagon Shop of Davidson & George; L. C. Reed, concrete stone works; Robert & Malernee, Plow Works; P. H. Hall, Hillyer &

Green, Stewart & Haynes, and J. L. Wiley, Brick Works. These four brick yards made more than 500,000 bricks per month. The Arkansas river carried a large volume of water, and there was much talk of a flour mill and various larger industries being built and operated by water power. Surveys were made by various men to establish a cane sugar factory in Garden City.

The first calaboose was built in May, 1885. It was 12x16 feet and 7 feet in the clear, and was built of 2x6 timbers, spiked together.

The Garden City Water Works was installed in the spring of 1886. It consisted of two pumps of a combined capacity of 1,500,000 gallons per day, two boilers, and an engine house, a stand pipe eight feet in diameter and one hundred and forty feet high. This stand pipe stood until April 28, 1896, at which time it was blown over by a strong wind.

The Garden City Bank was the first to be established in Southwest Kansas. It was opened for business about February 1, 1884, with a capital stock of $50,000. J. W. Rush was president; C. M. Niles, vice-president; and W. S. Bish, cashier. The First National Bank was organized in the spring of 1886. Authorized capital stock $200,000, and it started in with $50,000 paid up. The officers elected were Chas. E. Niles, president; Andrew Sabine, vice-president; C. E. Morrison, cashier; and W. S. Bish, assistant cashier. At that time it was the only National bank in Western Kansas. The Bank of Western Kansas was opened for business October 15, 1885. Capital stock $50,000. I. R. Holmes, president, and J. M. Dickey, cashier. The Finney County Bank was organized 1885. A. J. Hoisington, president; H. P. Myton, vice-president; A. H. Adkinson, cashier. Directors, Frederick Finnup, George H. DeWaters, A. Bennett, A. J. Hoisington and H. M. deCordova.

The Garden City Building and Loan Association received its charter in July, 1885. The capital stock of $1,000,000 was to be paid in weekly installments of twenty-five cents each. The directors were: Andrew Sabine, J. V. Carter, C. W. Morse, C. F. M. Niles, A. W. Stubbs, Geo. H. DeWaters, J. H. Borders, W. O. Finch, and W. E. Thralls. Dr. Andrew Sabine was elected president, and J. V. Carter vice-president.

Not all of the people who came to Garden City in 1885-86 were boomers. A great many substantial business firms were established at that time by men who have remained permanent residents since that time.

The name Hoskinson has been continuously and honorably identified with the history of the legal profession in Finney county since 1885. Andrew J. Hoskinson came to Finney county in 1885. He was a hard-working lawyer, giving the closest attention to the business that engaged his time and abilities. For some years he was a partner of William R. Hopkins under the firm name of Hopkins & Hoskinson. His two sons were Albert and Ralph, both lawyers.

The firm of McGee and Bill, General Hardware, was established in 1885, and E. C. Bill has been actively engaged in business since that time.

H. M. Knox has been a resident of Garden City since March 18, 1886. The capital of about $1,400 which he brought with him was invested in a store and bakery. Two generations of people, including most of the pioneers and all of the later residents knew his store under his individual name of H. M. Knox. Many pioneer Finney county people look back now and wonder what they would have done if it had not been for the credit extended them by H. M. Knox. He has been succeeded in activity by his oldest son, George S. Knox, who has spent his life in Garden City as a merchant. Other children of Mr. Knox are Dwight, Howard M. Junior, Edith and Ethel. Eugene died at the age of fifteen.

The Dickinson Jewelry Store is one of the oldest firms in Garden City. It was established March 9, 1885, by G. W. Dickinson. His son, C. E. Dickinson, took over the store in 1891, and has conducted the business continuously since that time.

B. F. Stocks began his career as a lawyer in Garden City in October, 1885, but his activities were not confined strictly to the legal profession. He entered the real estate field as a buyer and seller. His office was also a medium of making loans and abstracts. His son, Ralph C., was associated with him for many years until his death in 1922, and has now succeeded him in the business. Other children in the family were Herbert G., Edith, Brainard R., Ruth E., and Mary Belle.

James M. Dunn, Sr., opened his store in Garden City in the mid-eighties and operated it many years. For a number of years, later, it was under the management of his son, Frank M., Jr. At the present, J. M. Dunn and Donald of the third generation are conducting the business.

Miss Mary Hopper came to Garden City in 1885 and took a claim near Pierceville. She returned in February, 1886, to make settlement. Miss Hopper has devoted the greater part of her life to the school interests of Garden City and Finney county. Miss Hopper began teaching in Illinois in 1873, and was continuously connected with school work until 1927, making her a record of fifty-four years in service. Thirty-seven of those years were in the schools of Finney county. Her salary has varied from $25 to $125 per month. Miss Hopper is still ambitious at seventy-seven, but is now retired.

George O. Abbott who has lived in Garden City since 1882 and has witnessed most of its development, gives the following account of the first telephone system and electric light plant in Garden City:

"When the depression took place the country was

depopulated even more rapidly than it had settled up, and after a time the ones who still had faith in the country began gathering up some of the wreckage that lay mostly in real estate. An eastern trust company had come into possession of the Windsor Hotel and D. R. Menke was made their agent. In 1898 he persuaded them to make an appropriation to build a small electric light plant to light up the hotel, and as much of the town as would use lights. I was employed to operate the plant, look after the plumbing and heating systems, and in this way I became the first electric light and power plant operator in Garden City.

"Mr. Menke soon found that with his banking business, hotel and farming interests, he needed telephone service, and as an experiment, three telephone instruments were installed in the fall of 1900, one in the First National Bank, one in the Windsor Hotel office and one in the Santa Fe depot. This was the first telephone system in Garden City. The need of a more extensive system was apparent, and after careful deliberation, Mr. Menke purchased an automatic telephone switchboard of 100 instrument capacity, with seven phones connected to start with. R. M. Lawrence had No. 2 installed in his office, which was the first phone, because No. 1 would not work, and he has retained the same number throughout all the changes of the company. George Menke was in charge until he was obliged on account of poor health to change climate and Clarence Thomas became my assistant. The telephone exchange and the light plant expanded steadily until they were loaded to capacity. A new engine and dynamo were bought for the light plant, 1905, and a new manual call 250 drop switchboard for the telephone exchange."

When the first telephone line was built trees were growing on both sides of Main street. These interferred with the wires, but the citizens who had lived here and knew the value of trees in Western Kansas would not allow them to be cut, and the telephone poles were set down the center of the street.

The first long distance telephone out of Garden City was a line nine miles long, and was built in 1902 to ranches belonging to Bruce Holcomb, W. P. Gunar and Sam Leonard, all living northwest of Holcomb. J. A. Cobb lived on the Leonard place when the telephone was installed. Sam Austin built the line and was assisted by C. E. Dickinson. They received $175 for building the line. Another line was built a short time later to the Bullard, Burnside, and other ranches south of town.

One does not explore very far into the history of Finney county before coming upon the activity of those men who followed the profession of physician and surgeon. They began coming into this region as early as 1879 to offer service to the scattered population, for the dugouts and sod houses were often miles apart. In the years that followed they travelled over wide stretches of prairie on horseback or in buggy. There were no telephones, improved highways or automobiles. It involved tremendous physical toil and hardship to be a doctor in those days, but they never stopped to figure the cost to themselves, ministering with all their skill to any who called.

Dr. R. N. Hall was the first physician to locate in Garden City. He came in the spring of 1879. Dr. Morrison came next. Both of these men left in a short time for want of practice. Dr. H. S. Lowrance came to Garden City in 1881, and hung out his shingle as physician and surgeon. He had a large and lucrative practice and remained in Garden City several years. He married Miss Ida Rich of Garden City in 1884.

H. D. Niles, M.D., came to Garden City in 1885. He was a member of the firm of Huber & Company, druggists, and was a popular physician.

Joseph W. Holmes came to Garden City about 1883, and practiced successfully for a number of years.

Dr. Andrew Sabine came to Garden City July 1, 1884, coming here from Marysville, Ohio. He was a thoroughly competent and educated physician and surgeon, and had the love and respect of everyone. In later years he was connected with banking and other business institutions of the city, and engaged extensively in cattle ranching. He died in Garden City February 14, 1915. A great block of granite has been placed to mark his grave in Valley View cemetery, and the Andrew Sabine junior high school was named in his honor.

Dr. O. L. Helwig was a successful physician and surgeon in Garden City for a long term of years until his death. He first had a small hospital over Dunn's store for awhile, and then for several years he and Dr. Chas. Rewerts maintained a hospital in the building now used by Garnand's funeral home.

For a number of years after his graduation from the University Medical School in Kansas City, Dr. Chas. Rewerts was associated with his old friend, Dr. Helwig. In 1916 he built a modern 25-room hospital at 612 Fifth street. In 1928 he and Dr. O. W. Miner built the 50-room addition to the Rewerts-Miner Hospital, which will ever stand as a monument to the services of Dr. Rewerts. His death, which occurred suddenly December 17, 1930, caused sorrow to hundreds to whom he had ministered.

Loren V. Miner has the longest record of service in the medical profession of any in this region. He was born in Athens county, Ohio, March 14, 1860. He graduated from the Columbus Medical College in 1886. In search of a location, he first came to Garfield county and established himself at Eminence in 1887, and continued to live there long after Garfield county had lost its identity. Since 1913 he has lived in Sublette, and is still active in general practice. Oliver W. Miner has followed the profession of his father, and for a number of years has lived in Garden City, in connection with Dr. Rewerts of the Rewerts-Miner hospital.

Dr. R. E. Gray has been a druggist and successful physician in Garden City since 1885. Thinking he could give better service to patients living at a distance, he bought a Locomobile in the spring of 1901. This was the first car to be used by anyone in Garden City. It was a steamer, and until the doctor bought a condenser, it would run out of water about every ten miles, but at that he got over the county faster than with a horse and buggy.

Dr. G. L. Neal, a graduate of the New York Medical School, came to Garden City from Salem, Indiana, in May, 1886. He retired after twenty years of general practice at the age of seventy-six. Dr. Neal is now ninety-six years old and the oldest member of the Independent Order of Odd Fellows in the United States.

POSTMASTERS OF GARDEN CITY

David R. Menke, October 8, 1878, to June 16, 1881.
Norman C. Jones, June 16, 1881, to August 11, 1885.
Hiram N. Christian, Aug. 11, 1885, to February 18, 1886.
Lewis C. Martin, February 18, 1886, to April 19, 1890.
David W. Pitts, April 19, 1890, to May 15, 1894.
Enos L. Stephenson, May 15, 1894, to July 1, 1898.
Joseph C. Kitchen, July 1, 1898, to February 28, 1907.
Israel L. Diesem, February 28, 1907, to December 13, 1909.
Raymond E. Stotts, December 23, 1913, to August 5, 1922.
Charles I. Zirkle, August 5, 1922, and still serving.

J. E. Baker came to Garden City in 1885. For a number of years he engaged in banking and in the cattle industry. Since 1905 he has been continuously in the mercantile business.

History of the Garden City Fire Department

For several years after Garden City was started its only claim to city water works were town pumps and watering troughs in front of some of the business places on Main Street. For this reason it could have no fire fighting apparatus other than a volunteer bucket brigade.

In December, 1886, fire started in a restaurant in block 36, just north of the railroad tracks. In order to get water to fight the fire Carter Brothers of the Carter Brothers Hardware Company, aided by citizens, drove several pipes with sand points on the end into the ground and attached pitcher pumps, and in less than twenty minutes they were pumping water into buckets. But a bucket brigade on a fire like that amounted to nothing for the buildings were all frame. The fire continued to rage until it had swept the entire south half of the block.

Early in 1887 bonds were voted for the installation of city water works which were completed that summer, and soon after, the first fire apparatus was purchased. It consisted of two hose carts, a hook and ladder wagon, and 1000 feet of hose. A fire department was organized with fifty-four members and a chief, the names of whom were as follows: D. Rasure, Chief of the Volunteer Fire Department; Hook and Ladder Company, G. T. Sims, M. J. Sharpe, R. D. Love, W. C. DePew, Sam Presson, Oscar Richardson, J. B. Nichols, Eugene Austin, W. B. McKamey, J. Heylin, E. H. Murphy, J. Jackson.

Hose Cart No. 1, E. T. Tebbe, F. C. Platt, Will J. Pierce, Fred Cornell, John Ward, Frank Selby, Harry Snooks, George McMullen, Lee Chapman, H. U. Tebbe, Fred Dennis. Hose Cart No. 2, W. H. Meyers, J. F. Kirkpatrick, B. F. Hardesty, R. C. Martin, G. L. Miller, C.

Harding, George Martin, Will Davidson, E. C. Briggs, Harry McGee. Other members, B. Elder, W. H. Ferrill, G. K. Bass, Will Glascock, G. M. Seeds, W. O. Carter, Mose Conover, J. W. Whiteman, James Bandy, Perry Brown, W. Sharp, J. G. Angel, J. C. Wolf, J. D. Goldsby, S. H. Pate, B. J. Joy, Nelse Davenport, Walter Wernstine, Chas. Laux, Lee Motherhead, O. A. Harding.

In March of 1887, occurred the first great fire on which the new department had an opportunity to try its skill. A fire broke out in block 37 and swept the entire east half of that block along Main Street.

In May, 1887, another fire practically wiped out the business buildings along Main Street in block 23. On December 27, 1887, a fire burned several buildings in block 22. These fires gutted four of the principal business blocks.

On May 5, 1892, the fire department disbanded, and for the next year Garden City was without a fire department. It was re-organized March 7, 1893. The charter members of this organization were: G. K. Bass, Sam Craig, J. V. Rice, O. D. Johnson, George Mack, E. G. Finnup, Wm. Kirk, E. J. Leonard, W. S. Holbert, Frank Wolf, Ellis Titus, Will Householder, and E. B. Stotts.

The fire department has made many runs in answer to fire alarms during the past years, and has saved properties amounting to thousands of dollars, but some were of a nature that could not be controlled by ordinary methods. The following fires are those most disastrous:

November 18, 1894, the livery stable of John Stevens burned. Loss $1,200, and several head of horses were burned.

February 9, 1897, the Garden City Roller Mills burned. Loss about $8,000.

March 11, 1898, the Rink Building and five others burned. These were on the east side of Main Street in Block No. 9.

March 21, 1901, the North School Building was destroyed by fire. Loss $22,000.

November 10, 1903, the hose house burned with damage of $1,000.

April 5, 1905, the department answered three calls. The home of Mrs. Boggs was burned. It was too far from the fire plugs for the hose to reach it. The Finch barn was reported on fire, but it was under control when the firemen arrived. The third call came for the livery barn of R. C. Finch on lot 12, block 65. The horses, buggies, harness and building were a total loss.

March 23, 1910, the five-year-old daughter of J. H. Brown was burned to death when their home was destroyed by fire.

In September, 1911, the Red Lion Livery Stable was burned. Building and equipment a total loss.

July 28, 1916, a fire in the alfalfa mill at the sugar factory resulted in a total loss of $15,000, on account of no water available to fight it.

November 30, 1919, fire destroyed the Christian church.

October 18, 1924, J. B. Byars Dry Goods Store, loss $11,000.

May 26, 1927, D. A. Knox (Home Grocery), loss $3,500.

May 26, 1927, Garden City Telegram, loss to building $1,500; contents $8,000.

February 13, 1928, Garden City Telegram, loss $2,300.

April 14, 1929, the Elks Home was destroyed by fire. Loss, building $25,000, contents $1,000.

January 1, 1930, two children of M. R. Kiddo were burned to death in a fire at his residence.

January 11, 1930, Gano Elevator. Loss of building $18,000; contents $25,000.

August 30, 1930, Conard's Studio. Loss $14,000.

The following men have served as Chiefs of the Fire

Department at different periods since its organization: D. Rasure, W. O. Carter, Benjamin Blanchard, Geo. K. Bass, Sam Craig, Myron Hayes, George Dillon, Robert Counsell, George S. Glancy, S. A. Studebaker, W. P. Lightner, Gus Worlen, and E. H. Gentry.

Mayors of Garden City

C. J. Jones, January 26, 1883, to April, 1883.
George W. Ricker, April, 1883, to April, 1884.
H. M. deCordova, April, 1884, to April, 1885.
I. R. Holmes, April, 1885, to April, 1886.
C. G. Larned, April, 1886, to April, 1887.
D. A. Mims, April, 1887, to April, 1889.
J. W. Wallace, April, 1889, to April, 1890.
S. B. Barnes, April, 1890, to April, 1891.
Andrew Sabine, April, 1891, to April, 1893.
J. J. Munger, April, 1893, to April, 1895.
G. H. DeWaters, April, 1895, to April, 1897.
E. Davis, April, 1897, to April, 1901.
W. O. Carter, April, 1901, to April, 1905.
G. L. Miller, April, 1905, served until his death, Oct., 1908.
O. H. Foster, December, 1908, to April, 1910.
John F. Walters, April, 1910, to April, 1911.
Walter Harvey, April, 1911, to April, 1913.
D. R. Menke, April, 1913, to April, 1914.
A. H. Burtis, April, 1914, to April, 1918.
Wm. Wonn, April, 1918, to April, 1921.
H. O. Trinkle, April, 1921, to April, 1927.
Fred J. Evans, April, 1927, and still in office.

GARDEN CITY PUBLIC LIBRARY

The Ladies Library Association was organized in June, 1897. A membership fee of $2.00 per year was charged, and fines assessed on books over due. The members used various methods to obtain funds to buy new books, and many books were donated. Each member was allowed two books every week. One paper back and one board back. Every book in the library was covered with heavy paper in order to protect the bindings and the title was hand printed on the outside. They used a room on the second floor of the Buffalo Block, and the members of the association took turns in acting as librarian. It was open only on Saturday afternoon from 2 p.m. until 5 p.m.

The first officers were: Mrs. (Dr.) Frederick Cole, President; Sallie M. Finnup (Mrs. Geo. T. Inge) Secretary; Mrs. D. R. Menke, Treasurer. The executive committee was composed of the officers and Mrs. (Dr.) A. Sabine, Mrs. Wm. E. Hutchison, Mrs. W. O. Finch, Mrs.

Theodore Roosevelt in Garden City. He was returning from the Rough Riders' Convention at Las Vegas, New Mexico, 1899.

John E. Baker, Mrs. W. M. Kinnison and Mrs. Elizabeth Hoskinson.

In 1907 the citizens voted to have a tax levied to maintain a public library. Three years later a library board was appointed by the mayor and city council, and at that time (1910) the Ladies Library Association gave to the city its library, consisting of about 1,500 volumes. In 1911 the books were moved into the City Council Chamber, until a suitable building could be erected. A reading room was opened with a librarian in charge.

After satisfactory proof that the citizens of Garden City would do their part, a gift of $10,000 was received from the Andrew Carnegie Public Library Fund, for a building, and the erection of the present building began in October, 1916. The gift of the beautiful site where the building is located was made by George W. Finnup, which is but one of the many tokens of his generosity to the city. The formal opening of the library was October 4, 1917, and the complete cost was $11,500.

The Ladies Library Association are to be given thanks for the many books which filled the shelves at the opening, and for the gift of the fernery which occupies the window in the west reading room.

Thanks also are due to the citizens and women's clubs for donations, for the piano, and furnishings in the basement. And to the mayor and city council, who have voted a levy for the future maintenance.

Mrs. E. S. Weeks, Miss Josephine Kackley, and Miss Grace Blatchley served in turn as librarians until the completion of the new building. Miss Jeanne Severance was the first librarian after the building was completed, serving from 1917 to December, 1919. Mrs. Minnie Hanna has been librarian continuously since that time. She has lived in Finney county many years, coming here as a bride in 1891, and for fifteen years lived on a claim north of Garden City. When Mrs. Hanna took charge of the library, it had 2,000 volumes; in the past twelve years the number has been increased to almost 7,000. Many books have been donated. The largest donation was 190 volumes from B. F. Simons. Another large donation came from Hamer Norris of many volumes of bound magazines.

EARLY HISTORY OF THE GARDEN CITY SCHOOLS

An item in the Garden City Paper of April 3, 1879, which stated: "John Stevens has just completed his fine residence. His new bride has the best house in Garden City", is also the basis of Garden City school history. Mr. Stevens generously donated the use of one room in that house for school purposes, and the first school to be held was during the months of June and July, 1879. Sammy Krotzer was the teacher, and his salary was to be paid by private subscriptions from the patrons. Sammy was young and inexperienced, and not one of the slick kind; it was only because the patrons of the school were unable to pay what they had agreed, that he starved out and was obliged to quit before his term was finished, leaving his debts behind. For that reason it may be unfair to use the following item which appeared in the Garden City Paper of August 14, 1879:

"Sammy Krotzer, who has been teaching school at this place the past two months, left for the eastern part of the state last Sunday evening. We understand Sammy tried to get away without paying some of his bills. He was immediately telegraphed for at Dodge City, at which place he was caught by the sheriff. He was searched, but not finding sufficient amount of money on his person to hold him, that official took enough money for his trouble, and then turned him loose."

In October, 1879, Levi Wilkinson circulated a petition for a subscription school to be held during the winter months. T. J. Philpin was the teacher. The term was three months and the school was held in the Landis & Hollinger hall over the store. This was on lot 13 of block 36. Mr. Philpin was brought here by Mr. Armentrout, the manager of the lumber yard, and he was given room and board in the Armentrout home. In this way he was enabled to continue teaching even if he failed to collect any tuition. But he was also young and inexperienced. There were several big boys in the school who delighted to torment him, and he had no control over this element. The school went along for a few weeks without much order and it threatened to be a failure.

And then one morning, school was called as usual, but the "big boys" faced a new teacher. He was R. M. Morton, weighing about one hundred and ninety-five pounds. He was roughly dressed, with tobacco juice oozing out from the corners of his mouth, and he had lost a part of one arm. The boys were very much amused, and didn't try to conceal it, for the new man was a familiar character around town, and they had never thought of him as a school teacher. Elmer Weeks was one of the leaders of the bunch. He started a prank, and the other boys snickered. But almost at that instant Morton unexpectedly was standing by Elmer, and his stub arm punched the boy in the ribs with such force that he wilted back into his seat. From that time on, Mr. Morton had excellent order, and the term was finished with satisfactory results. He was a well-educated man, and a good teacher.

In the fall of 1880 a school district was organized including Garden City and vicinity, and money was to be received through a tax levy to defray expenses. Miss Alice Moore was the teacher, and the first to teach in Finney county with a certificate. The story of that school of 1880-81 is well told by her, in a letter to George Finnup, dated January 11, 1931:

"Father had asked for the school for me before I came. Mr. Wilkinson smiled his kindly smile, and Mr. Armentrout's black eyes twinkled rather wickedly when he asked me if I was sure I was over twenty. "You don't look eighteen," he said, "and the school so far has been hard to handle." I answered them that I would look older when I got a coat of tan, and if the directors would stand behind, I didn't fear getting along with the children. They said they would stand behind me all right, and I knew they would have done so had there been any need. Moreover, I think the big boys themselves would, if there had been need, have threshed each other, for everybody wanted a school. The third director was Joe Weeks, whom I never saw, but we had each other's good will.

"The directors asked me to go to Dodge City to the

teachers' examination to procure a certificate, so the district could draw the public money. Dodge City was then the bad man's town of the west, and it was a daring thing for a nice young girl to go there a stranger, and to pass the night at a hotel. But I did, kept strictly within the proprieties, and my purpose was accomplished.

"The school was taught over Landis and Hollinger store, and I am sure you remember the figure in wind-swept skirts (they reached to the ankles in those days) at the top of the out-door back stairs, ringing my mother's old dinner bell. I think there were about fifty pupils enrolled. I managed it pretty well, but my mother used to come over every afternoon after recess and hear again the primary classes for which I had not the time. I, not the district, paid her. In reality it was several years before I received the last payment on my warrants. But I drew twelve per cent interest to the date of payment.

"I was, and am yet, very fond of the children of that school. They were so willing to do as I wished. All moved on tip toe across the thin, shaky boards of the floor, to make it possible for Mr. Wilkinson to hear his customers in the store below. I remember there were several big boys who moved clumsily, but quietly in their big boots. I remember besides my brother Walter, John Simon and George Edwards. The two big girls I remember were Ella Worrell and Emma Simon with curling black hair. I was one of them at the parties, but they were all for dignity at school. John Simon used to say, 'I must have a dance with teacher before we go.'

"There were several smaller children from the Simon family and a little boy from the Edwards. There were two boys from that most excellent family, the Platts, and several young deCordovas, all with Spanish black eyes. There was a fine group of young girls who bunched together. Among them were Sallie Finnup, Ollie Menke, Lizzie Wilkinson, Nellie Armentrout and my sister

Marion. Ollie and Lizzie each had two younger brothers. There were Hopkins children and two Hopper boys, grandchildren of the Fultons. There was a fine bright boy, Ira, and his two sisters, Lizzie and Nora, from the Hayward family who operated the Pennsylvania Hotel. I am sorry I cannot remember the names as well as the faces of most of the children, but George, it was a half century ago. I almost forgot that I had Willie Jones in school, son of Buffalo Jones. He was as irrepressible as his father, a real nuisance in school; could keep a solemn face and have everyone twittering around him. He and your brother, Ed Finnup, were the same age.

"I can remember dealing out but one punishment. It was to Bert Hopper. Bert would eat apples in school; truly a crime in the face of all who could not afford the luxury. Finally, I kept him after school to stand by my desk to watch me eat his apple to the finish. That cured him. Brother Walter said I might at least have given Bert or him the core.

"Since then, my boy, I have known many schools with their boards, but never have I known a director so kind, so patient, so earnest for the public welfare as Mr. Wilkinson. We all have him to thank that we held the first successful school in Garden City.

"I remember the entertainment on Christmas, 1880. Mr. Morton helped in the singing. We gave a little play, and Link Fulton had the leading part. The hall was crowded. They were packed tight all around the little stage in the corner. The audience craned their necks over each other, their heads all but over topping those of the players, and the players may easily have had their toes trodden on. It was a grand success. I remember John (Mr. Biggs) solicitously asking me if I were not very tired after such a wonderful and exhaustive work.

"There may be a few alive who will remember the lyceum held in the same hall. The men about town took part and the debates were very good. I remember my father and Mr. Armentrout in debate. I hope your historian has the facts about Mr. Armentrout, a keen pioneer citizen, and the father of irrigation in Garden City.

"I remember the picnic the next summer held in the lumber yard. I suppose because the boards had once been in trees. I was with young Mr. Gore, a sheep man, when the news came that Garfield had been shot.

"I think the Hursts came that summer. I remember Albert was at our house when melons were ripe. Please remember me to his wife, she was such a pretty and neat young woman. Your Teacher Friend, Alice (Moore) Biggs, Winslow, Wash."

The next school was taught by Miss Olive Hurst in the spring of 1882. She gave excellent satisfaction as a teacher and the school was well attended. The term ended July 14, 1882, with an exercise in the afternoon consisting of recitations and reviews. Rev. Platt and Rev J. R. Lowrance made talks to the children. The school board was composed of B. F. Taylor, director; B. L. Stotts, treasurer; H. M. deCordova, secretary. This term was taught in a frame building on the east side of Main Street, in the first block north of the Santa Fe railroad tracks.

During the winter of 1882-83 a subscription school was taught by Rev. S. W. Foulk. He was assisted by Miss Agnes Baird. The older pupils had classes in the Congregational church, under Mr. Foulk, and Miss Baird taught in a separate room. The tuition was $1.25 per scholar.

A subscription school was taught in the fall of 1883 by J. W. Nelson. He was assisted by Carrie E. Miller in the primary department. This school was taught in a hall over the store of George T. Inge. Mr. Nelson remained in Garden City some time and married Miss Mayme Lowrance, daughter of Rev. J. R. Lowrance.

Beginning with January 3, 1884, Miss Delia Rude

taught a six months school which closed July 13, 1884. This was also a subscription school and was housed in an adobe building in the north part of Garden City near the present Garfield school. Miss Rude was an excellent teacher, and is still remembered by many in Garden City who were her pupils.

Finney county was organized October 1, 1884, and the first school district in the county was formed November 24, 1884, by Albert Hurst, county superintendent, but no school houses were built that year, as the laws of the state forbid districts levying tax or issuing bonds for building purposes until after a county had been organized one year.

A school was taught that winter in the Methodist church, beginning October 1, 1884, and closed March 17, 1885. R. S. Hill was principal with a salary of $65 per month. He was assisted by Miss Clare E. Dempsey, who received $40. Wm. J. Carter, D.D., who was at one time principal of the Garden City schools, says of Mr. Hill:

"Just how R. S. Hill reached Garden City, I never knew, but he rolled down from the mountains of Colorado, where in a mining camp he had risen from poverty to affluence, then struck bottom again, and landed in Garden City without a cent. He told me that much. It seems that he had known D. R. Menke years before, back in Illinois, and Dave stopped his pilgrimage with the gratifying information that Garden City needed a school. Mr. Hill had been a successful teacher before he attained riches in the mines of Colorado, and wealth having taken wings, he was more than willing to return to that work."

The first normal institute ever held in the county occurred during the month of July, 1885, in the Methodist church at Garden City. Albert Hurst, county superintendent, and Prof. and Mrs. J. M. Abbott of Silver Plume, Colorado, were the instructors. 117 were enrolled for the four-weeks' term. The greatest difficulty of the pioneer teachers had been the non-uniformity of text books. That burden was lifted during this institute by the adoption of uniform books for the county.

A meeting of the school board was held in the Congregational church August 20, 1885, for the purpose of selecting a site for a school house. J. W. Weeks, director; E. G. Bates, clerk; John A. Stevens, treasurer, were present. The proposition of Jones and Stevens was accepted, to-wit: John Stevens, 2nd addition, in block 38, lots 5, 6, 7, 8, 9, 10, for the sum of $75 each. By C. J. Jones, all the land in block one, Jones addition, adjoining the lots offered by Stevens, for the sum of $30 each. C. J. Jones was appointed to confer with contractors on plans and specifications for a building.

The committee, A. W. Stubbs, Rev. J. R. Lowrance, and E. B. Titus, who had been appointed to canvas the district, reported 140 petitioners in favor of voting $10,000 bonds for a school building. The bond election carried 333 in favor with 8 against. A large per cent of the votes were cast by ladies who were determined to have the school and they used all available vehicles to bring out voters.

The plans of Stevens and Thompson were adopted on account of its size and architectural beauty. The building to be 60x70, two story, divided into eight rooms and a 19-foot hallway through the center of the building. The entrance being through the base of a lofty tower. The contract for the construction was let to P. H. Hall for the sum of $10,765.

The walls of the building were of brick, burned in Garden City, and trimmed in stone. The building and apparatus when complete cost about $15,000. The building could not be completed until the next spring, so the Methodist church was again secured for the more advanced classes, and the Congregational church was used for those up to the third grade and fourth grade.

The school term began October 12, 1885, and closed

June 18, 1886. Four teachers were employed, R. S. Hill again serving as principal, with Ollie B. Mullins, Anna S. Wood, and Anna Van Pelt as teachers, each receiving $40 per month salary. Miss Mary Hopper and Miss Maggie Boyd began their long connection with the Garden City schools, by acting as substitute teachers the last two months for teachers who had to go on their homesteads.

In June, 1886, the first school building in Garden City was completed, and the following account of the big

The first school house in Garden City was completed in June, 1886. It was destroyed by fire March 21, 1901.

"house warming" appeared in a Garden City paper the next day:

"The chief center of attraction last evening was the high school building on Eighth street. The throng that filled its handsome rooms was unabated from six until eleven p.m. and largely represented the intelligence and culture of Garden City. Five large supper tables spread in the large upper room in the southeast part of the building were constantly being refilled with guests.

"The five tables were presided over by ten misses of the public school; Sallie Finnup, Tiny Bates, Effie Earp,

Anna Dunn, Ollie Menke, Mattie Pearce, Anna Miller, Clementine Adney, Mollie Langley and Anna Clark.

"The ice cream table, presided over by Miss Addie Adney, was particularly a center of attraction, and refreshing, owing to the heated atmosphere that pervaded the rooms. The cream was par excellence.

"The fruit stand was presided over by Misses Maud Gibson and Norma Wheeler, assisted by Miss Jesse Kitchen. They received much attention and patronage.

"Jacob's well in one corner of the room was a resort of the thirsty stranger, but we never knew that the original produced lemonade as this one did. Miss Minnie Hall, who impersonated the fair Jewess, 'Rebecca', drew up the cooling, refreshing draught. 'Jacob', personified by Ed Finnup, reclined beside the well, and took in the shekels."

Eight teachers were employed for the school of 1886-87. R. S. Hill, principal. Teachers, J. W. Newbern, J. C. Fugate, Ollie B. Mullins, Mary Hopper, Maggie Boyd, Nannie Stamper, Maud Amos, M. E. Pusey. Their salaries varied from $35 to $50, and the orders were discounted. This was the first term taught in the original Garfield school, which was on the same location as the present building.

It was destroyed by fire on March 21, 1901. The fire department was called to extinguish the flames at 5:30 a.m. On the way to the fire the firemen were almost exhausted from pulling against a heavy wind and deep sand on Stevens Avenue. Hose Company No. 1 was assisted in getting the apparatus to the fire by Albert Condra helping to pull the cart with his saddle horse. Regardless of the intense heat of the fierce flames, the fire brigade fought to save the burning building. Sheets of red-hot metal from the roof were carried a block away by the high wind. The Hook and Ladder Company and a number of citizens formed a bucket brigade to put out the fire set by these flying pieces of iron.

Superintendents of the Garden City Schools

R. S. Hill, 1884 to 1889, five terms.
S. H. Sanford, 1889 to 1890, one term.
T. C. Coffman, 1890-91, 1891-92, two terms.
P. S. Ayres, 1892-93, one term.
T. C. Coffman, 1893-94, 1894-95, 1895-96, three terms.
C. E. Johnson, 1896-97, 1897-98, two terms.
R. S. Ligget, 1898-99, one term.
A. C. Wheeler, 1899 to 1907, seven terms.
E. F. Ewing, 1907-08, 1908-09, two terms.
G. E. Brown, 1909-10, 1910-11, 1911-12, 1912-13, four terms.
Edward J. Dumond, 1913 to 1919, six terms.
C. G. Vinsonhaler, 1919 to 1927, eight terms.
Ira O. Scott, 1927, and still serving.

The first class graduated from the Garden City High School was in 1888. The members were: Vessie Davis, Edgar A. Smith, Lillian Gates, Clarence Adney and Hattie Ballinger.

Class of 1889: W. W. Reno, J. W. Gibson, E. G. Finnup, Nettie M. Lawrence, Zoe Hopkins, Anna Miller, W. J. Carter, Omer DeMetz, George H. Mack.

Class of 1890: Jas. W. Zimmerman, Mary Langley, Flo Craig, Mary Miller, Hiram L. Zimmerman, Myra W. Reeves, Mattie M. Pearce, Chas. Hambleton, and May F. Rich.

Class of 1891: Clementine Adney, Mary Baird, Ezra F. Baker, Mary Elvira Folsom, Lulu May Moon, Mollie J. Pearce and Bessie L. Yoder.

Class of 1892: Richard Joseph Hopkins, Cora Belle Dunn, Myrtle Lawrence, Robert J. Adney, Ola Parson, Ona Parson, Harry W. Menke, William C. Pearce, Benjamin Teitelbaum, Edgar B. Dunn, Albert Hoskinson, Lulu Huff, Lewis H. Titus and Samuel Levi Wilkinson.

Class of 1893: Nellie Glenn, Ollie E. Weeks, Elmer Weeks, Clyde Lawrence, Ethel Stotts, Eva Leibfried and Bert Hopper.

Class of 1894: Lizzie Truby Adair, Harry C. Diesem, Mary Ellen Foy, Lena Neal, Guy C. Seeds, Raymond E. Stotts, and Mamie G. Vinzant.

Class of 1895: Mary Frances Inge and Effie L. Kitchen.

Class of 1896: Ina Florence Holcomb, Walter R. Lawrence, Ora G. Ross and Ralph C. Stocks.

Class of 1897: Helen Lenore Folsom, Elmer Gregory, Mary Ida Hatcher, Jesse May Johnson and Ora Parson.

Class of 1898: Josie R. Fant, Earl Griggs, Lewis Griggs, Minnie G. Hatcher, Ada Huffman, Bertha Lawrence, Mary Millikin, Pearl L. Ross, Alta May Smith and Cora C. Wilkinson.

Class of 1899: Bessie Van Schoiack, Mary R. Crawford, Georgia Ann Smith, William Edwards, and Pardee Rhodes.

Class of 1900: Hettie C. Hatcher, Nettie P. Folsom, Jessie S. Griggs, Mary Lora Hopkins, Rhoda C. McCartney, Zella C. Pyle, Beulah F. Shaffer, Morgan P. Keleher, Jessie Edministon, Gertrude Fryar, Dennis D. Doty, Nellie Maud Dawson, and Lee Cook Diesem.

Class of 1901: Anna Clark, Vina W. Wright, Anna M. Keleher, Kate Hatcher, M. Edith Knox, Roy P. Thorpe, Vivian O. Hopper, Gertrude E. Burtis, Edna C. Wirt, Lelia VanSchoiack, Guy F. Pyle, Loa V. Lawrence and Arlington M. Lawrence.

Class of 1902: Eva Belle Baker, Abbie Dauthit, Emma V. Eskelund, Malissa P. Faulk, David H. Morgan, John Alfred Quinn, Ethel Alberta Reeves and Nellye Sharp.

Class of 1903: Leon H. Brown, S. Clarence Ford, Clarence Ely, Iva Gertrude Ford, Robert J. Craig, Alford Larmor, Gaylord Lawrence, Alfred Keffer, Ralph Irving Carter, George M. VanSchoiack, H. George Wolking, Daisy Bevan, Chester C. Doty, Nelle J. Hopkins and Richard Perry.

Class of 1904: Gertrude E. Bon Durant, Fred Scott

Dunn, Ruby O. Foulk, Francis A. Hulton, Helen Julia Morgan, Ethel Priestly, Bruce A. Risley, Frieda Schulman, Gertrude Jeanne Severance, Edith Myra Stocks, Myrtle F. Stringfield, Edna P. Warner and Henry Allen Whitfield.

Class of 1905: Lena M. Chapman, Albert Duckworth, Tom Eaman, Myrtle Hatcher, Gertrude Holcomb, J. Emmett Hopkins, Letha Hurst, Samuel Nite, Alineen Rea, Ruth Severance, Loren VanSchoiack, Gale W. Vinzant, Lucile Briggs Walls and Grace Warner.

To George W. Finnup, who for several years was a member of the Board of Education, is due a large part of the credit for the naming of the Garden City school buildings. The names he suggested were accepted by the Board of Education at a meeting July 6, 1925.

William Easton Hutchinson East Ward building, built in 1917, gives recognition to one of Garden City's most distinguished citizens. Buffalo Jones West Ward building, built in 1917, was named in honor of the man who homesteaded where the building now stands, and who was active in securing the first school in Garden City. The Junior and Senior High School was built in 1917. It was fittingly named "Sequoyah". This county was first named for Sequoyah, one of the greatest Indians who ever lived, and who was a great advocate of education. The Junior High School building, erected in 1910, was named the "Andrew Sabine Building" in honor of Dr. Sabine, who was the leading physician in this part of the state for many years, and gave his life unselfishly to suffering humanity. The Athletic field was named "Spencer Penrose Athletic Field" for Spencer Penrose. Largely through his efforts the sugar factory and its component industries were constructed. Since these enterprises have been in operation, there has been such an increase in the school population, it became necessary to build several additional school buildings and purchase the athletic field.

Early Church History

"No one can relate the true history of a church, for no one can measure the power of her prayers, the weight of her sermons, the reach of her influence, or the mute appeal of her silent tower pointing upward to God."

THE COMMUNITY CHURCH

THE story of the beginning of public worship is well recorded in the minutes of the first meeting before organization of the First Congregational Church in Garden City. The following is an exact copy as taken from the clerk's record, Vol. I, 1879.

"Garden City was first determined upon as a place for a permanent town by William D. and James R. Fulton, who were also the first residents of this place. They came here in March, 1878. The town continued to have a gradual growth, and sometime in the winter of 1878 and '79, Elder Spencer of Sherlock, Kansas, held a religious service, preaching a sermon. This was the first and only service until Rev. W. D. Williams of Sterling, Kansas, visited the place May 18, 1879. Preaching services were held morning and evening and a Union Sabbath school was organized in the afternoon. The attendance was so large and the interest so manifest that it was deemed expedient to continue religious services, and Rev. Williams announced that he would visit them again in three weeks. The services were held in the Landis and Hollinger store building, which was so nearly finished that by boarding up the front doors and arranging the work benches, and making temporary sittings of the lumber scattered around the building, the room was as comfortable as it was commodious."

Levi Wilkinson and W. H. Armentrout were appointed a committee to draft a constitution and by-laws, which they did on June 15, 1879, and on August 4, of the same year, the organization was completed with twenty-seven charter members from five different denominations. Permanent officers of the Congregational Church were elected. Rev. W. D. Williams, moderator; J. E. Edwards, Frank Rhoades, deacons; Levi Wilkinson, clerk; W. H. Armentrout, George Rock and C. M. Walters, trustees.

Rev. L. H. Platt was the first pastor of the new church, and began his pastorate November 15, 1879, and continued as pastor until July, 1884. For the first three years the services were held in the hall over Landis and Hollinger's store. During those first years they received from the Home Mission fund $300.00 a year and the same amount was supposed to be contributed by the local members for the support of the church.

The church was the social center of the community. For some time they had the advantage of a travelling library, and were supplied with good books and literature. An organ was furnished by C. J. Jones and the organist was a woman with exceptional musical ability and training. D. R. Menke played the violin and instructed George Finnup and other boys of the town. The town has never had a better song leader than Levi Wilkinson. He had a fine tenor voice and he loved to sing. He taught the children and led the young people in many splendid song services. There were special programs, and organizations for the women. The work of every department was carried on with interest and efficiency. N. M. Carter was the superintendent of the Sunday School and was a faithful worker. The attendance at all the church services was nearly 100% of the population of the community. Everybody who was able to be up, went to church. Business men, housewives, old and young, and the cowboys from far out on the range. The pioneers of Finney county were an educated, ambitious people, and they sought for the same culture in their new homes that they were accustomed to in the home towns they had left in the east.

The records of the church for July 10, 1881, show that a request be made of the Congregational Building Fund Society for a loan to build a church, and during the year 1882 the first church building in Garden City was built at the corner of Eighth and Fulton Streets.

During the eight years' pastorate of Lyman Hull, who became pastor November 5, 1889, he advocated a union of the struggling churches of Garden City, who were all drawing support from their respective Home Missionary societies in order to live. When Charles N. Severance became pastor a meeting was called November 1, 1897, to form a Union church. All denominations were in favor of a Union church, but they wanted the Union to be of their own creed. The result was that the Presbyterians withdrew. The United Brethern disbanded, but the Cumberland Presbyterians and the Congregational churches united with but three dissenting votes, under the name of the Union Church of Garden City, Kansas, on February 1, 1898. From that time on the services of the Union church were held in the Cumberland Presbyterian building, which is now the Community church. It was built in 1886, and remodeled under Rev. Brehm's first pastorate and again remodeled in 1929. After the Union church had been organized for some time, it became necessary, in order to affiliate with some state and national organization to add the word Congregational.

During 1928 a movement was started to organize a Community church. This was accomplished in October of that year, and within a few weeks after the organization was perfected, 75 members joined the new organization, 55 of whom had never before been affiliated with any church. In the summer of 1929 the church was remodeled inside and out, and was dedicated as a Community

Church by Rev. Charles M. Sheldon, preacher and author of international fame.

The membership of the Community church is not now the largest in Garden City, but the list still contains a large number of members who were original members, or descendants, and they are very earnest in still carrying out the efficient programs of the founders.

The following is the list of pastors as they have served the church: Rev. L. H. Platt, Nov. 15, 1879, July, 1884; Rev. Homer Thrall, Rev. Samuel Wood, Rev. Layman Hull, Nov. 5, 1889, Nov. 1897. Charles N. Severance, Nov. 1897. W. F. Harding, J. A. Henry, W. E. Brehm, F. B. Bates, L. C. Schnache, and H. O. Judd. Mr. Judd has been laboring faithfully for the church since the first Sunday in February, 1915.

The Charter members of the First Congregational Church August 4, 1879: J. S. Edwards, Mrs. Mary Edwards, Levi Wilkinson, J. C. Smith, Mrs. Rebecca Smith, John Creveling, Chas. Creveling, Elizabeth Knittle, Mrs. Kate Hall, Mrs. Elizabeth Walker, Frank Rhodes, Mrs. Maggie Stapleton, W. H. Armentrout, Mrs. W. H. Armentrout, Anna Armentrout, George Rock, Clarence McLaughlin, Wilber Elliott, Henry W. Crow, Mrs. Sallie Crow, J. B. Smith, Dora Smith, R. N. Hall, Martin J. Smith.

THE FIRST PRESBYTERIAN CHURCH

THE First Presbyterian Church of Garden City was organized March 14, 1886. The organization took place in the First Methodist Church. Rev. A. E. Thompson, pastor at Spearville, moderated the meeting. The charter membership numbered twenty-seven: John Johnson, Mrs. Louise P. Johnson, Miss Nettie Johnson, A. Bennett, Mrs. Minnie Bennett, Miss Belle Carver, Luther C. Reed, Mrs. Nannie A. Reed, Mrs. Eliza J. Piper, R. A. Baird, Miss Agnes W. Baird, Margaret E. Baird, Mary

Gertrude Baird, Walter G. Lynn, Charles E. Moore, R. M. Sayer, Mrs. Kate W. Sayer, Mrs. Fannie Dulin, J. W. Howell, Mrs. Annie M. Howell, Mrs. Lulu Howell, Mrs. Alva D. Howell, Willie W. Howell, T. E. Cameron, James D. Sankey, Mrs. Elizabeth Sankey and James F. Holmes.

Three months later the church secured its first pastor, Rev. David Kingery. "Services were held in the old skating rink," says Miss Anna Kingery, "a rough frame building seated with uncomfortable board benches. Later the owners of the rink converted this into a business and office building, and our people were out of a meeting place, but the Congregationalists courteously shared their building with us, the two pastors preaching alternately. As soon as the Stevens Opera House was completed, services were held there until the new church was ready for use. The first Sunday in February, 1887, the original building on the corner of Garden City Avenue and Spruce streets was dedicated."

In the fall of 1887 Mr. and Mrs. R. M. Lawrence came to Garden City. Mrs. Lawrence, who is the oldest living member of the church, says: "We found the church new and nicely furnished. A new red ingrain carpet, the gift of the Ladies' Aid Society, covered the entire floor. The furniture was new, seats well varnished, and an organ. There were eighty members in the church, a good choir, Sunday School, and the Ladies Aid and Missionary Societies. The church was in a flourishing condition."

Then followed years of discouragement. People began to leave Garden City, and the church membership decreased. About this time the appalling discovery was made that the church, which had been supposedly free of debt, had to assume an obligation of $900. It happened this way: Mr. Johns of Burrton, a friend of Rev. Kingery, donated some property to the new church. This was sold for $1,200 and the amount applied on the new building.

Only one payment was made, however, when the boom collapsed and the sale fell through. This was a great calamity considering the condition of the church. This debt hung over the church for many years. The interest was paid by the Ladies' Aid and the principal reduced a little each year until better times came and the debt was cleared. Possibly this debt was a blessing in disguise, as it became the tie that bound the handful of members together, as they "shared each other's woes", and shed the "sympathizing tear".

Says Mrs. Lawrence: "Those were lean years in which we sometimes had a minister, but oftener did not. We always had a Sunday School and a prayer meeting, which was conducted by the men and sometimes by the women, with much faltering and trembling. But the indebtedness which we considered as unfortunate was really the means of keeping us together, as we had to have socials, suppers and entertainments to get money to pay on the debt." At one time in 1891 the membership was reduced to eighteen, yet they felt honor bound to pay off the debt, and that kept them from disbanding.

Among the names to be mentioned with reverence is that of R. M. Lawrence, who for nineteen years, until his death in January, 1908, was the leading character in the church. As deacon, elder and Sunday School superintendent, he inspired the church in times of doubt and uncertainty.

One element never to be forgotten was the gratuitous assistance given the church for thirteen years by the Board of Home Missions, without whose aid it would have been impossible to have maintained the church.

The original building was erected in 1886-87. It was a small but comfortable frame structure, 30x40 feet, with an ell, 14x18 feet. This was adequate for the purposes of the congregation until the winter of 1906, when the building was enlarged.

In 1906 a manse was erected at a cost of $3,300. The building committee consisted of R. M. Lawrence, C. E. Sexton and Mrs. A. Hurst.

On June 8, 1928, the congregation voted to erect a new church building on the corner of Seventh and Pine streets. On March 17, 1929, they voted to name the lower auditorium "Rogers Hall" in honor of Mrs. J. F. Rogers, who has given so freely and largely to the new church fund. June 2, 1929, the new church was dedicated at the morning service. This new building is of Gothic architecture which is carried out in the inside finish, furniture and fixtures, and represents an expenditure of $72,000, including pipe organ and fixtures. The building committee was composed of Walter J. Stroup, chairman; E. Stoeckly, W. A. Maltbie, George Knox, and J. H. Burnside. Members of the session: H. M. Hope, clerk; Albert Hurst, Eugene Stoeckly, Dr. Sanford Bailey, Samuel A. Guthrie, W. A. Maltbie, Wm. Easton Hutchinson, W. T. B. Herriott, R. P. Downing and W. W. Glascow.

The following pastors have served the church: David Kingery, June, 1886, to September, 1887; C. K. Lehman, January, 1888, to July, 1888; H. R. Schermerhorn, September, 1889, to February, 1891; W. M. Dougherty, August 18, 1891, to March, 1894; W. E. Browning, March, 1895, to March, 1896; F. D. Breed, July, 1896, to October, 1896; H. B. Allen, May, 1897, to October, 1897; A. L. Speer, 1898, six weeks; F. G. Moore, March, 1899, to April, 1900; O. M. Gillette, July, 1900, to April, 1902; Wm. Bullock, November, 1902, to April, 1906; A. S. Davis, September, 1906, to November, 1913; E. M. Scott, May, 1914, to Aug. 1920; T. A. Clagett, February, 1921, to November, 1922; H. H. Rhule, D.D., March, 1923, to May, 1930; R. B. Twitty, September 1, 1930—.

THE FIRST BAPTIST CHURCH

REV. A. S. MERRIFIELD preached in the Methodist church Sunday, November 1, 1885, and in the afternoon he organized a Baptist church with seventeen members. I. R. Holmes, T. M. Dickey, Walter Shobe, C. J. Feurt and W. T. Guerrance were elected trustees. The charter members were: T. M. Dickey, Mrs. Mollie Dickey, E. M. Hatcher, Mrs. Madie Hatcher, L. V. Smith, Mrs. Frata Smith, Jas. W. Wallace, Mrs. Kate B. Wallace, Mrs. Dessie Mothershead, Enoch Johnson, Mrs. T. F. Doty, W. H. Keck, Mrs. W. H. Keck, Mrs. Sarah Perrine, Miss Emily L. Mills, Miss Mary Mills, Mrs. Nellie Wilson.

For the next two years they held a cottage prayer meeting in the homes of the members. They planned to build a house of worship in the spring of 1886, but it was almost two years before another pastor visited the congregation.

On January 24, 1887, Rev. W. W. Willis, District Missionary for the Baptist church in Southwest Kansas, had charge of a service in the Cumberland Presbyterian church. A number of meetings were held in this church. T. M. Dickey was the first moderator, J. W. Wallace clerk, E. M. Hatcher treasurer. Services continued to be held in the homes.

Rev. Willis was called as first pastor in October, 1887. He preached half time and his salary was between $400 and $500 annually. Services were held in the Y.M.C.A. hall for awhile and other halls were rented from time to time, and the Friends church was used for two years. The present building was dedicated March 23, 1902. The following pastors have served the church. W. W. Willis, P. G. Shanklin, J. C. Abbott, Ira Cain, J. C. Denham, J. J. Griffin, N. C. Self, J. C. Burkholder, H. D. Allen, H. R. Baker, U. P. Ewing, F. C. Ward, D. P. Gaines, E. G. Stout, G. W. South, W. W. Marr, J. S. Umberger, M. C. Humphrey, J. J. Griffin.

Mrs. L. V. Smith is the only charter member still living in Garden City.

HISTORICAL SKETCH OF METHODIST CHURCH

THE first Methodist sermon in Garden City was preached in a billiard hall in January, 1882. Rev. H. S. Booth, a superannuated member of the New England Conference, was the organizer and first pastor. He lived at that time 35 miles northeast of Garden City. He was invited here to preach by J. S. Edwards and B. H. Taylor. The organization was effected on February 19, 1882. The charter members were: Mr. and Mrs. J. S. Edwards, Mr. and Mrs. B. H. Taylor, Millie Fulton, Frances Hopkins, Anna Martin, Elizabeth G. Smith, Mary Augusta Booth, Mr. and Mrs. L. C. Pearce, and six probationers. A union revival meeting was held the following winter after the organization, and resulted in thirty-five accessions to the Methodist church. A constant growth in members and interest was manifest. At the end of Rev. Booth's pastorate in 1885 the membership had reached 113. In 1884 the agitation for a church building began. The official board saw no prospect of raising more than $400 for that purpose. Rev. Booth started out to see what could be done, and in two days he had over $800 subscribed and before the year was up, an edifice was completed at a cost of $2700, $700 of which was raised on dedication day. Bishop Ninde preached the sermon. The following is the list of pastors and times they have served this charge.

H. S. Booth, 1882-1885. Stephen Brink, 1885-86. Paul Jones, 1886-87; during his pastorate the building was enlarged and was rededicated by Rev. H. D. Fisher. M. Bamford, 1887-91. A. T. Burris, 1891-92; A. P. George, 1892,93. C. F. Williams, 1893-95. D. S. Hoover, 1895-97. Geo. W. Irwin, 1897-98. F. C. Fay, 1898-1902. L. M. Riley, 1902-1907. J. W. Kirkpatrick, 1907-1909. C. F. Sharpe, 1909-1910. W. B. Barton, 1910-1913. W. H. Moore, 1913-1915.

W. W. Enyeart, 1915-1917. S. M. Van Cleve, 1917-1920. D. A. Leeper, 1920-1922. N. S. Gardner, 1922-1925. H. R. Runion, March to October, 1925. S. W. Keller, 1925-1928. R. C. Walker, 1928 to present.

The original church edifice, erected in 1884 on the northwest corner of Eighth and Chestnut streets, was used until during the pastorate of Rev. Wm. B. Barton in 1910, although it had been enlarged twice and yet long outgrown by the steadily increasing membership and Sunday School. The present church was immediately commenced on the same lots, the services being held meanwhile in the high school, now the Andrew Sabine Junior High. The basement was first finished and roofed over, being used until 1914, when the superstructure had been completed under the ministry of Rev. W. H. Moore and was dedicated by Rev. Thomas Iliff, celebrated church financier from Denver. The pipe organ was not installed until 1921. Just after the World War the old parsonage on the same lot had been sold off and the cottage across the alley on Ninth street purchased and improved for a parsonage. The church's plans include a modern parsonage on the vacant lot south of this one and also a church school building just behind the church.

THE FIRST CHRISTIAN CHURCH

REV. A. C. McKEEVER came to Garden City May 8, 1884, to organize the First Christian Church. He was pleased with the town and determined to make his permanent home here, and in all the years since that time he has never changed his voting place. He drew up the following article which was signed by the charter members:

"We, the undersigned members of the Christian Church living in Garden City and Finney county, Kansas, being duly assembled in the First Congregational Church of said city, on Wednesday evening, May 20,

1884, Rev. A. C. McKeever presiding, do hereby subscribe our names as charter members of the First Christian Church of Garden City, Kansas. Asking the forgiveness of all our past sins, we pledge to God and to each other a faithful and active co-operation for the spiritual good of each other and glory of the cause of our blessed master; finding ourselves individually and collectively to be governed by such officers and such laws as are to be found in the New Testament Scriptures for the guidance of the church of Christ and the individual members of the same. Signed: Wash Baxla, J. P. Wallace, J. W. Holmes, O. P. Reeves, W. R. Grace, C. E. Walton, Gilbert Holmes, Frank Watson, Cora Holmes, Hanna Baxla, A. C. McKeever, Mrs. Ethel B. McKeever, Virginia Holmes, Mrs. C. J. Jones, F. M. Baxla, William Hanen, Virgil Holmes, Charles Rude, Delia Rude, Alice Rude, Eliza Carlton, Zulpha Handy, Nancy J. Grace, Mrs. Dawes, L. D. Smith, M. L. Smith, Ella Hanen, Emma Grace, Martha E. Newby, Mary A. McDonald.

Cora Holmes, the daughter of Jane Holmes, was the first to be immersed in Finney county. This baptismal service occurred at a lake south of Garden City May 12, 1884. The first church building was erected in the fall of 1886. Rev. McKeever was the pastor from 1884 to 1895.

The church flourished until 1889, at which time Rev. McKeever issued three hundred and twenty-five letters in one day to members who went to the opening of Oklahoma. It happened that Dick T. Morgan, who prior to that time had been living in Garden City, staked a lot in Guthrie, Oklahoma, just across the street from the one staked by the Church Extension Board of the Christian Church. The next week Mr. Morgan put up a notice on his lot, asking all the people from Garden City to meet him there the following Sunday morning. Two hundred Garden City people responded to the invitation, and they went across to the church lot and organized the First Christian Church of Guthrie.

On November 30, 1919, the first building was destroyed by fire. The present building was erected on the same site in 1920.

The church records were lost in the fire which destroyed the building in 1919, and the following list of pastors is as correct as can be obtained at this time: A. C. McKeever, Rev. Bowen, Victor L. Goodrich, Rev. Ingram, Rev. Carr, Rev. Vaughn, Cecil Pearse, J. G. Slick, J. R. Robertson, M. O. Dutcher, Rev. Underwood, O. E. Palmer, Rev. Findley, L. C. Montgomery, R. C. Leonard and J. E. Rains. The last three named each served for a number of years.

The Financial History of Garden City

By George W. Finnup

IN the boom days of 1885, 1886 and 1887 Western Kansas settled up with a rush that came like a great tidal wave.

The men were generally young or middle-aged, some single, and many were soldiers of the Civil War which had then been over about twenty years, and they could prove up the land earlier by being allowed the time they served in the war. The great object was to get a piece of beautiful land by living on it five years, or else commuting by paying out on it after being on it six months; this cost $2.50 per acre within the railroad limit of ten miles, or $1.25 per acre if the land was outside the limits; many mortgaged their land as soon as they could get a title by proving it up. There were many loan companies here after the business and many arranged for their loans before they made proof on their land at the United States Land Office, which was then at Garden City.

When this grand rush started there were very few people living west of Dodge City in Western Kansas, so it was quite a job at that time to organize the counties so they could handle business, start the towns, townships, and school districts, lay out roads and get things in running order. Most of the people were strangers to one another, and it soon became apparent that it was no child's play to settle up a new country. Much speculation developed in these boom days, mostly in town lots in the towns being laid out which became rivals of one another for county seat honors. The people became careless and reckless about going into debt, and voting bonds, and many never expected to stay to help pay for the indebtedness when it had to be settled.

When the boom stopped, everything became flat and one could not sell property because the bubble had burst and very few had any money. With the dry years following it created an unusual condition. On top of all that, Oklahoma was opened for settlement and it had been looked upon by many as a "promised land" for many years. April 22, 1889, was the grand opening and thousands of people rushed in there from this part of Kansas, so that many of the towns and most of the lands were deserted and left with mortgages, bonds and debts. Then followed a long, long struggle which only a few now here went through with from beginning to end. The second Oklahoma rush was to the Cherokee Strip, farther west, which opened on September 16th, 1893.

Thousands of quarters of land and thousands of city lots and buildings would not bring in enough rent to pay the taxes and they went to tax deed and often would not bring the amount of the taxes against them. Nearly all the mortgage companies had failed and most of those lands were in default, also, for the taxes. The county commissioners of every Western Kansas county compromised the taxes for what they could get in order to get the property back on the tax rolls so it would begin paying again.

When all this disaster came, the towns, school districts, townships and counties that did not receive their taxes quit paying interest on their bonded indebtedness. There was no money in the country. Most of the people were poor, buildings were vacant in towns, and on the farms and they were unpainted, neglected and abandoned. Hundreds of the buildings were torn down or moved from the towns into the country to take the place of sod houses, dug-outs, or small shacks. This condition lasted many years. Nearly all counties, towns, school districts and townships issued warrants for current expenses, which were sold at a discount and some were not paid for many years. The discounts ranged largely on the time they had to run. The counties having railroads through them held up pretty well, but those off the railroad, their warrants and bonds sank as low as fifty cents on the dollar, and sometimes less.

Only those who went through those days can understand them now. The years of 1893, 1894, 1895, 1896, 1897, 1898, 1899, were so bad that even a good county like Pratt County had seven straight failures at that time, and how the people stayed is something for discussion today. But after 1900 there has never been a total failure in that county, or in many other counties.

For different reasons Garden City was the leading town in Southwestern Kansas but it had become very hard up and it reflected the condition of the country. The total wealth thirty years ago of real and personal property of Garden City did not then equal the value of the automobiles alone in Garden City today.

Garden City in one way and another accumulated quite an indebtedness even though the city councilmen and the mayor drew no salary for their services at that time, and the city clerk's salary for awhile was only $10.00 per month. Garden City managed to keep going by keeping its credit, reducing its expenses to a low minimum, and paying for and redeeming its warrants for operating expenses; but the city had out many bonds for building the water works and a few other improvements, besides a tree judgment, in which an old council of the city had allowed a party $1.35 for every tree that would live a certain length of time, and at the same time C. J. (Buffalo) Jones offered to do the same thing for 35c a tree. The city litigated for some years and finally got a large judgment against it bearing 7% interest, and it had to be paid by direct levy. The litigation also made added expense as there were attorneys to pay, court costs, and the credit of the city was more or less injured. Our city bonds had been in default for several years on interest and the holders of same could put them in judgment at any time and have a direct levy made. The city had fallen in population from the high-water mark of over 6,000 down to 1,300 to 1,500, and along in 1901 and 1902, things began to pick up a little.

According to the records in the office of the Auditor of the State, the assessed valuation of Garden City at that time was as follows:

1900
Value of town lots	$97,786.00
Personal property	49,845.00
Value of railroad property	15,190.00
Total of all taxable property	$162,821.00

1901
Value of town lots	$97,569.00
Personal property	57,937.00
Value of railroad property	16,154.00
Total of all taxable property	$171,660.00

1902
Value of town lots	$82,078.00
Personal property	48,020.00
Value of railroad property	15,613.00
Total of all taxable property	$145,711.00

We will leave our story now for a few minutes, and go forward about thirty years, and show the valuation of Garden City for 1931, with a population now of about 6,500 people.

1931
Value of real estate in city	$3,548,730.00
Personal property	1,016,976.00
Public Utilities	373,932.00
	$4,939,638.00

Intangible, which includes money, notes, accounts, tax-sale certificates, judgments, etc. 527,296.00
─────────── $5,466,934.00

The last item takes a 50c per hundred rate.

Now we will go back again to thirty years ago, to the debt settlement. The three leading builders of the city had been C. J. Jones, John A. Stevens, and Frederick Finnup. Jones had lost everything and had gone elsewhere to engage in other enterprises, as he was never idle. Stevens had lost practically everything, and was blocking up a little ranch by getting tax-deeds to several sections of land in north Haskell County. Frederick Finnup was still holding his property, but it had depreciated in value for years, and was not saleable.

The reader can easily see that we had gone through a long struggle of hard times and disaster. The city debt including its part of the school district and county indebtedness about equalled the assessed valuation of the city at that time. We had to make a new start in order to stay and induce new people to come.

The writer of this article was familiar with conditions, and had been working for a year or more, hoping to work out a solution of the city's difficulties, and was finally successful.

A man came here from Topeka to start a second bank, but did not succeed; however, through his acquaintance the writer got in touch with a party in Topeka who had connections there with the leading bank, and the State Treasurer at that time, and had him to come to Garden City and talk over the situation. The writer had located the old bonds in the East which were in default on interest, and which could be purchased for fifty cents on the dollar. The tree judgment could be purchased for seventy-five cents on the dollar, but the immediate cash was necessary to secure that. After taking the matter up with the city administration and the city attorney, arrangements were made to refund the entire indebtedness. Local business men formed a pool and subscribed according to their ability and borrowed the money and gave their notes to the First National Bank (of which W. B. George was the manager) and bought this judgment. With this secured, arrangements were made to settle the bonds through the Mulvane Bank in Topeka. These arrangements were completed a few months later when the bank paid off the bonds and the holders of the judgment and the city issued new bonds running thirty years for $66,000.00 bearing $4\frac{1}{4}\%$ interest, and out of this sum the brokerage fees were paid to the Topeka men, thus retiring the entire city indebtedness, and wiping out considerable of the principal, and reducing the interest charges from over $7,000.00 a year to a reduced sum of $2,805.00 per year. This settlement was made during the year of 1902. No other municipality in Western Kansas ever secured such a settlement to the people of the community, and it is doubtful whether any other man living was in a position to make this connection and secure this settlement. The writer did not ask or receive a dollar for his services in this transaction, nor in any other transaction involving the good of Garden City or Finney County.

When this heavy cloud which had been hanging over the city was cleared away, it restored confidence and people could invest and live here without being taxed too heavily.

GARDEN CITY POST NO. 257

Garden City Post No. 257 was organized July 14, 1883, by Senior Vice-Commander H. M. Millard with 19 charter members: M. E. Wolf, J. T. Pearce, J. L. Dunn,

J. G. Byington, G. R. Moon, H. M. Wheeler, L. C. Pierce, F. M. Bishop, B. F. Smith, John Simon, Geo. Brittain, L. C. Hopkins, John Clark, W. R. Hopkins, J. Huffman, J. J. Munger, F. Finnup, E. G. Bates, N. J. Earp.

Past Post Commanders, and the Years They Served as Such

1883 H. M. Wheeler	1902 A. M. Hopper
1884 J. J. Munger	1903 J. L. Seeds
1885 J. W. Weeks	1904 C. G. Colburn
1886 Geo. R. Moon	1905 Zeph. Roberts
1887 W. R. Hopkins	1906 H. W. Crow
1888 James G. Unger	1907 W. T. Eggen
1889 D. A. Mims	1908 W. S. Johnson
1890 Fred Finnup (E. L. Hall)	1909 J. R. Stillwagon
	1910 W. D. Evans
1891 C. A. Brown	1911 S. W. Horner
1892 W. P. Cowhick	1912 E. F. Smith
1893 T. E. Weeks	1913 W. R. Hopkins
1894 E. B. Titus	1914 H. W. Crow
1895 B. W. Lemert	1915 B. C. Henshaw
1896 J. L. Dunn	1916 Geo. A. Day
1897 E. Davis	1917-1918-1919 A. M. Hopper
1898 G. S. Boyd	1920-1921-1922 Courtland Brown
1899 L. N. Eggers	
1900 W. E. Trull	1923-1924 L. A. Dockum
1901 C. J. Powers	1925-1926 B. C. Henshaw

This Post had a total enrollment of 292 different comrades as their quarterly, later semi-annual, and finally only annual reports indicate, and also show that they reported as many as 97 members in 1891 and almost as many for several years earlier and later.

GEORGE W. FINNUP

George W. Finnup was born at Vevay, Switzerland County, Indiana, which was located on the Ohio River half way between Cincinnati and Louisville. Across the river one could see the lights of Carroll County, Kentucky. He attended the public schools in Vevay, and seldom missed a day. He arrived in Garden City with the family in 1879. He attended subscription school here a few months a year until 1882, and then attended one term at Washburn College in Topeka in the fall of 1883. At that time the college was some distance from the town. Many years later, Mr. Finnup was the first man to take a life scholarship in Washburn, which is being used by worthy students.

On January 1, 1884, he went to work in his father's store and lumber yard, and in a few years took the

GEORGE W. FINNUP
Active in Western Kansas affairs for many years, but whose chief hobby is in perpetuating the memory of the early settlers of this part of the state.

management of it, and continued until the death of his father. In 1892 his brother, E. G. Finnup, came into the firm and was identified with it until the death of his father. Over thirty years ago George W. Finnup became interested in land, and in the following years handled it on a large scale. Up to the present time he has owned 495 town lots in Garden City besides city property in other towns. In Finney County, which is the second largest county in Kansas in area, he has owned and handled 624 quarter sections of land, or about 99,840 acres, which is about 12 percent of the total area of the county. In Kearny County, adjoining Finney on the west, he has owned about 22,500 acres, and in Hamilton County, on the west of Kearny, about 21,420 acres. The total acreage in these three counties lacks 240 acres of being 900 quarters. In 1914 he had a 40-section sand-hill pasture southwest of Holcomb, which was ten miles long, and he owned about half of this, which was deeded land, and the balance was forest reserve.

In checking up the records of these lands in Kearny County in June, 1931, C. A. Loucks of Lakin, writes Mr. Finnup, "I doubt if there is another man in the state, or in several states for that matter, that has owned as many acres of land that you have, and I do not think only in the matter of acres, either, but of the enormous amount of money it must have taken to handle it; and then, too, the handsome profit which you have made, but I know of no one who has labored harder, and more faithfully, and is more entitled to whatever profit you have made; and I am also thinking what a wonderful amount of good you have done by selling these people land on the easy terms which I know you have disposed of it."

In addition to land in these three counties, he has owned land in a number of other counties in Kansas, as well as in several other states, including over 10,000 acres in Colorado. In recent years he has developed thousands of acres of his land for wheat and row crops, including some alfalfa, and has built some substantial buildings on Main Street in Garden City. For many years when land was cheap and slow selling, he made a market for most any piece of land offered him in this county. About thirty years ago he handled some cattle, but in a couple of years gave it up as he could not do it successfully and live in town.

After the death of his father and mother in 1914 he decided that life was short and that one could not live forever, so he began a constructive program for the benefit of the people of Garden City and Finney County, and the surrounding counties, which he has carried on for some years, and which included a fine park in Garden City, a fund for helping keep up the church properties and beautifying them, libraries in a number of counties so the children as well as their parents could have good reading in the winter evenings, spelling contests, and many other helpful and inspiring benefits.

Mr. Finnup takes as much interest in Garden City and Finney County affairs as he does in his own business, and has given much time and money trying to build railroads and to further the development of the country in different ways. Mr. Finnup has remarked: "Much of one's life is spent, when one is public-spirited, in trying to do too much, and ingratitude, one of the world's besetting sins, is often the result. One must have an iron constitution to stand the strain, and some of these efforts are never appreciated as one would like to see. Selfishness and dishonesty are two of the world's greatest curses, and any man or woman blessed with talent and prosperity owes an imperfect world much to make it better, and life happier. The love of money is the root of all evil, but money used for the benefit of humanity is a wonderful thing. Rockefeller says that public acclaim is much greater than great riches."

For many years Mr. Finnup could have travelled around the world and had considerable money left, on the amount of taxes he has had to pay on his lands and lots.

Considering the time, the cause, and the leadership since the Civil War, Blaine in the Republican party, and Bryan in the Democratic party have been his choice of the public leaders.

Mr. Finnup was married in Garden City June 26, 1902, to Alta May Smith, and they have two children, Frederick and Isabel May, who live at the home at 321 Ninth Street, Garden City, Kansas.

Reading right to left: R. W. Hoskinson, Chas. I. Zirkle, J. W. Hope, William H. Thompson, William Jennings Bryan, W. G. Darby, R. E. Stotts, E. G. Finnup, Simon E. Zirkle, E. E. Brysselbout, Gus Burgheim, F. G. Austin. This picture was taken near Garden City June 6, 1912. William J. Bryan was the Democratic candidate for president. He took the seat on the hay-rake and J. W. Hope, a standpatter Republican, and W. G. Darby, a Bull-Mooser, picked up the tongue. Mr. Bryan remarked, "Now, boys, this is just the way it is going to be after the election."

C. J. (BUFFALO) JONES

Charles Jesse Jones, more familiarly known as "Buffalo" Jones, was born in Tazewell county, Ill., in 1844. He was the second son of a family of twelve children, and from the time he was strong enough to pick up a bucket of chips at the woodpile until he had attained his majority, it was work, work. His father was a famous hunter, both from love of the sport and from necessity. Mr. Jones attributes a great deal of his own inclinations to his early home experiences. He developed a genius for taming wild animals and seemed to have a power of subduing fractious beasts to his will. Naturally he became an expert rider when very young, which served him so admirably on the Great Plains in later life when in pursuit of the buffalo so closely connected with his name.

His early education was very much restricted. The district school was a log building with rough slab benches. and it was his privilege to attend only two or three days a week, or when it was too cold to work. He was twenty-one when he decided to enter the Bloomington university, which he attended for two years. On account of eye trouble he had to give up his school work and decided to go west.

In 1866 he left his old home and started out. He stopped at Troy, Kansas, and for the next five years was engaged in the nursery business at that place. In 1869 he married Miss Martha J. Walton. But Mr. Jones was not contented to remain where the country was all taken up by small farmers. The winter of 1871 he left his home in Troy on horseback to seek a new location where more game and cheaper land could be had. For several weeks he pressed on westward through winter storms until he reached Osborne county, and entered on government land about the center of the county January, 1872. The following April he returned to Troy and was accompanied on his return by his wife and child. This was a severe undertaking for his young wife who had been reared amidst the luxuries of eastern communities; but like all pioneer American women, she cheerfully followed the fortunes of her husband, accepting whatever hardships might befall.

Mr. Jones remained on his land in Osborne county awhile, but did not like farming. He removed to Sterling, Kansas, where he lived until 1879, when he became interested with the Fulton brothers in promoting Garden City. R. J. Churchill has said of C. J. Jones:

"Most men went west to grow up with the country; Jones went west to grow the country up; others might take the milk pail and stool and sit down in the middle of the pasture and wait for the cow to come around to be milked; Jones would jam the old cow up in the corner and milk her. With Jones it was always, 'What next?' Jones was a born booster; he lived a booster; he died a booster and was buried like a booster, without a stone to mark his grave."

The name C. J. Jones has already been mentioned many times in connection with the development of Southwest Kansas. Aside from his business activities, Mr. Jones was passionately fond of hunting and capturing wild animals, and during the years he lived in Finney county he found time to go on several big hunts, especially on expeditions to capture buffalo calves. He was accompanied on these trips by men who were famous hunters. John H. Carter, Lee Howard, Charles Rude, J. A. Ricker, Dick Williams, Wm. Terrill, Governor St. John, and on one trip by Emerson Hough. His first buffalo calf hunt was in 1886, and they succeeded in capturing fourteen calves. His second buffalo calf hunt was in May, 1887. On this trip they captured only three calves. On the third trip, extravagant preparations were made for the hunt. His companion was John Biggs, a typical cowboy and a brave hunter. They left in the spring of 1888 and captured thirty-seven buffalo calves, and Mr. Biggs arrived in Garden City July 6, with thirty-two head. The cost of this trip was $1,825.

Mr. Jones had many horses, but his favorites were: Gray Devil, a wild horse; Kentuck, a thoroughbred, and his old buffalo horse, Jubar, which he said never failed him.

In 1891 he sold five pair of buffaloes to C. J. Leland, a wealthy English nobleman, for a great price and delivered the animals to England himself.

His daughter, Mrs. Jessie Jones Phillips of Chicago, has supplied a brief sketch of the years of her father's life after he left Garden City: From 1890 until 1893 he lived in Nebraska. When the Cherokee Strip was opened for settlement in 1893 he made the race and staked a claim adjoining Perry, Oklahoma.

In 1897 he was sergeant-of-arms in the Oklahoma legislature at Guthrie.

In June, 1907, he started for the Arctic region to hunt wild animals. He succeeded in capturing five musk-oxen calves and started back to the United States. But the Indians or Eskimos cut the calves' throats while Jones was asleep. It was their belief that all game would leave the country if the musk-oxen were taken out alive. Mr. Jones was very much disappointed, but returned with many other fine specimens of animal heads and skins which he donated to public museums.

1898 and 1899, worked on "Buffalo Jones' Forty Years of Adventure", which was then published.

1900-1902, worked on invention for irrigation purposes.

1902-1905, game warden of Yellowstone Park, appointed by President Roosevelt. He accomplished a great deal with wild animals which had become unruly from petting (principally bears); introduced the herd of buffaloes which has greatly increased; exterminated many lions which were jeopardizing the elk and other harmless animals. The buffaloes he drove in on horse back from Utah and other states at great personal discomfort. Wild life increased steadily in the park from this time.

1906, he started a large ranch on government land north of Grand Canyon in Arizona, for the preservation of buffalo and cross-breeding of buffalo and domestic cattle.

1907, started Zane Gray on the road to fame as an author by financing a trip to this region, which Gray made famous.

1908-1909, lectured with motion pictures on his lion hunts in Arizona.

1910, organized an expedition to Africa for the purpose of roping and making motion pictures of all wild animals which Col. Roosevelt had hunted the year before. The expedition was a great success.

1911-12-13, lectured on this African trip; established a sheep ranch in New Mexico for crossing Persian sheep with domestic.

1914, organized second trip to Africa for the purpose of capturing a live gorilla. He was seized with jungle fever, and carried on a stretcher to the last boat which left the French Congo, after war was declared.

1915, lectured and worked on irrigation invention.

1916, developed water elevator in San Antonio, Texas, and Denver, Colorado. Had major operation but seemingly recovered.

1917, stricken in San Antonio, and never recovered full strength. Died October 1, 1919, at the home of his daughter in Topeka, Kansas.

The triumphant days of Mr. Jones in Garden City were clouded by the death of his two sons, one ten and the other thirteen. He had previously lost two little girls at Sterling, Kansas. The daughters of C. J. Jones who are still living are Mrs. Olive Whitmer Heath, psychiatric worker in the Veterans' hospital at Coatsville, Pa., and Mrs. Jessie Jones Phillips of Chicago.

The complete life and works of C. J. Jones are detailed in the following books: "Buffalo Jones' Forty Years of Adventure," compiled by Henry Inman; "Lassoing Wild Animals in Africa," by Guy H. Scull; "The Last of the Plainsmen," by Zane Grey.

FREDERICK FINNUP PARK

Frederick Finnup Park consists of 104 acres adjoining Garden City on the south and east of Highway 83 along the north bank of the Arkansas River and within the city limits. The deed to the park came as a gift to the city from George W. Finnup May 8, 1919. It was dedicated to the memory of his father, Frederick Finnup. In further recognition of the service Frederick Finnup gave to the community, sixty business men and professional men of Garden City voted unanimously at the regular meeting of the Chamber of Commerce in January, 1928, and later the city commissioners passed an ordinance to set side May 8, as a city holiday to be observed annually. At the request of the members of the Finnup family, the day is celebrated in memory of all pioneers of Western Kansas.

Rev. A. C. McKeever said in an address on Finnup Day, May 8, 1930:

"George W. Finnup, son of Frederick Finnup, indeed a son of a worthy sire, has erected a monument in your midst in honor of his father; this monument has been accepted by your city and county, and by the different organizations thereof, and it shall stand as a monument to Frederick Finnup who came here in 1879 and entered at once into the activities of the community. He gave his service to the development of the city and made many sacrifices of his time and means to make Garden City a good place to live. When George W. Finnup, in his desire to erect a monument to the memory of his dearly loved and revered father, gave this plot of ground to Garden City, and the city in its desire to honor its former citizen, has developed the beautiful park and playground known as Finnup Park, and has set aside May 8 to be known as Finnup Day. We, as citizens and friends, feel that it is most fitting and the people of Garden City, of Finney county, and people traveling through our city are all benefitted and blessed."

FREDERICK FINNUP

Frederick Finnup was born in Germany December 27, 1840. He came with his parents to the United States at the age of five years. His boyhood days were spent in Cincinnati, Ohio, where he learned the trade of varnisher and cabinet maker, receiving as pay for his labor the first year, $1.50 weekly; the second year $2.00 weekly; the third year $2.50 weekly and the fourth year, $4.00 weekly, with a $25 bonus at the end of that time.

He was united in marriage to Minnie Lohmann February 11, 1866, at Vevay, Indiana. Mrs. Finnup was born at Wulften, Germany, August 16, 1840. Their children are George W., Sallie M., wife of George T. Inge, and Edward G., all born in Vevay, Indiana, and all living now in Garden City.

On April 17, 1861, Frederick Finnup enlisted in Company E, Ninth Ohio Volunteer Infantry, under Colonel Robert McCook, of the noted "Fighting McCook" family. The regiment was all German, had a regimental band, and was drilled by a major who had been in the Prussian army. They were in nine battles and many minor engagements. Mr. Finnup was in the battle of Chickamauga September 19 and 20, 1863, one of the decisive battles of the war, under General George H. Thomas. Of the 249 men in the 9th Ohio, 48 were killed, 185 wounded, and 16 missing. After this battle General Thomas remarked: "Whenever you meet the 9th Ohio, lift your hats from off your heads." But Mr. Finnup never leaned on his army record or sought office in civil life. He laid aside his uniform and went to work.

For about thirteen years after the close of the war he engaged in the furniture business at Vevay, Indiana. On account of his wife's failing health he made a trip west to look for a new location. He decided to settle somewhere along the Santa Fe railroad in the Arkansas valley. He met C. J. Jones at Ellinwood, Kansas, who painted a wonderful picture of the town they were starting at Garden City, and of the surrounding country with its "mountain showers". Mr. Finnup was interested and came on to Garden City, arriving April 14, 1879. The men of the town were out fighting a prairie fire, and Mr. Finnup went straight from the depot to join the men who were to become his fellow citizens, in an effort to protect the interests of Garden City. And from that time on he faced the hardships and stood by the pioneers when the storms and difficulties arose.

Mr. Finnup immediately built a two-story frame building with imitation stone front, 40x50 feet, on lots 15 and 16 in block 23, and covered by deed No. 1. This was his place of business where he carried a line of general merchandise with a lumber yard in connection in the rear until December 24, 1888. At that time he moved into a two-story brick building, 34x110, adjoining his original building on the south, which he had built in 1886. He continued in business in this location until the time of his death. The twelve rooms above his store were occupied as a home by the family for nearly thirty years. In 1882 he built a concrete building of two stories on the west side of Main street, north of the railroad right of way, on lot 18 in block 36, and it was occupied by the United States Land Office. Mr. Finnup was the largest builder in Southwest Kansas up until the boom day and his two-story buildings stood out like land marks in the whole surrounding country.

In November, 1879, the family moved to a homestead one mile west of Garden City, the southeast quarter of section 14, which he purchased from Tom Hurdle for $500.00, a big price for a relinquishment in those days. He finished a two-room sod house which was plastered both inside and out, with a good shingle roof. It was referred to as the "White House" by local people and by travellers on the old Santa Fe Trail which passed a few rods north of the house. In the spring of 1880 he set out many trees, hauling water in barrels to aid in digging the holes. Some of the trees are still living. The family lived on the homestead twenty-six months. The store was closed part of this time as there was no business.

As the country developed Mr. Finnup's business increased and became quite large. For many years he built various business houses of brick, and also other properties. He was ready at all times to carry and help anyone who was deserving and needed assistance, by extending credit or loaning money, but he seldom signed notes or bonds. He handled some stock and land, and a great many bonds of Western Kansas. He was the largest individual tax-payer in the county from its beginning until his death, and was the oldest merchant in Garden City when he died. He gained success by giving good service and value received at all times, coupled with hard work. But he realized that success would not have been possible without the confidence and good will of so many loyal customers and friends of the early pioneer days, who suffered hardships and privations to make this treeless plain habitable, and laid the stepping stones for many who are enjoying prosperity today.

Mr. Finnup died April 6, 1914, and his faithful wife and loyal helpmate died August 7, 1914. Both were in their seventy-third year, and they rest side by side in Valley View cemetery.

THE SANTA FE RAILROAD THROUGH SOUTHWEST KANSAS

The history of Southwest Kansas dates from the building of the Santa Fe railroad. The construction work was scarcely completed before cattlemen and homeseekers began following this "trail of iron" and settling along its right of way.

The route established by the Santa Fe Trail early suggested the feasibility of establishing a grand trunk railway essentially over the same route which the instincts of pioneer trade had already selected. And the organizers of the Atchison and Topeka Railroad Company had this in mind when they incorporated by the act of the Territorial Legislature February 11, 1859. But the terrible drouth of 1860 paralyzed every enterprise of the Territory of Kansas, and then after that followed the war of the Rebellion.

The company was re-organized and a new charter granted March 3, 1863, under the name Atchison, Topeka and Santa Fe, which absorbed the rights and franchise of the A & T. On February 9, 1864, a grant of land was transferred from the state to the Atchison, Topeka and Santa Fe, giving them alternate sections for a distance of ten miles on each side of the proposed road, on condition that it should be finished before the expiration of ten years from the act of approval.

Work of building the railroad began at Topeka in October, 1868. It was completed to Dodge City in August, 1872, and on to the western state line December 23, 1872. It followed substantially the course of the old Santa Fe trail through this region along the north bank of the Arkansas river. The line was placed in operation to Granada, Colorado, May 10, 1873.

There was no money in operating the road at that time for several years afterwards. During the winter of 1873 and '74 one man had charge of the track from Larned to the state line. He went west on the 5 o'clock train in the morning and returned on the 8 o'clock train the next evening. He rode on the platform of the rear car, and if anything wrong was noticed, the train was stopped and he made repairs. The first rails were iron, the engines small and the cars and coaches of wood construction. The passenger coaches had brakes on the end, that turned by hand, and there were no vestibules.

Peter Tellin was one of the first engineers on a Santa Fe passenger train into Dodge City, and continued on the line for many years. He is now nearly blind, but has a vivid recollection of those first years of railroading in this region, and said recently:

"In 1874 soldiers were stationed at Sherlock and Kendall. That summer we had to carry two loaded rifles in the engine cab and six in the baggage car for protection against the Indians. We were always afraid the Indians would attack the trains.

"During the summer of 1874 I hauled the Syracuse colony (they came from Syracuse, N.Y.) from Dodge City to Syracuse. There were twelve cars. Besides the passengers, the train was loaded with horses, wagons and farm implements. In about three years, they were nearly all starved out. The drouth and grasshoppers took everything. Nearly all had to leave. The Santa Fe helped them to get land in eastern Kansas. A number of them settled around Strong City.

"Game was plentiful in those days. Buffalo, antelope and deer. The buffalo did not last long. I saw my last herd in 1878. At that time I saw what was called the main herd. I don't know how many there were. We just had to run the train through the herd, making all the noise we could, and running very slowly. They could not run, as there were too many in the herd. One time, Buffalo Jones, who was mail agent on our train, jumped off near where Garden City is now, to shoot some buffalo. I did not see him jump off as he thought I had, so the train went on without him.

"The winter of 1874 was very cold. I was told that over 1,000 head of cattle drifted in to the north bank of the Arkansas river, all the way from the Colorado line to Dodge City. For 21 days that winter the line was blocked between Dodge and Granada and no regular trains were run. The snow laid on the ground for six weeks. There was a large herd of antelope around Sherlock, and they got so poor you could go right up to them and they wouldn't move."

During the summer of 1875 Lieut. Spencer of the 17th Infantry, stationed at Fort Larned with a detail of five or six soldiers, went west every morning and returned in the evening as a guard. There was only one train each way a day and that was freight and passenger combined. Larned was the end of the freight division. In 1874-75 the cattle shipped over the Santa Fe were all loaded at Great Bend. That was the cattle town of the valley, and it was a lively place with all the good and bad that Dodge City had the name of having. There was no settlement south of the river except occasional cattle ranches, and the great herds came over the trails straight to Great Bend or passed north to the Union Pacific. It made little difference in those days where the herds crossed, as there was nothing to intrude on but Indians and buffaloes. From Dodge City to the state line there was next to nothing in the way of stations. Pierceville made a start, but the Indians filed a contest and ruined the town in 1874.

Cambell M. Johnston, now of Garden City, entered the service of the Santa Fe in June, 1882. His uncle, Thomas Sherlock, was a director of the road, and through him young Johnston secured a job as clerk in the offices at Dodge City. He remained there as cashier for six years, and then was agent at various stations, including Coolidge and Lamar. Mr. Johnston recalls an incident that happened the first morning he took up his duties in the depot.

"I noticed a tall, good looking young fellow walk upon the depot platform, dressed from Stetson hat to high-top boots in most expensive cowboy garb, but for all that he looked like a tenderfoot. He swaggered along clicking his long spurs, just drunk enough to act smart. He took a position on the platform and every time anyone came along the trail that passed the depot, he would twirl his hat, jump up and crack his heels together and clap his hands. Then he would shout at them: 'Approach me! Approach me! I am wild and woolley and full of fleas. I dare you approach me!'

"Before long a cowboy from off the plains came jogging along. His mind was apparently deeply absorbed in his own business, but he heard the taunt directed at him from the man on the platform. His horse stopped instantly and he watched with silent regard the performance of the dude cowboy for a few minutes. Then without a word he gave a spring and landed upon the splendid-appearing cowboy and proceeded to mop up the platform with him, and did not seem in the least excited or elated over his victory as he got on his horse and rode on his way. The man who had been so boastful got up and shook himself, entirely sobered, and remarked that he guessed he got what he deserved."

Pliney C. Pegan, a pioneer resident of Garden City, went to work for the Santa Fe railroad in 1885 and continued with them until he retired on a pension in June, 1930. For twenty-five years he was a passenger conductor on Nos. 5 and 8 between Dodge City and Denver. He traveled about 72,000 miles a year while on this run, and was never responsible for a wreck or a bad accident. He is now seventy-five, and lives in Denver, Colorado. Mr. Pegan came to Great Bend soon after the Santa Fe reached that point. He had many thrilling pioneer experiences. He says:

"When I first came to Great Bend I lived with F. M. Dodge who was the second man to settle in Barton county. His home was in a dugout on the Walnut, four miles north of Great Bend. It was in line with the herds of buffalo as they moved to the salt marshes while traveling north and south. One season the main herd came thundering across the prairie, and for three days and nights they passed the dugout in a solid, continuous mass."

On September 29, 1883, about 12:30 a.m., an attempt was made at Coolidge, Kansas, to rob the eastbound "cannonball" passenger train on the Atchison, Topeka & Santa Fe railroad. The train arrived at Coolidge on time but was detained about ten minutes by a hot box. Conductor S. F. Greeley gave the signal to start and as he did so, noticed several men walking along the depot platform just ahead of him. One of the party jumped on the platform between the express and mail cars and another jumped into the side door of the express car, which was open. The conductor called to the man entering the express car, asking what he was doing there. He was answered by a shot from a pistol, but it missed him. The robber fired a second and third shot both directed toward expressman S. S. Peterson, who was asleep on his couch in the car. He jumped up at once and returned the fire, the assaultant retreating to the other end of the car where he made his escape and disappeared in the darkness.

In the meantime others of the bunch proceeded to the engine and commanded John Hilton, engineer, to pull out. Hilton had his hand on the lever and as he turned to look at his visitor, he was shot through the body and died instantly. The robber now directed his attention to fireman George Fadel and shot him through the neck, and then jumped from the engine and made his escape. The plan of the robbers was to capture the train and run it out to a point where confederates were in waiting. Telegraph wire had been tampered with so as to prevent messages being sent east or west.

Special trains were sent to Coolidge from Las Animas, Colorado, with the sheriff and a posse and from Dodge City with deputy sheriff Dave Matthews, Billy Combs and Nelson Cary. The Santa Fe officers made every effort to find the men who were connected with the crime and offered a big reward, but they failed to even find a clue.

Many of the first settlers in Southwest Kansas were enabled to remain on their homesteads by doing section work, and in taking care of pumps at the water tanks. Others were employed to walk the tracks, until steel rails were laid. The Santa Fe extended every reasonable inducement to get settlers interested in coming and in remaining in this region.

THE GARDEN CITY, GULF & NORTHERN RAILROAD

Railroad building in Western Kansas has not all been confined to large companies. Some roads have been promoted and build by local men. Among these railroads was the Garden City, Gulf and Northern, now a part of the Atchison, Topeka & Santa Fe system. Ground for this road was broken July 8, 1908. The company was organized by Basil M. McCue, who came to Finney county from Hasting, Nebraska, in 1904, and became extensively engaged in the real estate business.

A petition was filed with the county commissioners April 4, 1907, asking the county to subscribe one hundred and ninety thousand dollars to the capital stock of the proposed railroad, which was to be built from Garden City to Scott City. A bond election was held later and carried 693 for and 158 against. The road was finished and trains were running over it before December 31, 1908. E. A. Tennis was general manager of the road.

A grade was later built through the sand hills south of Garden City to the Haskell county line, but that section of the road was never completed. In 1910 and 1911 Mr. McCue extended his railroad north from Scott City to Winona, a distance of 53 miles. This section of the road was later abandoned and the steel taken up. Gillispie station on the Garden City, Gulf & Northern railroad, was named for F. A. Gillispie, a representative of the Garden City sugar company, and Tennis station for the general manager of the road. The townsite of McCue, now Friend, was named in honor of the builder of the railroad. After operating the railroad for two years Mr. McCue sold it to the Atchison, Topeka & Santa Fe for $500,000.

THE GARDEN CITY-WESTERN RAILROAD

The Garden City Western railroad was built in 1915. The officials are: J. Stewart, president; Spencer Penrose, vice-president; F. A. Gillispie, secretary-treasurer, and W. B. Benson, general freight agent. The road is fourteen miles in length, and was built primarily for the purpose of serving the beet and alfalfa district. But there has been a big increase in wheat acreage in the northwest part of the county, and the railroad now ships many carloads of grain every year. There are three principal stations or loading points on this line. Wolfe station has in addition to beet and alfalfa loading equipment, a 15,000-bushel-capacity elevator, owned by Tom Daniels of Deerfield. At Lowe Station the Everly Grain Company has a 15,000-bushel elevator. This point also has large stockyards and a grocery store. Peterson is also a beet-loading station.

RAILROADS THAT WERE CHARTERED BUT NEVER BUILT

Several railroads have been surveyed through Finney county, and bonds voted by the citizens to help promote them, but they were never built and the bonds were never issued. The surveys and half-finished grades were abandoned by the promoters, and their story is almost forgotten.

The charter of the Nebraska, Garden City and Southwestern railroad was filed with the Secretary of State March 8, 1886. It was to be built from Red Cloud, Nebraska, to the coal fields of Colorado, and Garden City was to be the most important intermediate point on the railroad.

A vote was cast at the Garden City township election September 27, 1886, for the purpose of subscribing $50,000 to the capital stock of the Kansas, Texas and Southwestern railroad. The election carried, seven hundred in favor and two against. The road was to be constructed from Garden City to some point on the Union Pacific, and also south to some indefinite point.

June 28, 1887, a petition signed by Porter D. Perry and 106 other persons in Terry and Pleasant Valley townships, asking for a special election to vote upon a proposition to subscribe $21,000 to the capital stock of the Garfield-Pawnee Valley and Colorado railroad company. The election carried by seventeen votes.

A petition signed by C. J. Jones, J. A. Stevens, and 651 other resident taxpayers was presented to the board of commissioners May 31, 1887. They were asking the county to subscribe $120,000, to be issued in $1000 bonds, to the Denver, Garden City and Southwestern railroad, which was to be built from some point in Meade county to Garden City, and north to the Finney county line. They also asked for the same amount to be issued to the Garden City Nickel Plate, which was to be built from Garden City to some point in Ness or Lane county. A right of way for this road was secured, surveyed and several miles of grading completed.

The Nebraska, Kansas and Southern was surveyed through the county in 1907. The town of Burham was platted in Garfield township, and the road completed from Garden City to a point seventeen miles northeast. The project failed to go any farther, and the stockholders lost all their investment.

THE GARDEN CITY SUGAR COMPANY

Since 1905 the Garden City Sugar Company has had much to do with the development of the Arkansas river valley in Southwest Kansas, and no other one concern has spent more money in improvements in Garden City and surrounding territory. The sugar company has led the way in the progress of the great irrigation system in the Garden City district. It has built the sugar factory, an alfalfa meal mill, the Garden City Western railroad and an electric power plant. It has built electric power lines through the valley and made it possible for individual farmers to develop their lands with irrigation and to operate their pumping plants with electricity. During the past twenty-five years all of Western Kansas has had its ups and downs, its dry years of short crops and its setbacks on account of other conditions beyond the control of man. But the sugar factory has been in operation every year, and has put into circulation on an average of more than a million dollars a year.

The first movement toward securing a beet sugar factory at Garden City was as follows, and is told by D. R. Menke: "The land we sold to the sugar company was bunched up by Charles Schneider, Ed Wirt and myself early in the spring of 1902. We first purchased the Great Eastern Ditch and then bought about 12,000 acres of land including the townsite of Deerfield in Kearny county, Kansas. Nearly all of this land consisted of abandoned farms along the Great Eastern Ditch and nearly all of it was unimproved. Later on we interested George W. Swink of Rocky Ford, Colorado, and sold him a fourth interest. Mr. Swink was one of the promoters of the Rocky Ford sugar factory.

"After carrying the matter along for about six months we found we needed some outside people to help finance our project. With the assistance of W. B. George, cashier of the First National Bank of Garden City, we succeeded in interesting the shareholders of his bank, who were all bankers in small towns in Missouri. These people secured the money needed and took an interest with us at cost and expenses. In May, 1905, Mr. Swink got in touch with Oliver H. Shoop, R. P. Davie, J. R. McKinnie and others of Colorado Springs, Colorado, and these people looked over our project May 29 and 30, 1905. A proposition was made to us which was approved by our shareholders within ten days and a contract entered into about the middle of June, 1905. Mr. Shoop signed the contract for his company and Mr. George as secretary and I as vice-president for our company. A part of the agreement was to build a sugar factory at Garden City."

E. C. Sharer has written a brief sketch of the establishment of the Garden City Sugar Company and its earliest operations:

"During the spring of 1905, George W. Swink of Rocky Ford, and Harry L. Lubers of Las Animas, Colorado, interested J. R. McKinnie, Verne Z. Reed and Oliver H. Shoop of Colorado Springs, in the purchase of 20,000 acres of land located near Garden City. A trip was made to Garden City to look over the land and water rights. Some of the land was under various irrigation ditches, and some was located above the ditches. The price of the land was very cheap and the water rights were included, which were of a very uncertain value. In course of a very short time, R. P. Davie and E. C. Sharer of Colorado Springs became interested and a deal was made to acquire the holdings of the syndicate owning the property.

"The location for a good reservoir was found to store water under the Great Eastern Ditch. The Amazon Ditch was being improved and with the pumping plants along the valley in Finney county it seemed possible to contract enough acreage for beet culture to supply a factory of a tonnage of about five hundred tons daily. During previous years enough beets had been grown to demonstrate the kind of soil and the length of the growing season, and to prove the sugar content. With these proven conditions the Colorado syndicate began to look for capital to build a sugar factory. Spencer Penrose, Chas. M. MacNeill, Dawson Hawkins and F. A. Gillespie came down to look over the plans and possibilities of a beet sugar factory.

"After a thorough investigation, plans were made to

finance a sugar factory, improve ditches and build a reservoir. Ultimately a much bigger and better factory was built than was originally planned. E. H. Every of Colorado Springs interested a number of men to buy securities; among them were Wm. J. Palmer of Colorado Springs and Governor Dodge of Denver, Colorado.

"Garden City and land owners of Finney county responded in a splendid manner, and helped in the promotion in every way. The Santa Fe railroad officially contributed equivalent to half the cost of the freight. This amounted to a considerable item and was most helpful at the inception of the enterprise. What was then needed was farmers, beet growers and dairymen. In time a number of people moved into the county and bought land, others came in and leased land. Garden City enjoyed a splendid growth, and soon became one of the most prosperous towns in Western Kansas."

James Craig says: "I would like to say something of the men who made it possible to have a sugar factory at Garden City. Such men as R. M. Lawrence, D. R. Menke, George Finnup, E. G. Finnup, J. E. Baker, W. M. Kinnison, George Boyd, H. V. Lawrence, and many others who gave of their time and money.

"When the sugar factory interests finally decided to locate the factory at Garden City they asked the people to give them a bonus of $30,000 and secure them 12,000 acres of beets. The next thing was how to raise the bonus. A committee was appointed to take donations of land or money with D. R. Menke, chairman, E. G. Finnup, secretary, and James Craig, treasurer. Some gave money, and many gave ten acres of land and some forty or more acres of land. The sugar company agreed to take the various tracts of land at a fixed price. The deeds were made to the holding committee and after the factory was built the transfers were made to the sugar company."

Expenditures for 1930

Sugar beets	$298,680.68
Fuel oil	36,659.87
Lime rock	20,556.80
Coke	7,624.08
Beet seed	25,375.65
Machinery and electrical supplies	70,667.89
Alfalfa hay (for alfalfa meal)	9,328.32
Freight (in-bound only) on above	129,975.19
Freight, out-bound, finished product, over	100,000.00
Supplies purchased from local merchants	64,805.57
Local payroll (exclusive of Mexican beet labor)	157,500.00
Paid Mexicans for labor on beets	108,240.63

Taxes

Finney county—		
School district No. 1	$ 9,709.36	
Holcomb consolidated schools	15,827.07	
All others	27,066.42	52,602.85
Kearny county		4,714.75

Grand Total	$1,086,732.19

FORMER RESIDENTS OF FINNEY COUNTY WHO BECAME EMINENT

Wm. M. Thompson—elected to the U.S. Senate from Kansas, 1912.

John H. Cotteral—appointed judge of the U.S. Federal Court in Oklahoma. Resided in Garden City from 1885 to 1889. Appointed by President Roosevelt.

Richard J. Hopkins—appointed judge of the U.S. District Court for the District of Kansas by President Hoover, 1930. Was representative from Finney County, lieutenant governor, attorney general, associate justice of the Kansas Supreme Court at time of appointment as federal judge. Resided at Garden City since 1879.

Henry F. Mason—elected associate judge of the Kansas Supreme Court, 1903, and held the office until his death in 1927. Had been a member of the Kansas legislature from Finney county. Was a resident of Finney county since 1887.

Wm. Easton Hutchison—appointed associate judge of the Kansas Supreme Court on the death of Henry F. Mason by Governor Paulin. Was judge of the District Court.

Wm. McD. Rowan—Colonel of the Kansas Militia for many years, was made colonel in the regular army during the world war, now attached to the prohibition enforcement department of the government at Omaha. Retired from the army with the rank of brigadier general.

Clarence E. Abbott—Colonel of New Mexico state militia during the trouble on the Mexican border, colonel in the world war, now Judge Advocate in the army. Lived in Garden City for a number of years while his father, Hon. A. J. Abbott, was judge of the District Court. Was appointed U.S. District Attorney for New Mexico.

Charles W. Morse—resided in Garden City from 1885 to 1890 when he removed to Salt Lake City, Utah, and was elected Judge of the District Court.

Dick T. Morgan—resided in Garden City from 1885 to 1889. Removed to Oklahoma and was elected to Congress.

L. J. Pettyjohn—came to Garden City in 1895 as clerk of the Kansas Court of Appeals. Is at present a member of the Federal Land Bank Board at Washington.

During the world war the following held commissions in the army overseas: Wm. McD. Rowan, Colonel; J. J. Haskell, Major; Raimond Walters, Captain; S. M.

Daugherty, Lieutenant; and James Homer Harriott. John Lowderman and O. H. Warner, aviators, but not overseas.

Jesse J. Dunn—judge of the Supreme Court in Oklahoma, 1908.

A. G. C. Bierer, judge of the Supreme Court in Oklahoma, 1894.

Clifford R. Hope, representative in United States Congress, 1930.

The Early History of Scott County

ONE of the most important archæological relics of early life in Kansas is the ruins of an old pueblo north of Scott City in the Scott county state park. Scientists have agreed that these ruins are the long lost remnants of the pueblo El Quartelejo, which was established about 1702 by some adventurous Pueblo Indians from the town of Picuries in New Mexico. Originally it was a stone and adobe building of 32 by 50 feet, and was divided into seven rooms.

Probably this was the first walled house constructed within the present borders of Kansas. The ruins were visited in 1898 by Profs. S. W. Willston and H. T. Martin of the Kansas University, who derived many interesting facts and recovered numerous relics. In it were found stone, flint and bone implements, mealing stones, potsherds, a quantity of charred corn and other things used and found in an Indian pueblo of the Rio Grande, New Mexican type. There is no record or evidence that Spaniards or other whites had anything to do with its construction or ever lived there, and it seems that the Pueblo Indian owners of El Quartelejo were soon persuaded by the Governor of New Mexico to return to their former home.

A few nomadic stockmen held their herds along the Beaver and White Woman creeks at an earlier date, but civilization began when the first permanent settlement was made in Scott county in October, 1884, by Mrs. M. E. De Geer and her daughter, Mrs. I. L. Eastman (later Mrs. Frank H. Miller). These brave women from Chicago, Illinois, selected and filed on claims where Scott City now stands, and built a cabin which was shared with many newcomers the following severe winter. Frank H. Miller also came from Chicago in October, 1884, for the improvement of his broken health. He hauled lumber from Garden City to construct Mrs. De Geer's cabin, and remained through the winter of 1884-85. Charley Waite came in February, 1885, and a month later was followed by John Keeve. These Chicago boys came for a broader field of enterprise and to enjoy the fine climate of the plains. They were brave, self-helpful young men, well reared, but equally well suited to the rough work of pioneering. Hon. S. W. Case came in October, 1884, and located his claim on a part of the present town-site of Scott City, and in the early spring of 1885 opened the

Pioneer home of Mrs. M. E. DeGeer, built in 1884. The first building in Scott City and County.

pioneer store of the county. In March, 1885, Mrs. De Geer began the publication of the "Western Times" and from this time the county filled up rapidly.

Scott county was created by an act of legislature in 1873, and named in honor of General Winfield Scott. For several years it had no population, and so needed no local form of government, but it was attached to Ford county for judicial purposes. Very soon after people began to settle there, a petition signed by the required number of citizens was presented to the board of county commissioners of Finney county requesting that Scott county be organized as a municipal township and attached to Finney county for judicial purposes. Scott county was organized as a township of Finney county, and Scott Center (the present Scott City) was designated as the place of transacting public business. A township election was held in Scott Center July 7, 1885, and the following officers were elected: Trustee, Charley L. Waite; Treasurer, C. R. Swan; Clerk, M. H. Bailey; Road Overseer, W. E. McLain; Justice of Peace, S. W. Case and Joseph Hollister; Constable, Ira J. Wolf.

In June, 1886, Charles Reed was appointed enumerator of Scott county by the governor, and after taking the census, it was found that it had the required number of inhabitants (1,500) to proceed with a county organization. Eugene McDaniel, A. H. Kilpatric and M. Cunningham were appointed commissioners, and Charles Reed county clerk. The county was declared organized July 5, 1886, and that day the appointed commissioners and county clerk met in special session with Eugene McDaniel chairman. An election was called to be held August 10, 1886, and at that time the following officers were elected: Charles Reed, County Clerk; W. R. Hadley, Treasurer; B. F. Griffith, Register of Deeds; S. T. Burgess, Clerk of the District Court; J. F. Daniels, Sheriff; Lulu Boling, County Superintendent; Dr. J. F. Bond, Coroner; Eugene McDaniel, Commission of 1st District; H. M. Connor, Commissioner of 2nd District; C. Garrett, Commissioner of 3rd District. The county seat was located at Scott Center by unanimous vote.

The county has an area of 720 square miles and 460,800 acres, with an elevation of 3,000 feet. Four-fifths of the county is smooth, and reaches away before the vision like the placid surface of a waveless sea. Here and there are fine reaches of billowy prairie, with long graceful slopes dipping gently into valleys; long reaches of low-laying bottom lands skirt the clear-winding streams, which are generally flanked by low hills and occasional picturesque bluffs. In the center of the county a few miles to the south of Scott City, is the famous White Woman basin, a tract of low, bottom land, 25,000 acres in extent. It is a black alluvial deposit of great depth. In this basin the White Woman suddenly sinks into the earth and takes its subterranean course along and beneath the basin where it is forever lost to sight. The annual overflow of the river, which has its source in the foothills of Colorado, floods the basin with its surplus waters which quickly sink again into the bed of the lost stream. It is claimed that so strong is the current of this subterranean river, at flood time, that the sound of its swift waters can be heard distinctly some distance from the mouth of several of these sink holes, and the listener is left to wonder when and where these wild waters shall again see the light of day.

Several stories have been told as to why this basin was called the White Woman, and perhaps all are wrong, but the following story is a favorite. The towns of Friend and Shallow Water lie close together in the basin of White Woman river and people living there say this is how the basin got its name. "The family settling at Shallow Water and the lone man who settled at Friend were neighbors for that day. And the daughter of Shallow Water meant to marry the bachelor of Friend. The level Navajo, twelve miles north to south and less than 100 miles east to west, was ordinarily a dry-bed stream, and the lovers were wont to meet midway between their homes. But when the snow melted and came down from the mountain ranges far to the west the stream became a raging torrent. On a lonely night the waters came down with a rush and the man was swept away in the swirling torrent. The girl's mind was weakened by her loss, and every night she walked along the basin, looking for her lover. The wraith is seen there now, it is said, and those who in an older day met the white-robed 'something' presumed to be the spirit of the lady in search of her lover, christened it, 'the Valley of the White Woman'."

The Beaver and the White Woman, both clear streams, with numerous spring brook tributaries reaching out in different directions, have always supplied pure water for the stockman. The county also embraces many fine flowing springs, and wells of both hard and soft water are easily obtained at fifteen to fifty feet depth for irrigation purposes. Quarries of building stones are found in certain sections of the county, including the white-, gray- and cream-colored magnesian limestones. Native timber was limited to small belts and groves along the streams.

Scott City is the county seat and chief town in the county. It was founded in September, 1885, by the Scott City Town Company, composed of Dr. Hall, F. A. Parsons, S. W. Case, Mrs. M. E. De Geer, Mrs. F. A. Parsons, Mrs. I. L. Eastman, W. E. McLain, Mrs. D. F. Hall and Messrs, Sangster and Swan, who filed their charter in that month and soon after laid out the town. They changed the name from Scott Center to Scott City at this time. There was never any county seat fight in Scott county, as Scott City was located in the geographical center of the county and from the very first held the key to the situation. The spirit of clique and discord and division that ruined many Western-Kansas towns, never entered Scott county.

In 1886 the town had three weekly newspapers, four banks, a board of trade, two hotels and fifty other business concerns. The Masonic, Odd Fellows and Good Templers' lodges, and a post of the Grand Army of the Republic, the A.K.W.R. society and the Women's Christian Temperance Union had flourishing organizations. The ladies of the Woman's Christian Temperance Union erected a two-story building in 1886. The lower story was

Views of Main Street in Scott City, 1886. Top, looking north; Bottom looking south, from the junction of Main Street and DeGeer Ave.

Birdseye views of Scott City in 1886

leased to the county for official and clerical uses, and the hall above was used for literary and social gatherings. They also provided a free library and reading room for the public. The officers of the W.C.T.U. were: Mrs. M. L. Parsons, president; Mrs. Mary E. Clark, secretary, and Mrs. I. L. Eastman, treasurer. The Methodist church was the first edifice of worship erected.

Scott City had many land and loan men in 1886. Dr. D. F. Hall laid out a 104-acre addition to the northeast division of the original townsite and sold many business and residence sites. Frank H. Miller became largely interested in both city and country property, and in 1886 established the Traders' Bank. Mr. Miller made a handsome fortune in handling Scott City property. The Scott City Real Estate Company with Frank A. Capps, president, and Charles Clark, secretary, opened a land and loan office. Thompson, McNabb & Landis, real estate and loan agents, did a large business. The Western Kansas Land and Loan Company was organized by James H. Camfill, but in 1887, sold his interests to Tom Kennedy of Harper, Kansas. The land department of the company was conducted by Messrs. S. L. Hughes and P. H. O'Gara. Smith, McLain & Company, land and loan agents and land attorneys, with W. O. Bourne as junior member of the firm. Mr. Bourne had a fine suburban claim. Morse & Perry, real estate and loan firm, began business in 1887. Kelley & Fitts also did a capital business in real estate and farm loans.

Johnson Brothers & Service, whose bank was founded in February, 1886, by Johnson Bros., was the pioneer banking house of the county and was a strong, well-organized concern. The Scott County Bank was incorporated in 1886 by Samuel M. Jarvis, R. R. Conklin, C. G. Larned, H. J. Hunt, F. A. Parsons and J. D. Jarvis, and opened its doors with a capital of $50,000. The Traders Bank was organized in 1886 by Frank N. Miller and friends, was shortly re-organized, the new incorporators being ex-Governor George W. Glick and S. B. Glazier, of Atchison, W. L. C. Beard, M. J. Keys and Frank H. Miller. The fourth bank was opened in 1887 under the firm name of McKnight & Nicholson.

Prominent among the professional men were Traverse Morse, attorney; Messrs. Hadley and Hubbell, the former attorney for the county, the latter county superintendent of schools. The medical profession was finely represented by Dr. J. F. Bond, who was the first doctor

Dr. J. F. Bond, first doctor in Scott City

to settle in Scott county Dr. Ira W. Bouldin, and Dr. Arbuthnot, physician and druggist, whose partner in the drug business was Mr. Eggleston, a breeder of thoroughbred horses, and farmer.

NEWSPAPER HISTORY

The Western Times was the pioneer paper of Scott City and county. It was founded in the spring of 1885 by Mrs. M. E. De Geer and subsequently conducted by Mrs. Kate Russell. In August, 1886, M. J. Keys became the owner with E. B. Herrington as local editor. The name was changed to "The Sentinel", and was an excellent Republican paper. The second newspaper to be founded was "The Herald" in November, 1885, by Hon. S. W. Case. This was an influential Democratic journal, with Frank A. Capps as local editor and business manager. The third newspaper was established in the spring of 1886, and was called the "News". It was edited and managed by Sam H. Kelley.

DISCONTINED

Scott City—
  Common School, Dec. 1887-1888 (monthly)
  Coyote, Oct. 1910-1911 (monthly)
  Republican, Dec. 22, 1893-1896
  Scott County Herald, April 1886-1888
  Scott County Lever, Feb., 1889-1891
  Western Times, 1886

Grigsby—
  Chronicle, April 20, 1900-1902
  Scorcher, Nov. 26, 1886-1887

Pence—
  Phonograph, Oct. 15, 1887-1889

The Republican was founded in 1909 by Morris and Van Kirk, editors and publishers. February 16, 1911, Miss Ella J. Starr became the editor and publisher. This paper has been discontinued.

Scott county now has one newspaper, The News Chronicle, published weekly at Scott City by E. L. Epperson, editor and publisher. This paper is a continuation of the following: Scott County Herald, founded in Nov., 1885, by Hon. S. W. Case, with F. A. Capps editor, and Mrs. S. W. Case corresponding editor; consolidated in 1888 with the Sentinel, which was founded in 1886 by M. J. Keyes; continued as the Sentinel-Herald with D. F. Hall, editor, and J. M. Beadles, managing editor; in 1891 name changed to Scott County Lever, J. C. Starr, editor and publisher; consolidated in 1892 with Scott County News which had been founded in 1886 by Sam H. Kelley, J. C. Starr continued as editor and F. L. Crampton, manager. It was called the Scott County News-Lever; the name was shortened in 1903 to Scott County News, J. C. Starr, editor and publisher; consolidated in 1909 with Scott County Chronicle, which had been founded at Grigsby as the Chronicle, with W. E. Baxter, editor and publisher; the Chronicle was bought by E. H. Epperson, and for a year and a half was edited by him on his homestead, ten miles east of Scott City. Mr. Epperson moved to Scott City in 1902, and the name of the paper was changed to the Scott County Chronicle.

Among the progressive business men of the booming town of 1885-86 were the following: Charles Clark, manager of the Chicago Lumber Yard; George Little took charge of the Kansas Lumber Yard May 18, 1886; H. Miexsell & Company operated the Buffalo Drug house; the hardware trade was represented by W. Meisenheimer; Crane & Coltrane, flour, feed, baled hay, etc.; Brady Brothers opened the second store of general merchandise, and were leaders in business and social circles; West & Wright, general merchandise; The Grand Central Hotel was owned and managed by P. A. Sexton; Messrs. Gibson & Gillespie, lumber merchants.

The Santa Fe and Missouri Pacific railroads were both built to Scott City in 1887, each putting forth great efforts to be the first to reach that point and thus to gain the right-of-way. The Missouri Pacific won in the race, and the first train over that road steamed into Scott City July Fourth, 1887. The whole town and county turned out for a big celebration in honor of the event. A few days later the Santa Fe railroad was completed to Scott City.

Other prominent people who made permanent settlement in Scott county in the pioneer days of 1885 were:

Frank M. Cutler, Jake and Mattie Armantrout, C. W. Dickhut, J. W. Lough, Spencer H. Hull, Ada L. Hull, Mrs. Louise Hull, Mr. and Mrs. J. C. Render, A. D. Hull, John Deaton, Mrs. Sue Lancaster (formerly wife of Eugene McDaniel who died in 1887), C. J. Van Antwerp, George Norman and M. M. Bush. R. S. Stone has always been a Scott county booster, although he now resides in Garden City.

Many came to Scott county in 1886 and 1887. The following list is very incomplete: Nora (Potter) Petefish, Mr. and Mrs. J. W. Ludlow, Milt Piper, Mrs. M. H. Steele, Mr. and Mrs. Omar Fleenan, Mrs. C. A. Easley, I. S. Ruth, H. E. Dague, J. A. Hollister, David D. Beck, Mrs. Florence H. Beck, F. L. Grosjean, J. P. Bush, P. V. Seward, F. H. Mahler, Mrs. Charles Watkins, Nellie (Sprague) Cook, John Kittle, Charles Harkness, Bert Ding, Mrs. J. T. Deaton, C. W. Proudfoot, Mr. and Mrs. W. S. Manker, and Wm. Lenahan.

The beginning of pump irrigation in Scott county is largely told in the story of J. Wesley Lough. He arrived in Scott county in October, 1885, and located 11 miles south and west of Scott City. His homestead was the northwest quarter of sec. 18, twp. 19, range 33. In coming to Kansas, Mr. Lough travelled by railway to Garden City, bringing only some household goods. From Garden City he was carried to his homestead location in a freight wagon. He had just enough money to buy a team, and he bought a wagon by giving a mortgage partly on the wagon and partly on the team, and with this equipment he started his career in Western Kansas.

At this time, three buildings and some tents comprised the town of Scott City. The only water on the town site came from a dug well, and was dipped up in a bucket drawn up hand over hand. Mr. Lough paid $34.10 for the material that entered into his first habitation. Around this rough frame he put up sod walls, and the roof of the single room was covered with dirt, tar paper and sod, and this served as his home for two years. During that time, he did more freighting than farming, but broke up about 100 acres for himself and many acres for other settlers. Hot winds prevailed and Mr. Lough became discouraged and moved to Colorado. He farmed in Colorado for nine years before returning to Scott county, and this time his main business was stock raising until he discovered that the lake of water beneath the land might be utilized for irrigation.

His initial effort to develop the subterranean water resources was made in 1909. The first well was drilled as a result of financial cooperation among about twenty-five men of the Scott City community. The location for the test was Elmer E. Coffin's land two miles south of town. The drilling was done by Billy Wilson. The well came in with an abundance of water, and thus established the contention of Mr. Lough in favor of irrigation. Mr. Lough drilled the second well himself on his own farm. The fifteen-inch bore reached the water strata at a depth of thirty-five feet. The next step was to find a satisfactory pump. Mr. Lough visited Houston, Chicago, New York and finally at Elizabeth, New Jersey, bought a steam engine which when tried proved too small. Another engine of the same type was bought, and still a third, but all proved too light for the work to be done. These engines have long been discarded, and these experiments cost a great deal of money.

In his earlier efforts he used a twenty-two horsepower engine, but then decided to install an engine of thirty-six horsepower. He went to Ohio and bought two such engines. These were capable of doing the work required, but the expense of operating them was too great. He next bought an oil engine and it solved the problem of cheap and successful pumping. Mr. Lough's next progressive step in pump irrigation was to erect a plant on the home farm, twelve miles southwest of Scott City, costing $50,000, operated with electricity made on the farm, and pumping enough water every twenty-four hours to irrigate 320 acres. It was started to work in the spring of 1917.

Mr. Lough's interest and experiment in irrigation projects have brought him prominently before those interested in irrigation. What he has achieved is not for himself alone, but opened a new era for the western part of the state.

Mr. Lough married Miss Flora B. Smith on May 3, 1884. Their children are Aughty, Audry, Stella, William D., Mace and Freda.

Elmer Elsworth Coffin has been a resident of Scott county since May 14, 1886, and it would be difficult to name a citizen who has contributed in greater degree to the progress and welfare of Scott City and Scott county. He has always been active in business affairs, in agriculture and his career has been representative of the best type of pioneer ability.

When he decided to come to Kansas, he disposed of his Indiana interests, and made the journey to Garden City by railroad, and then by stage to Scott City. Upon his arrival he pre-empted the northeast quarter of section 24, township 17, range 33. He immediately built a sod house of one room, using a curtain for a partition. He soon after took a homestead adjoining his pre-emption, and built a dugout 12 by 14 feet, as his place of abode to live in the following winter, and in this dugout his first son was born. The next summer he built a three-room frame house. Mr. Coffin engaged in raising stock and feed, and the same summer that he came to Scott county he opened the first butcher shop in Scott City. Later he turned his attention exclusively to the stock business, buying, raising and shipping horses for fourteen years to Connecticut, where they were used for farming purposes. In addition to introducing the Percheron and Clydesdale horses in this section, Mr. Coffin shipped in many sires of this class and thus improved the class of horses in the county.

Mr. Coffin was one of the promoters of the Garden City, Gulf & Northern Railroad from Garden City to Scott City, and assisted in promoting the Colorado, Kansas & Oklahoma Railway, a road running from Scott City to its connection with the Union Pacific at Winona, and was a director of both roads. He has twice been mayor of Scott City, has been a member of the city council, and a director of the commercial club. He has served several years as county commissioner, and was very active in helping to secure the present fine high school building by circulating a petition through the county.

To Mr. and Mrs. Coffin the following children have been born: Pearl, who is the wife of G. E. Anderson; Herbert, Blanche, Philip, Alfred, Edwin, and Jennie, who is the wife of Charles Wymer.

Charles Wesley Dickhut was only a small boy when his parents moved to Kansas from Illinois. They made the entire trip in a wagon, and after arriving in Kansas, Charles W. worked out by the month, frequently for twenty-five cents a day. He remained at home until he was twenty-two, and his wages were turned to add to the family possessions. In 1885 Mr. Dickhut went to Scott county and filed on a homestead six miles east and three south of Scott City. He built a frame house 14 by 24 feet of rough boards. He started with two teams and a cow, but subsequently he did his farm work with only the cow and one horse hitched together for a team, and in various other ways he passed through the fire of adversity, but he did well as a farmer, and in 1886 married Miss Mary E. Childers, who helped him to stick to his chosen career.

In 1903 Mr. Dickhut came to the vicinity of Scott City

where he prospered by combining general crop raising with live stock. His private affairs did not altogether take his time and attention. He helped promote the Citizens Bank of Scott City, and has contributed some substantial buildings to the city. He has held several public offices in the county and no one could be a more thorough believer in liberal and higher education for the young, and the Scott County High School was started while he was on the Board of Commissioners.

The children of Mr. and Mrs. Dickhut are: Clarence W., Clifford R., Edna and Edwin, the last two being twins.

Elmer H. Epperson came to Scott county in 1886, and entered a homestead near Grigsby and proved it up. Mr. Epperson's first home was a shed which he used until he could build a sod house. When he first arrived he was compelled to set his family out on the prairie, while he took the wagon and drove to Pierceville, Kansas, on the Santa Fe railroad, to haul back building material. While he was away his family on the homestead was visited by a severe rain and hail storm. On his return from Pierceville, Mr. Epperson went to work at once to build a sod house. It was 12 by 22 feet, covered with boards and tar paper and then sodded. The house was floored and plastered with native lime. This was their home until 1902.

In 1900 Mr. Epperson engaged in the newspaper business on his farm, starting The Chronicle, which he conducted at his country home until July 1, 1902. During his first month in the paper business, he rode the header thirty days in succession, and in the meantime put out a weekly issue of his paper. In 1902, he was awarded the county printing and moved his plant to Scott City, and at this time, gave up farming. Mr. Epperson engaged in this business continuously until his death in 1930, although his son became the manager after 1909.

Through his paper Mr. Epperson contributed most effectively to the advancement of Scott City. In October, 1913, he was appointed as postmaster of Scott City to succeed James Morris. Mr. and Mrs. Epperson were the parents of seven children: Anna M., Lena D., Lora R., Caroline, Elmer L., who became partner with his father in the newspaper business; Gertrude, Albert R., and Florence Merle.

T. A. J. Carbould is one of the most interesting and perhaps the most travelled man in Southwest Kansas. He is not one of the earliest pioneer settlers in Scott county, yet he was the pioneer in that region in his profession. He came to Scott City in 1893, a graduate, registered veterinarian, the only one between Hutchinson, Kansas, and Pueblo, Colorado. Western Kansas was still a great horse country, and Mr. Carbould's work among sick and injured animals kept him traveling across the prairie. His whole life has been one of thrills and adventure. He was born on a British warship on the sea in 1864. When four months old he was taken to Australia where he spent the first ten years of his life, and was then sent to England. When 14 years of age he was appointed to His Majesty's Service at Worchester as a naval cadet. After four years he was transferred to H.M.S. on "The Thunderer", an old wooden-walls sailing vessel, as mid-shipman. During the years 1886-87-88 he was in service on the British White Fleet, which made a three-year tour of the world, stopping at every principal port in foreign countries and those of the British possessions. At the end of this term he left the service and went to Canada. There he joined the Scarlet Riders of the plains, better known as the Royal Nor'west Mounted Police. After serving three years and ten months he was wounded in a skirmish with renegade Rocky Mountain Indians. He was forced to leave the service and it was at this time that he took up his residence with his cousin, Arthur Brain, a wealthy rancher in Scott county.

In 1899 he enlisted again in the British army and served two years and four months in the Boer War in South Africa. During his service he was badly wounded while saving a comrade, and was awarded a silver medal for his bravery, which was pinned on his breast by Queen Victoria just before her death. This medal is the most prized of all his relics and trophies. In 1903 Mr. Carbould returned to Colorado, where he followed his profession as a veterinary. In 1915 at the beginning of the World War he joined the Blue Cross, serving as veterinary both on transports and at field bases for the British army until the United States entered the war, and then he was transferred to the American service. He went across the Atlantic seven times during this war and once afterwards. He was discharged in 1920, but held a government position in Mexico for two years. Since 1922 he has lived quietly at Scott City.

THE SCOTT COUNTY STATE PARK

The official opening of the Scott County State Park occurred June 12, 1930. The park consists of twelve hundred acres, and is composed of the most rugged scenery in Kansas. The lake covers 110 acres, and the large concrete dam is a splendid work of engineering. The Steele Memorial, located on a high bluff within the park area, was dedicated on the opening day. It was made possible through the contributions of more than one thousand persons throughout the United States. It honors Mr. and Mrs. Steele, pioneer residents and former owners of the properties on which the park is located.

TELLS OF TIME WHEN METEOR FELL IN SCOTT COUNTY

By J. K. Freed

FLORIDA had its land boom; Texas had its oil boom; Kansas too had its boom but it was of a different kind. It came straight out of the west and went straight for you—for you, and not the other fellow, while you tried to hide behind something if it were only a barbed wire fence. But as well try to hide from an earthquake as from it. In a single second you remembered more of your shortcomings than you ever before would admit. I have looked down as cold and cruel a gun-barrel as any drunken cowboy ever toted, and I smiled and jollied him until he forgot his business, but this was a case where tact and diplomacy did not count. You could only await developments.

When it was forty miles west and twice as far above the earth it exploded with a terrific boom. In rapid succession these fragments exploded again and kept coming toward you. Though it was ten o'clock at night it was, for a moment, as light as day. The doors and windows in Scott City and at Syracuse seventy-five miles away were rattled. It seemed the whole world shook. This was followed by a fierce cannonading which gradually grew fainter and fainter until it died away in the distance, like rolling thunder. Then came the whistling of rocks like bullets or heavy hail, and intense humming or whirling like that of an airplane going a hundred miles an hour. This ended with a dull thud and all was over. Again that calm peacefulness so characteristic of a cloudless night on the western plains prevailed.

With the people, calmness was not so quickly restored. Some did not know much about meteors, what they were, where they came from, or what they were likely to do. Those who were indoors did not see the fireworks and did not know what all the noise meant. A neighbor was returning from town where he had "met with the boys". He rushed into the house exclaiming, "Good God, Maggie! It was as big as a haystack afire, and it came straight for me and didn't miss me by forty feet!" He has since been a sober and God-fearing man. The meteor was the talk of the neighborhood for a time. Some days later I was riding over the prairie and saw a black rock sticking out of the ground. "Huh!" I thought, "that is funny to find a big chunk of coal out on the prairie all by itself. Guess I'll just take it along as a curiosity." Before I got home I happened to think of that meteorite and then I decided I had really "roped in" a piece of the sun, moon or some other world. I felt as important as a United States senator.

Some time later I was plowing with five horses to the gang plow. My field was a mile long and as level as a base-ball diamond. My team felt a little too frisky so for safety's sake I set the plow a notch deeper and I soon had them down to the right pace. I thought I was doing some of the finest plowing that had ever been done when zip! my plow reared up and sent me sprawling through the air. I landed beside the team with the plow upside down beside me. The team was too surprised to run, while I sat there, talking to myself. As I remembered it, that conversation ran something like this: "What can all this mean? Haven't I plowed hundreds of acres and never struck a rock or stump within ten miles of here? Was it dynamite?" I then walked back to where the plow had left the ground but I failed to find a thing, even a hole in the ground, so I took my jack-knife and cautionsly began digging. Then I found I had run against one of those nuggets from the sky. It weighed about twenty pounds.

Strange things sometimes happen! We found that a four-pound rock plowed up by my son six months before this one fell was also a meteorite but one of an entirely different structure. It had evidently fallen years before for it was covered with rust. I do not know just why two different meteorites should choose this particular farm for a landing field, for there have been only about 900 falls known to the scientific world in the last 5,000 years. I believe there is no case like it on record.

Herbert T. Hineman is one of the earliest settlers in Lane county, having entered his homestead there in 1885, and settled permanently in 1886. He and his young wife were conveyed to this pioneer home in a wagon which was drawn by Tom and Jerry, a most responsive yoke of oxen, with whom as Mr. Hineman has remarked, "we resided for over six years". In addition to his team and wagon he possessed two cows and $7.50 in cash.

Kanza Kennel. Wolf Hounds. George Hineman, Dighton, Kansas

Mr. and Mrs. Hineman resided on their homestead, the northwest quarter of sec. 23, twp. 20, range 29, for five years. Their home consisted of two rooms made of sod and plastered with native lime.

In November, 1890, they moved to their present home. On this farm he devoted himself to the raising of grain and feed, and to building up a herd of livestock, particularly to the horse industry. The range was open and a horse could be produced almost without cost. Later he began raising the pedigreed Percheron. Mr. Hineman has made a success with horses, but his greatest fame has come as a raiser of jacks. In 1904 he began this business by purchasing "Mammouth Jumbo", and with this individual his line of noted jacks started. "Kansas Chief" won the world's championship at San Francisco Exposition in 1915. Mr. Hineman exhibited eleven head of jacks and janets there and won twenty-eight ribbons with them.

Mr. Hineman has a ranch of many hundred acres all fenced and cross fenced, and in addition to livestock is now growing large acreages of wheat. He is also largely interested in various business concerns in Dighton, Kansas. He was elected as sheriff of Lane county in 1902 and served in that capacity for four years, during which time there were but four juries empaneled and only one murder case tried. There was no jail at that time and no apparent need for one. To Mr. and Mrs. Hineman were born two children, George and Albert.

Mr. Hineman said recently in a speech at a pioneer settlers' picnic: "Our pioneer days on the broad, expansive plains, where one could see for fifty miles in the distance, were the happiest days of my life." He faltered. "No, I'll take that back. When I look about me today and see the faces of my old friends and neighbors and see sitting close to my side the first teacher of my boys, Mrs. Isabel Wolf Johnston, whom we have always loved as one of our family, I think of her motherly care and fine moral and intellectual teaching. I am compelled to say, with my family and grandchildren all about me, these are my happiest days, and I feel the love of God and nearer to eternal happiness."

CPSIA information can be obtained
at www.ICGtesting.com
Printed in the USA
BVHW050937131221
623915BV00002B/115

9 781013 691171